EVERYTHING

YOU NEED TO KNOW ABOUT...

Low-Carb Cooking

PATRICIA M. BUTKUS

David & Charles

A DAVID & CHARLES BOOK

David & Charles is a subsidiary of F&W (UK) Ltd.,

an F&W Publications Inc. company

First published in the UK in 2004

First published in the USA as The Everything® Low-Carb Cookbook,

by Adams Media Corporation in 2002

Project Manager Ian Kearey

Cover Design Ali Myer

A catalogue record for this book is available from the British Library.

ISBN 0 7153 1953 1

Printed in Great Britain by CPI Bath

for David & Charles

Brunel House   Newton Abbot   Devon

Visit our website at www.davidandcharles.co.uk

David & Charles books are available from all good bookshops;

alternatively you can contact our Orderline on (0)1626 334555 or

write to us at FREEPOST EX2110, David & Charles Direct,

Newton Abbot, TQ12 4ZZ (no stamp required UK mainland).

Contents

Introduction

WELCOME TO THE WORLD OF LOW-CARB COOKING! There are many reasons why you might choose to decrease the number of carbohydrates you consume. Whether it's a choice based on dietary needs or a weight-loss plan, *Everything You Need To Know About Low-Carb Cooking* is the perfect cookbook to help you reduce your carbohydrate intake. Different people have different dietary needs, and they are as varied as the recipes in this book. This book offers you more than 300 great-tasting recipes that are low in carbohydrates but not low on flavour.

What Is a Carbohydrate?

In a word, fuel. All energy in food comes from carbohydrates, proteins or fatty acids. Carbohydrates are high-energy chemical compounds that are found in foods like breads, pasta, cereal and vegetables. There are two types of carbohydrates – sugars (also called simple carbohydrates) and starches (or complex carbohydrates).

Simple sugars are absorbed directly into the bloodstream fairly quickly after you eat them. That's why you get a quick burst of energy from a chocolate bar, followed by a crash as your blood sugar level drops once the sugars are absorbed.

Starches are digested into simpler sugars, which are further converted into glucose. Glucose is the main source of energy for the cells of the human body. Because it takes longer for the body to break down and digest these carbohydrates, the sugars enter the bloodstream at a fairly constant rate.

Your body uses the energy it needs and stores the rest for later use. When you eat more carbs than your body needs, the high glucose levels cause your body to produce more fat to store the excess energy.

Diets that consistently contain more carbohydrates than the body needs can lead to health problems such as obesity and, in some cases, diabetes. Research has also suggested that diets high in starch contribute to atherosclerosis and heart disease, the number one cause of death in Great Britain and the USA.

So while it is important to have carbohydrates in your diet, controlling your intake to reasonable levels is always smart. *Everything You Need To Know About Low-Carb Cooking* gives you over 300 recipes for every occasion that will keep you low on carbs but high on taste!

Nutritional Analyses

Every recipe is rated to reflect the carbohydrate amount and includes specific carb counts. Using a reputable, internationally recognized computerized nutritional analysis program, I determined the total carb count on a per serving basis. Several of the current popular programs for calculating carbs subtract the fibre content before reporting the carb count. My analysis is based on the full carb amount; no compensations have been made. If you're counting net carbs, recipes containing ingredients with fibre will have lower carb counts than indicated here.

It's very difficult to determine accurate fat content in final recipes, especially given that much of the fat used during cooking doesn't remain in the final dish. Keep in mind that 1g of fat equals 9 calories.

You will notice two ratings used throughout the book for each recipe. Every recipe has a carb level identified as 'Low' or 'Moderate'. Although the moderate recipes have a higher level of carbohydrates, they are still low-carb recipes.

- **LOW** – These recipes all contain 10g or fewer of carbohydrates per serving
- **MODERATE** – These recipes all contain between 10g and 20g of carbohydrates per serving

Eating healthily is an important part of your lifestyle. These recipes make it easy to eat well while still controlling your carb intake. Enjoy.

Easy Appetizers

❖ **Indicates Easy Recipe** ❖

Party Cheese Balls

Serves 25
Carb Level: Low

Per serving:

Carbohydrate:	2.1 g
Protein:	8.0 g

This recipe produces two balls – keep one in the freezer for surprise get-togethers.

225g (8oz) cream cheese, softened
375g (12oz) blue cheese, crumbled
454g (1lb) sharp Cheddar cheese, shredded

1 tbsp Worcestershire sauce
1 tbsp finely chopped onion
Salt and white pepper to taste
220g (7oz) pecan chips, toasted

Using a wooden spoon or food processor, mix together all the ingredients, *except* the pecan chips, until smooth. Shape the mixture into two balls, about 454g (1lb) each. Roll each ball in the pecan chips to coat. Chill quickly. Keep in the refrigerator and serve chilled. The extra ball may be stored in the freezer, double-wrapped in cling film, for up to 1 month.

Yam and Chorizo Crisps

Serves 10
Carb Level: Low

Per serving:

Carbohydrate:	6.1 g
Protein:	9.3 g

These are great served with a Mexican-style dinner.

185g (6oz) goat cheese, softened
150g (5oz) spicy salsa
225g (8oz) chorizo sausage

1 medium yam, peeled, quartered, sliced and marinated (see page 5)
Salt and white pepper to taste
Coriander leaves for garnish

1. Combine the goat cheese and salsa in a small bowl. Use the tines of a fork to blend until incorporated; set aside. Slice the chorizo into 3mm ($1/8$ in)-thick slices. Heat a non-stick sauté pan over medium-high heat. Add the chorizo and cook, uncovered, until lightly browned on both sides. Remove with a slotted spoon onto paper towels.
2. To assemble, place about ¾ teaspoon goat cheese mixture on each yam crisp. Top with a slice of the browned chorizo and garnish with fresh coriander leaves. Serve immediately.

Crabmeat on Red Pepper Strips

80ml (½fl oz) mayonnaise
2 green onions, finely chopped
½ plum tomato, seeded and chopped
1 tbsp chopped fresh parsley and tarragon combined
2 tsp fresh lemon juice
½ tsp grated fresh lemon zest
Pinch of cayenne pepper

225g (8oz) crabmeat, flaked
Salt and freshly ground black pepper to taste
2 large yellow, red or green peppers, cut into 50 x 25mm (2 x 1in) strips
Fresh chervil sprigs for garnish

Mix together the mayonnaise, green onions, tomato, chopped parsley and tarragon, lemon juice, lemon zest and cayenne in a medium-sized bowl until blended. Add the crabmeat and toss lightly to coat. Season with salt and pepper. Spoon 1 or 2 teaspoons of crab mixture onto each pepper strip. Garnish with chervil sprigs.

Serves 4
Carb Level: Low

Per serving:

Carbohydrate:	9.6 g
Protein:	11.8 g

Serve in individual strips as an appetizer, or place three strips on a bed of greens as a starter course.

Hot Artichoke Dip

320g (11oz) tin artichoke hearts, rinsed, drained and chopped
2 cloves garlic, crushed
60ml (2fl oz) mayonnaise

Dash of Worcestershire sauce
55g (2oz) grated Parmesan cheese
Salt and white pepper to taste

1. Preheat the oven to 180°C, 350°F, gas mark 4.
2. Combine all the ingredients in a 1l (32fl oz) ovenproof glass dish and bake uncovered for 25 minutes. Serve hot with crisps or vegetable chips.

Serves 10
Carb Level: Low

Per serving:

Carbohydrate:	5.0 g
Protein:	2.1 g

Try this recipe with the guilt-free Yam Chips (see p 5) for a perfect pairing.

Spinach and Ricotta Dip

Serves 12

Carb Level: Low

Per serving:

Carbohydrate:	2.1 g
Protein:	0.9 g

This is a great party recipe – easy to make in advance.

300g (10z) frozen chopped spinach, thawed and drained
60g (2oz) ricotta cheese
80ml (½fl oz) mayonnaise
60g (2oz) chopped green onions
80ml (2fl oz) sour cream
3 tbsp lemon juice

1 tbsp grated onion (including juice)
Dash of Worcestershire sauce
Salt and freshly ground black pepper to taste
Chopped parsley for garnish

Combine all the ingredients, *except* the parsley, in a food processor and blend until smooth. Adjust seasoning to taste. Transfer to a bowl and chill thoroughly. Top with chopped parsley. Serve with fresh trimmed vegetables or toasted bread rounds.

Mushrooms with Mediterranean Stuffing

Serves 10 (about 30 mushrooms)

Carb Level: Low

Per serving:

Carbohydrate:	3.0 g
Protein:	2.7 g

Everyone loves no-cook recipes during the summer. This is a favourite for making in advance.

160ml (5fl oz) low-fat cottage cheese
90g (3oz) feta cheese, crumbled
1 tbsp freshly snipped dill
1 tsp lemon juice
½ tsp olive oil
¼ tsp dried oregano

Salt to taste
30 medium mushroom caps, cleaned and de-stemmed
Fresh dill sprigs for garnish

Combine the first seven ingredients in a small bowl and mix until blended thoroughly. Spoon about 1 teaspoon of filling into each mushroom cap. Garnish with fresh dill sprigs and serve.

Spicy Yam Crisps

1 yam, peeled, quartered and thinly
   sliced
50ml (2½fl oz) freshly squeezed
   lime juice

½ tsp chilli powder
¼ tsp ground red pepper
Salt to taste

Place the yam slices in a shallow glass dish and toss with lime juice; allow to marinate for 30 minutes at room temperature. Drain the crisps and transfer to a serving platter; sprinkle with chilli powder, pepper and salt. Serve immediately with your favourite dip.

Serves 10

Carb Level: Low

Per serving:

Carbohydrate:	2.2 g
Protein:	0.3 g

Yam crisps are a great alternative to potato crisps. Use as a base for canapés – they are also great with Mexican dips.

Ham Cornets

225g (8oz) cream cheese,
   softened
1 tbsp Dijon mustard
1 tbsp chopped fresh tarragon

Salt and freshly ground black pepper
   to taste
10 slices good-quality ham, cut into
   thirds
30 water biscuits or crackers

Mix together the cream cheese, mustard, tarragon and salt and pepper in a small bowl until blended. Place about ½ teaspoon of the cream cheese mixture at the short end of a ham slice and roll into a cornet shape. Repeat with the remaining slices, reserving a small amount of the cream cheese mixture. To assemble, smear a very small amount of the cream cheese mixture on each biscuit as a 'glue' to secure the ham cornet. Top each biscuit with the cornet and serve immediately.

Serves 15

Carb Level: Low

Per serving:

Carbohydrate:	7.6 g
Protein:	17.8 g

A quick stop at the delicatessen counter and you're ready with the main ingredient for these savoury bites.

Open Mushrooms
with Warm Garlic Flan

Serves 6

Carb Level: Low

Per serving:

Carbohydrate: 6.4 g

Protein: 14.0 g

This is a classy first course worthy of an intimate dinner with good friends.

6 large open mushrooms
2 tsp chopped chives
 for garnish

Marinade:
250ml (8fl oz) olive oil
2 cloves garlic, crushed
½ tbsp finely chopped fresh rosemary
½ tbsp finely chopped fresh oregano
½ tbsp finely chopped fresh basil
Juice of 1 lemon
1 tsp salt
½ tsp black pepper

3 tbsp balsamic vinegar
2 tsp soy sauce

Garlic flan:
250ml (8fl oz) double cream
3 cloves roasted garlic, cut in half
3 egg yolks
½ tsp powdered, unflavoured
 gelatin
Pinch of salt
Pinch of white pepper
Pinch of grated fresh nutmeg
Butter, softened

1. Remove and discard the stems from the mushrooms. Clean the caps using a damp paper towel.
2. In a medium-size bowl, whisk together all of the marinade ingredients. Add the mushroom caps and leave uncovered for 2 hours at room temperature.
3. Preheat the grill to high heat.
4. Grill the mushrooms for about 3 minutes on each side; let cool. Cut the mushrooms into 12mm (½ in) slices and set aside.
5. Preheat the oven to 180°C, 350°F, gas mark 4.
6. To prepare the flan: bring the cream and garlic to a simmer in a small saucepan over medium-low heat. Transfer the mixture to a blender or food processor and add the egg yolks, gelatin, salt, pepper and nutmeg; purée until smooth.
7. Using 125g (4oz) buttered ramekins, pour in the custard to the top. Place the ramekins in a baking pan and fill it with 12mm (½ in) of water. Bake for about 1 hour or until the custard is set.
8. Position each ramekin in the centre of a salad plate. Serve the slices of mushroom around the flan and garnish with chopped chives.

Artichoke Hearts with Herbed Cheese

Tin artichoke hearts, rinsed and
 drained
225g (8oz) cream cheese,
 softened
1 tbsp chopped fresh herbs (parsley,
 basil, chives, etc.)

Salt and freshly ground black pepper
 to taste
30 fresh radish slices

Slice the artichoke hearts into 30 neatly trimmed slices. Mix together the cream cheese, herbs and salt and pepper in a small bowl until smooth. Use a pastry bag to pipe a small rosette of the cream cheese mixture (about $\frac{1}{2}$ rounded tablespoon each) onto each artichoke slice. Top with a radish slice and serve immediately.

Serves 15
Carb Level: Low

Per serving:	
Carbohydrate:	1.0 g
Protein:	1.3 g

Tinned artichoke hearts are good to have on hand when you need a quick appetizer with an elegant look.

Parmesan Crisps

100g ($3\frac{1}{2}$oz) shredded (not grated)
 Parmesan cheese

Freshly ground black pepper
 to taste

1. Preheat the oven to 170°C, 325°F, gas mark 3. Line a baking tray with greaseproof paper.
2. Place rounded teaspoons of the shredded cheese on the parchment, equally spaced with about 50–63mm (2–2 $\frac{1}{2}$ in) between each mound. Lightly flatten each mound with your fingertips to a circle about 38mm ($1\frac{1}{2}$ in) across. Sprinkle with pepper. Bake, checking after 3 minutes until the cheese just starts to melt and very lightly begins to brown. Remove immediately and transfer the crisps to a rack to cool. Store in airtight containers.

Serves 15
Carb Level: Low

Per serving:	
Carbohydrate:	0.2 g
Protein:	2.2 g

Check the crisps while baking – the colour should just start to turn golden. Overcooked cheese has a bitter aftertaste.

Caponata

Serves 15
Carb Level: Low

Per serving:

Carbohydrate:	6.9 g
Protein:	2.3 g

This is a delicious dip for crisps or fresh trimmed vegetables.

125ml (4fl oz) olive oil
6 medium courgettes, cut into
    12mm (½ in) pieces
200g (7oz) medium-diced onions
1 red pepper, seeded and
    medium-diced
6 cloves garlic, peeled and finely
    chopped
200g (7oz) diced fresh tomatoes
125ml (4fl oz) tomato purée

30g (2oz) capers, drained
60ml (2fl oz) balsamic vinegar
Salt and freshly ground black pepper
    to taste
90g (3oz) coarsely chopped
    walnuts, toasted

Heat the oil in a large non-stick sauté pan over medium-high heat.
Add the courgettes and cook, stirring frequently, until lightly browned
on all sides, about 5 minutes. Add all the remaining ingredients *except*
the nuts and simmer for about 15 minutes, stirring frequently to prevent sticking. Season to taste, cool and transfer to a glass or ceramic
serving bowl. Cover and refrigerate overnight. Serve at room temperature, garnished with the walnuts.

Grilled Pineapple and Avocado Chutney

1 pineapple, peeled, cored, and cut
   into 25mm (1in) thick rings
1½ tbsp vegetable oil
Salt and freshly ground black pepper
   to taste
2 small avocados, halved, stoned and
   cut into 12mm (½in) chunks
3 tbsp fresh-squeezed lime juice

½ tbsp jalapeño pepper, crushed and
   seeded (about 1 small pepper)
15g (½oz) coarsely chopped fresh
   coriander leaves

Serves 8	
Carb Level: Moderate	
Per serving:	
Carbohydrate:	11.6 g
Protein:	1.3 g

Serve the chutney the same day it is prepared (or the avocado will discolour).

1. Prepare a charcoal grill or preheat a gas grill to high. Make sure the grill grate is clean and lightly oiled to prevent sticking. You can also use an indoor grill pan for this recipe.
2. Brush the pineapple rings lightly with oil and season with salt and pepper. Place on the grill for about 8 minutes on each side or until browned and caramelized. If you are using an indoor grill pan, you may need to cook them longer on each side. (The grill pan does not get as hot as an outdoor grill.) Allow the grilled pineapple to cool. When cool enough to handle, cut them into 25mm (1in) chunks. Transfer them to a bowl.
3. Add the avocado to the pineapple along with the lime juice, jalapeño, salt and pepper and coriander; mix well to combine, and serve.

Olive Tapenade

220g (7oz) calamata olives, stoned	½ tsp lemon zest
2 cloves garlic	Freshly ground black pepper
1 tbsp lemon juice	to taste
60ml (2fl oz) olive oil	

Combine all the ingredients in a food processor; process until blended. Store refrigerated in airtight containers.

<table>
<tr><td>Serves 12</td></tr>
<tr><td>Carb Level: Low</td></tr>
<tr><td>Per serving:</td></tr>
<tr><td>Carbohydrate: 1.3 g</td></tr>
<tr><td>Protein: 0.0 g</td></tr>
</table>

This is a savoury topping for Parmesan Crisps (see p 7). Great for olive lovers.

Mock Caviar

2 aubergines, about 454g (1lb) each	Salt and freshly ground black pepper
60ml (2fl oz) olive oil	to taste
8 cloves garlic, with skins on	
1½ tbsp chopped parsley	

1. Preheat the oven to 220°C, 425°F, gas mark 7.
2. Split the aubergines longways and brush the cut surface with olive oil. Place on a baking sheet with the whole garlic cloves. Bake for 30 to 40 minutes or until tender. Remove from oven and allow to cool.
3. Scoop out the flesh from the aubergines and transfer to the bowl of a food processor. Trim the root ends from the garlic cloves and squeeze out the garlic pulp; add the pulp to the aubergines. Add the remaining ingredients and process until smooth. Store refrigerated in airtight containers.

<table>
<tr><td>Serves 12</td></tr>
<tr><td>Carb Level: Low</td></tr>
<tr><td>Per serving:</td></tr>
<tr><td>Carbohydrate: 4.4 g</td></tr>
<tr><td>Protein: 0.8 g</td></tr>
</table>

This is a great topping for Parmesan Crisps (see p 7) or cucumber slices.

Pesto Aubergine Caviar

1 large aubergine
1 red pepper, seeded, stemmed and
*   finely chopped*
1 tbsp olive oil
Salt
60ml (2fl oz) pesto, homemade or
*   prepared*

1 large lemon
30g (1oz) fresh grated Parmesan
*   cheese*
Freshly ground black pepper
*   to taste*

Makes 150g (5oz)
Carb Level: Moderate

Per serving:	
Carbohydrate:	12.3 g
Protein:	5.4 g

This very versatile spread works great as a dip for vegetables or as a creative topping for roasted meats such as lamb.

1. Preheat the oven to high.
2. Wash and dry the aubergine, cut it in half and place on it on a baking sheet cut side down. Cook for a few minutes until the skin blisters and chars, checking several times and adjusting the position of the aubergine halves to make sure the skin cooks evenly.
3. Reduce the oven temperature to 200°C, 400°F, gas mark 6. Bake the aubergine for 50 minutes.
4. Meanwhile, sauté the red pepper in the olive oil over medium heat until tender; sprinkle with a pinch of salt and set aside.
5. Remove the aubergine from the oven and allow to cool for about 10 minutes. Scoop out the flesh and place in a food processor. Discard the remaining skin.
6. Add the pesto to the food processor. Use a citrus zester to get ¼ tsp lemon zest; add to the processor. Juice the lemon and add to the processor. Process the contents until fairly smooth.
7. Transfer to a bowl. Stir in the cooked red pepper and grated Parmesan cheese. Add salt and freshly ground black pepper to taste. Cover until cold and refrigerate.

Chinese-Style Paste

Serves 12	
Carb Level: Low	

Per serving:

Carbohydrate:	0.9 g
Protein:	1.3 g

Use this paste on top of sesame rice crackers for a delicious pairing with a Chinese meal.

125g (4oz) cream cheese
1 tbsp wasabi
½ tbsp grated root ginger
½ tbsp oyster sauce

1 tbsp tamari sauce
Chilli flakes to taste

Place all the ingredients in the bowl of a food processor; process until blended. Store refrigerated in airtight containers.

Jalapeño Paste

Serves 12	
Carb Level: Low	

Per serving:

Carbohydrate:	2.3 g
Protein:	1.6 g

Use this paste on top of Spicy Yam Chips (see p 5) for a tasty pairing with a Mexican meal.

6 jalapeños
2 tbsp olive oil
125g (4oz) cream cheese
1 tbsp chopped coriander leaves

1 tsp lime zest, finely grated
Salt and pepper to taste

1. Preheat the oven to 200°C, 400°F, gas mark 6.
2. Rub the jalapeños with olive oil and roast on a non-stick baking sheet for about 30 minutes, or until they turn dark brown. Transfer to a bowl and cover tightly with cling film. Allow to stand for 15 minutes or until cool. Seed and skin the peppers. Mash the flesh together with the remaining ingredients in the bowl of a food processor; process until blended. Store refrigerated in airtight containers.

Sausage Appetizers

454g (1lb) pork sausage meat
225g (8oz) grated Cheddar cheese
125g (4oz) margarine, softened
185g (6oz) plain flour

1 tsp paprika
Salt and freshly ground black pepper
   to taste

1. Preheat the oven to 180°C, 350°F, gas mark 4.
2. Form the sausage meat into fifty 25mm (1in) balls. Place on a non-stick baking tray and bake for 15 minutes. Transfer to paper towels to cool and drain.
3. Combine the remaining ingredients using the flat blade of an electric mixer. Wrap approximately 1 tablespoon of the dough around each sausage ball. Place the balls on an ungreased non-stick baking tray and bake for 10–12 minutes, until golden. Spear with toothpicks and serve hot.

tips **Food Safety**
Food safety is based on the simple principle of 'Hot foods hot – cold foods cold'. One of the best investments you can make is to buy a quality freezer thermometer, refrigerator thermometer and oven thermometer. Check them frequently to make sure they are working properly.

Serves 25
(makes 50 pieces)

Carb Level: Low

Per serving:

Carbohydrate:	6.2 g
Protein:	6.0 g

These savoury little bites are served hot from the oven – perfect for a cold-weather party.

Basic Party Dip
and Five Variations

Serves 15	
Carb Level: Low	

Blue Cheese Dip

Per serving:	
Carbohydrate:	1.9 g
Protein:	3.2 g

Dill Dip

Per serving:	
Carbohydrate:	1.9 g
Protein:	3.0 g

Dips are an easy appetizer to prepare in advance – then just add them to a garnished platter of crisps or trimmed vegetables.

125g (4oz) cream cheese, softened
360ml (12 fl oz) sour cream
Salt and freshly ground black pepper to taste

Mix together all the ingredients until smooth. Add the ingredients from one of the following variations. Keep tightly covered and refrigerated until ready to serve.

Blue Cheese Dip

1 recipe basic dip
125g (4oz) blue cheese, crumbled
½ tbsp minced fresh onion
1 tbsp lemon juice
125ml (4fl oz) buttermilk

This dip is great served with crackers, crisps or fresh vegetables.

Dill Dip

1 recipe basic dip
1 tbsp dill weed
½ tbsp crushed fresh onion
½ tbsp onion salt or celery salt

This dip goes well with fresh vegetables.

Basic Party Dip
and Five Variations (continued)

Seafood Dip

1 recipe basic dip
125g (4oz) cooked prawns and crab, chopped
15g (1/2oz) dry onion soup mix
2 tbsp chilli sauce
1/2 tbsp horseradish.

A delicious accompaniment with water biscuits, yam crisps or toasted party bread.

Creamy Onion Dip

1 recipe basic dip
45g (1 1/2oz) dry onion soup mix
1 tbsp snipped fresh chives.

This dip goes well with crisps or fresh trimmed vegetables.

Picante Dip

1 recipe basic dip
185g (6oz) salsa
30g (1oz) fresh coriander leaves, chopped
185g (6oz) stuffed olives, chopped

This dip is great with tortilla chips or fresh trimmed vegetables.

Serves 15	
Carb Level: Low	
Seafood Dip	
Per serving:	
Carbohydrate:	1.5 g
Protein:	1.4 g
Creamy Onion Dip	
Per serving:	
Carbohydrate:	3.2 g
Protein:	1.7 g
Picante Dip	
Per serving:	
Carbohydrate:	2.1 g
Protein:	1.5 g

Warm Spinach and Artichoke Dip

<table>
<tr><td>

Serves 8

Carb Level: Moderate

Per serving:

Carbohydrate:	10.9 g
Protein:	5.4 g

Be sure to use plain, not marinated, tinned artichoke hearts.

</td><td>

1 tbsp butter
100g (3¹/₂oz) sliced fresh mushrooms
1 small onion, chopped
30g (1oz) chopped yellow and/or
    red pepper
2 tsp plain flour
¹/₈ tsp ground nutmeg
250ml (8fl oz) milk
45g (1¹/₂oz) chopped fresh spinach
430g (14oz) tin plain artichoke
    hearts, well drained and chopped
30g (1oz) grated Parmesan or
    Romano cheese

</td><td>

1 tbsp dry white wine
1 tsp Worcestershire sauce
Several dashes hot pepper sauce

</td></tr>
</table>

1. Heat the butter in a medium-size sauté pan over medium heat. Cook the mushrooms, onion and peppers until they are tender. Stir in the flour and nutmeg. Add the milk all at once. Cook, stirring continually, over medium heat until thick and bubbling.
2. Stir in the remaining ingredients; cook, stirring, until heated through. Transfer to a soufflé dish and serve immediately. You can refrigerate the dip and when you are ready to serve, reheat in a 220°C, 400°F, gas mark 6 oven for about 20 minutes or until bubbling.

Five or Fewer Ingredients

❖ **Indicates Easy Recipe** ❖

Japanese Salmon

Serves 4
Carb Level: Low

Per serving:

Carbohydrate:	9.6 g
Protein:	38.5 g

Use the freshest salmon available and a low-sodium teriyaki sauce to get the best flavours.

Four 185g (6oz) centre-cut salmon fillets
125ml (4fl oz) teriyaki sauce

3 bunches spring onions
Freshly cracked black pepper
Salt to taste

1. Remove any bones from the salmon. Place the salmon in a shallow casserole dish. Cover with teriyaki sauce and allow to marinate in the refrigerator for 5 to 10 minutes.
2. Rinse the spring onions and trim off and discard the root ends. Reserve six, split the remaining spring onions in half longways, and trim off and discard all but 25mm (1in) of the green tops. Cut the onions into 25mm (1in) pieces. Place the trimmed spring onions in a non-stick frying pan uncovered, with enough salted water to cover. Bring to a boil, then lower the heat and cook uncovered until the spring onions are soft, about 3 to 5 minutes. Drain and keep warm.
3. Remove the salmon from the marinade and reserve the marinade. Press ¼ teaspoon of the coarsely ground black pepper into the skinless side of each salmon fillet. Heat a very large non-stick frying pan or two smaller ones until almost smoking. Cook the fillets skin side up and uncovered over medium-high heat for 3 minutes. Turn over and cook for another 3 minutes, or until the skin is golden brown and crispy, then turn to very low heat.
4. While the salmon is cooking on low, finely dice the remaining spring onions and add them to the reserved marinade. Add the marinade and 60ml (2fl oz) water to the pan(s) with the salmon. Increase the heat and cook uncovered until the salmon has reached serving temperature. Season with salt and pepper to taste. Serve immediately with the boiled spring onions.

Steamed Clams
with Coriander-Garlic Essence

48 littleneck clams
125g (4oz) unsalted whipped
* butter, well chilled and*
* cut into pieces*
¼ tsp whole black
* peppercorns*
½ tsp salt

30g (1oz) coarsely chopped
* coriander leaves, plus extra,*
* finely chopped, for garnish*
1 clove garlic, crushed

Serves 4
Carb Level: Low

Per serving:	
Carbohydrate:	2.3 g
Protein:	2.6 g

Be sure you put an empty bowl on the table for the shells.

1. Scrub the clams well under cold running water. Discard any clams with open or partially open shells. Place the clams in a large heavy pot along with 125ml (4fl oz) water and all the remaining ingredients.
2. Bring the mixture to a boil. Cover the pot with a tight-fitting lid and cook over high heat for 6 to 8 minutes, shaking the pot back and forth every so often to cook the clams evenly. Remove from the heat when the clam shells open up.
3. Transfer the clams to four large, flat soup plates and pour the broth over them. Garnish with the chopped coriander and serve immediately.

Clam Facts
(tips)
When buying hard-shell clams in the shell, make sure the shells are tightly closed. If the shell is open slightly, tap it to see if it snaps shut. If the shell does not close tightly, discard the clam.

Chipotle Prawns

Makes about 32 pieces
Carb Level: Low

Per serving:	
Carbohydrate:	0.4 g
Protein:	6.2 g

Chipotle peppers are actually dried smoked jalapeños. You can find them in the Mexican food section of your supermarket.

32 uncooked medium prawns
3 tbsp unsalted butter
1 heaped tbsp chopped tinned
  chipotle peppers in adobo sauce
1 small bunch coriander, chopped

Salt and freshly ground black pepper
  to taste

1. Clean and de-vein the prawns, leaving the tails on if possible.
2. Melt the butter in a 305mm (12in) non-stick frying pan over medium heat. When the butter is bubbling and starting to foam, add the chipotle peppers and prawns, and increase the heat to high.
3. Stirring constantly, cook the prawns until just firm, no more than 4 minutes. Do not overcook. Sprinkle with coriander and salt, and toss.
4. Put the prawns and sauce on individual plates or a platter, and serve hot.

tips **Unsalted Butter**
Many cooks prefer unsalted butter because it can be heated to a higher temperature than salted butter and does not contain as many impurities. It is more perishable than salted butter because it does not contain any preservatives, and it should be stored in the freezer if you are not using it right away. Butter can be frozen for up to 6 months.

Creamy Garlic and Fennel Soup

14–16 cloves garlic, peeled and
trimmed
500ml (16fl oz) double cream
2 large fennel bulbs

½ tsp salt
Finely ground white pepper

Serves 6–8	
Carb Level: Low	
Per serving:	
Carbohydrate:	6.2 g
Protein:	2.0 g

This is a great prepare-ahead recipe – refrigerate until ready to reheat and serve.

1. Place the garlic and cream in a medium-size pot with a cover and bring to a light boil over medium heat. Lower the heat, cover and gently simmer for 30 to 40 minutes, until the garlic cloves are very soft.
2. Trim and clean the fennel by cutting off the stalks and wispy sprigs (fronds) from the bulbs, and reserve for later use. Cut the bulb in half longways and use a small sharp knife to cut out the root. Keep the fronds refrigerated, wrapped in a very moist paper towel. Retain the stalks and bulb portion and discard the root trimmings.
3. Cut the bulb portion and the darker stalks into 12mm (½ in) pieces. Place in a colander and wash thoroughly to remove any dirt, then drain well.
4. Add the fennel and 750ml (24fl oz) of water to the garlic-cream mixture. Bring just to the boil, reduce the heat and cover. Simmer for another 40 minutes, until the fennel is very soft.
5. Transfer to a blender or food processor and purée in several batches until very smooth (doing so carefully, because the mixture is very hot). Return to the pot and add the salt and white pepper to taste. Heat for several minutes until the soup thickens a bit; adjust seasoning to taste.
6. Finely chop the fennel fronds and scatter over the soup for garnish. Serve hot, or keep refrigerated and gently reheat before serving.

Buying Garlic

Older garlic cloves will appear wrinkled and spotted, maybe even sprouting, and are bitter. Make sure the cloves have an unblemished, even ivory colour, and are firm to the touch, which indicates they are fresh.

Peppered Swordfish

Serves 4
Carb Level: Low

Per serving:

Carbohydrate:	3.0 g
Protein:	34.1 g

The flesh of the steaks should be gleaming and bright. Spotting, browning or any discolouration indicates fish that is ageing.

Four 185g (6oz) swordfish steaks
60ml (2fl oz) extra-virgin olive oil
Salt and freshly ground black pepper

2 medium red and 2 medium
yellow peppers

1. Lightly brush each side of the steaks with some of the olive oil, seasoned lightly with salt and freshly cracked black pepper. Sprinkle a little bit of salt on each side of the swordfish steaks. Refrigerate while preparing the peppers.
2. Cut the peppers in half, discarding the stems, seeds and whitish inner membrane. Cut the peppers into long, thin strips, no more than 6mm (¼in) wide and about 38–50mm (1½–2in) long.
3. Heat the remaining oil in a large, heavy non-stick frying pan on medium-high heat. Add the peppers, about ¼ teaspoon black pepper and ¼ teaspoon salt. Cook uncovered, stirring occasionally, until the peppers are soft and lightly browned, about 20 minutes. Set aside and keep warm.
4. Heat the same frying pan until very hot, almost smoking. Add the swordfish and cook over medium-high heat so that the fish is browned on the outside but moist on the inside, about 4 minutes per side; turn the steaks once through the cooking process. (Check they are done by cutting into the centre of the steaks with a thin-bladed knife: the flesh should be flaky with no translucence remaining.) Heat the peppers if necessary and serve on top of the steaks. Garnish with more freshly ground black pepper if desired.

tips **What Are Capers?**

Capers are the flower bud of a bush that is native to the Mediterranean and parts of Asia. Capers range in size from tiny, known as the nonpareil variety, from southern France, to the Italian caper which is as large as the tip of your little finger. Capers are generally packed in brine and should be rinsed before using. They are a tasty addition to many sauces and condiments.

Roasted Chicken Stuffed with Herby Goat's Cheese

90g (3oz) fresh basil leaves (about 2 large bunches)
225g (8oz) fresh goat's cheese, preferably flavoured with garlic and herbs, well chilled

1 tbsp butter
Freshly ground black pepper and salt to taste
2kg (5lb) roasting chicken

Serves 6
Carb Level: Low

Per serving:	
Carbohydrate:	0.9 g
Protein:	52.4 g

The roasted chicken can be prepared a day in advance. Refrigerate and just warm lightly before serving.

1. Preheat the oven to 180°C, 350°F, gas mark 4.
2. Rinse the basil leaves and pat dry with paper towels. In a food processor, combine the basil, goat's cheese and freshly ground black pepper; process until the basil is incorporated and the cheese is smooth (the mixture may turn a pale green); set aside.
3. Make sure the giblets are removed from the inside cavity of the chicken. Rinse the chicken inside and out, and pat dry with paper towels. Using poultry shears, cut off the wing tips of the chicken. Starting at the neck of the chicken, slip your fingers under the skin of the breast, carefully separating the skin from the flesh. Continue downward and, with your index finger, separate the skin around the thighs.
4. Using your fingers or a spoon, push the cheese mixture under the skin to cover the entire breasts and thighs as evenly as possible (press on the skin to distribute evenly). You will have a layer of cheese approximately 6mm (¼in) thick under the skin.
5. Rub the outside of the chicken with butter. Sprinkle the entire chicken, including the internal cavity, with salt and freshly ground black pepper. Truss the chicken by tying the legs together with a 150–200mm (6–8in) piece of butcher's twine. Roast on a rack in a heavy, shallow baking pan, uncovered, for about 1½ hours or until a meat thermometer inserted into a thigh reads 70°C, 160°F. Check on the chicken every 30 minutes during the roasting time and baste with pan juices. (Make a tent with tin foil to cover the chicken if the skin becomes too brown before the proper internal temperature is achieved.)
6. Remove from oven and let rest for about 10 minutes. Carve as desired, but it is best if cut into quarters, with the backbone removed.

Balsamic-Marinated Beef Sirloin

Serves 6
Carb Level: Low

Per serving:

Carbohydrate:	2.0 g
Protein:	40.3 g

This delicious recipe is also great grilled. Any extra balsamic glaze also works well on roasted vegetables.

Six 300g (10oz) 25mm (1in) thick beef sirloin fillets
125ml (4fl oz) extra-virgin olive oil, plus extra for grilling
125ml (4fl oz) plus 2 tbsp balsamic vinegar

1 tbsp very finely chopped fresh rosemary
Salt and coarsely ground black pepper

1. Place the meat in a shallow casserole dish. Mix together the olive oil, the 2 tablespoons of balsamic vinegar, and the rosemary in a small bowl; pour over the fillets, turning the meat to ensure the steaks are evenly coated. Marinate in the refrigerator, covered, for 2 hours, turning the fillets after 1 hour.
2. Remove the fillets from the marinade. Sprinkle salt and pepper on both sides.
3. Coat a grill pan or sauté pan lightly with oil. Preheat the pan until very hot, almost smoking, and cook the fillets for about 3 to 4 minutes on each side for medium-rare. (Increase cooking time by 2-minute increments per side for each of medium, medium-well and well-done.)
4. Place the remaining balsamic vinegar in a small saucepan and cook over medium heat until reduced to about half (60ml/2fl oz).
5. Let the fillets stand for a few minutes after they have cooked, then drizzle with a little of the reduced balsamic vinegar; serve immediately.

(tips) **Olive Oil**
The difference between extra-virgin olive oil and other types of olive oil is mostly in the taste. Extra-virgin olive oil is from the first pressing of the olives. It is fruitier and more intense in flavour than other olive oils. It is best in vinaigrettes and chilled soups, or drizzled over any dish. Other olive oils are usually better to cook with because they have a higher smoking point.

Roasted Tomato Onion Soup

4 large ripe tomatoes
8 medium onions, unpeeled
5 tbsp extra-virgin olive oil, divided,
    plus extra for garnish
125ml (4–5fl oz) water

125ml (4fl oz) double cream
Salt and freshly ground black pepper
    to taste

Serves 6 (makes about 5 cups)	
Carb Level: Moderate	
Per serving:	
Carbohydrate:	19.2 g
Protein:	3.2 g

Use fresh tomatoes from a farmers' market, if possible, for the best flavour.

1. Preheat the oven to 120°C, 250°F, gas mark ½. Bring a large pot of water to a boil. Fill a medium-sized bowl three-quarters full with cold water and ice; have it ready next to the hob.
2. To skin the tomatoes, make a small **X** in the bottom of each tomato using a small, sharp knife and cut out the core, keeping the tomato whole. Plunge the tomatoes in the boiling water for 1 minute. Using tongs, remove the tomatoes from the boiling water and drop them into the bowl of ice water; let them sit for a couple of minutes. (This process is called *blanching*. It stops the tomatoes from cooking any further.) Drain the tomatoes and peel off the skin using a small paring knife (it should come off very easily).
3. Cut the tomatoes in half and place cut-side down on a large baking sheet. Place the whole, unpeeled onions on the baking sheet with the tomatoes. Drizzle 2½ tablespoons of the olive oil over the tomatoes and onions, using your hands to coat them well. Sprinkle the tomatoes with salt. Roast for 3 hours.
4. Remove the skins from the onions and place five in a food processor along with the tomatoes; process until very smooth. Add 125–160ml (4–5fl oz) water and the remaining 2½ tablespoons of olive oil, and process again.
5. Transfer to a bowl and slowly add the cream, stirring well to mix. Add salt and freshly ground black pepper to taste. Cut up the remaining peeled onions and spoon them over the top of the soup along with a drizzle of olive oil for garnish. Serve hot or at room temperature. (If not serving right away, you may need to add more water, as the soup will thicken.)

Sage- and Pancetta-Wrapped Prawns

<table>
<tr><td colspan="2" align="center">**Serves 4**</td></tr>
<tr><td colspan="2" align="center">**Carb Level: Low**</td></tr>
<tr><td colspan="2">Per serving:</td></tr>
<tr><td>Carbohydrate:</td><td>1.7 g</td></tr>
<tr><td>Protein:</td><td>46.4 g</td></tr>
</table>

Pancetta is a cured Italian bacon that is not smoked. It is available from Italian specialty stores and some supermarkets.

20 uncooked large prawns
10 slices thinly sliced pancetta
28 fresh sage leaves

80ml (2½fl oz) sherry vinegar or
  cider vinegar

1. Remove the shells and tails from the prawns, and de-vein them. Cut the slices of pancetta in half. Tear the sage leaves from the stems.
2. On a flat surface, lay out a half slice of pancetta. Place one large or two small leaves of sage on top, then place one prawn across the pancetta and sage. Roll the pancetta around the prawn and secure it closed with a toothpick (exposing the tail and head ends of the prawn). Repeat with the rest of the prawns.
3. Heat a medium-size non-stick frying pan on medium-high. Place half the rolled prawns in the pan (the pancetta should sizzle). Cook until the pancetta is light brown and crispy on each side. Place the prawns on paper towels to drain, and cover to keep warm. Repeat for the other half of the rolled prawns.
4. Immediately after all the prawns have been cooked, keeping the pan on the flame, pour in the sherry vinegar and cook down to a syrup-like consistency. Place the prawns on a platter and pour the hot reduced vinegar over them. Serve immediately.

Smoked Trout and Watercress Salad

6 small smoked trout fillets
3 large bunches fresh
    watercress

Salt
6 tbsp walnut oil
Freshly ground black pepper

Serves 6
Carb Level: Low

Per serving:	
Carbohydrate:	0.2 g
Protein:	16.8 g

Smoked trout is available in the refrigerated section at better fish and seafood counters.

1. Carefully the remove skin, if any, from the trout fillets. Cut each fillet in half longways; set aside. Wash the watercress and pat dry in paper towels. Trim off all but 25mm (1in) of the stem.
2. Bring 750ml (24fl oz) of water and ¼ teaspoon salt to a boil. Add half the watercress. Cook for 1 minute. Reserving 180ml (6fl oz) of the cooking liquid, drain the watercress immediately in a colander under cold running water.
3. Place the cooked watercress in the bowl of food processor and process slowly, adding (at a drizzle) the warm cooking water only until you have a thick paste. With the processor running, slowly add 4 tablespoons of the walnut oil. The dressing should be smooth and fairly thick. Add salt and freshly ground black pepper to taste. You will have about 180ml (6fl oz) dressing.
4. To assemble the salads, place portions of the remaining fresh watercress in the centre of six large chilled plates. Drizzle a little dressing over the watercress. Place two smoked trout pieces criss-crossed on top of the watercress. Drizzle the remaining dressing around the salad and across the centre of the trout. You can also serve the salad on a large platter and arrange the trout fillets in a star shape.

tips Simple Success with a Few Ingredients

Quality ingredients are the key to success with recipes that use only a few items. Buy fruit at the peak of ripeness, use only the freshest fish and choose high-quality cheeses. You won't be disappointed.

Spanish Stuffed Veal Chops

<table>
<tr><td>Serves 4</td></tr>
<tr><td>Carb Level: Low</td></tr>
</table>

Per serving:

Carbohydrate:	0.7 g
Protein:	37.3 g

This is a great grilling recipe. Using a tooth-pick to secure the filling makes the chops easier to turn while cooking.

Four 300g (10oz) 25mm (1in) thick veal rib chops
Salt and freshly ground black pepper to taste
225g (8oz) sheep's cheese
125g (4oz) coarsely chopped pimento-stuffed green olives
1 bunch chervil, leaves chopped

1. Preheat the grill. With a sharp knife, cut a 50mm (2in) wide horizontal pocket in the side of each chop. The pocket should be about 38–50mm (1½–2in) deep. Season the chops lightly on each side with salt and freshly ground black pepper.
2. Remove the rind from the cheese and discard. Cut the cheese into 6mm (¼in) cubes. Place the cheese, olives and chervil in a bowl and lightly season with salt and freshly ground black pepper; toss until evenly mixed.
3. Stuff each chop with about a quarter of the cheese mixture. Secure closed with a toothpick if necessary. Grill for about 3 minutes per side for medium-rare. (Increase cooking time by 2-minute increments per side for each of medium, medium-well and well-done.) Serve immediately. Top with any remaining cheese and olive mixture.

tips **The Vegetable Everyone Loves to Hate**
Brussels Sprouts – *a 60g (2oz) serving contains 2.6g of carbohydrates. Brussels sprouts are believed to have been cultivated in 16th-century Belgium. It is best to store unwashed sprouts in an airtight container for up to 3 days – any longer, and a strong, undesirable flavour will develop. Brussels sprouts are a cruciferous vegetable, high in vitamins A and C and a good source of iron.*

Tuna Steaks
with Wasabi-Coconut Sauce

*450g (13oz) tin unsweetened
  coconut milk*
½ tbsp wasabi powder
Salt

*Six 150g (5oz) 25mm (1in) thick
  tuna steaks (ahi or yellowtail
  sushi grade)*
Freshly ground black pepper

Serves 6
Carb Level: Low

Per serving:	
Carbohydrate:	2.5 g
Protein:	40.6 g

This sauce has a kick – you may want to serve it on the side if you don't know the tastes of your dining guests.

1. Mix together the coconut milk and wasabi powder in a saucepan using a wire whisk until the wasabi is thoroughly dissolved. Stand at room temperature for 30 minutes.
2. Bring the coconut-wasabi mixture to a simmer, whisking constantly. Lower heat to medium and reduce mixture to 375gm (12fl oz). This will take approximately 5 minutes. Add ¼ teaspoon salt and stir. Remove from heat.
3. Season each side of the tuna steaks with salt and freshly ground black pepper. Place two large non-stick frying pans over high heat. When very hot, almost smoking, add the tuna steaks. Cook for 2 minutes and turn. Cook for 1 to 2 minutes more, until the tuna is browned on the outside but still rare on the inside.
4. Remove the tuna from the pans and let stand for 1 minute. Reheat the coconut-wasabi sauce gently over low heat. Cut the tuna on the bias into 12mm (½ in) thick slices, pour the sauce over the fish and serve immediately.

Wine and Cheese Fondue

Serves 6
Carb Level: Low

Per serving:	
Carbohydrate:	3.5 g
Protein:	45.5 g

This is a great savoury fondue. Use a good-quality wine to enhance the flavour of the cheese.

900g (2lb) Gruyère cheese
1½ tbsp plain flour, divided
500ml (16fl oz) Chardonnay or
    other dry white wine

Salt
Freshly ground white pepper

1. Using a sharp knife, remove the rind, if any, from the cheese. Grate the cheese using the large holes of a box grater. Mix with 1½ tablespoons of the flour.
2. Place the floured cheese in a heavy medium-size saucepan (or fondue pot). Add the wine and ¼ teaspoon salt, and bring to a simmer, stirring frequently. Lower the heat to medium and stir vigorously with a wooden spoon until the cheese is completely melted, about 5 minutes. Add the remaining flour, stirring constantly. Cook for about 2 minutes, until the floury, starchy taste is gone.
3. The sauce should be smooth, thick and creamy. If it is too thick, add more wine that has been warmed first. Adjust seasoning to taste. Serve with fresh strawberries and grapes, vegetables or cooked chicken breast strips.

tips **Tuna Steaks**

When using fresh tuna steaks as a grilled entrée, consider grilling an extra steak and making your own grilled tuna salad. Season and cook the tuna steak until just done throughout, but not dried out. Allow to cool, wrap tightly and refrigerate. To make the salad, lightly flake the tuna and mix with your favourite dressing. You can make a mesquite-flavoured tuna salad by using a dry spice rub on the tuna before grilling. Experiment and add different flavouring ingredients such as capers, fresh dill, chopped chives or minced spring onions.

Lemon-Spiked Pineapple Smoothie

1 medium-size ripe pineapple
6 tbsp freshly squeezed lemon
*   juice, plus thinly sliced lemons*
*   for garnish*

Sugar substitute (optional)

Serves 6
Carb Level: Moderate

Per serving:	
Carbohydrate:	13.1 g
Protein:	0.4 g

1. Peel the pineapple and cut out the core. Cut the fruit into small pieces. Place in a food processor and process to a fairly smooth, pulpy consistency. Transfer to a large pitcher.
2. Add the lemon juice, 750ml (24fl oz) of cold water, and ¼ tablespoon at a time of sugar substitute to the desired sweetness, stirring until dissolved. Chill for several hours and serve in glasses over ice with a thin slice of lemon for garnish.

(tips) Just Plain Nuts

Toasted chopped nuts are always a nice addition to simple poultry and fish dishes. Here are the carb and protein counts per 60g (2oz) for some of our favourite nuts:

You can buy fresh pineapples already trimmed at larger supermarkets. Remember to check the freshness date when using this time-saving step.

	Carbohydrate	*Protein*
Almonds	*7.2g*	*7.1g*
Walnuts	*3.8g*	*7.6g*
Peanuts	*5.9g*	*9.4g*
Cashews	*9.2g*	*5.3g*
Pecans	*4.9g*	*2.1g*
Macadamia nuts	*4.6g*	*2.8g*

Pineapple-Ginger Smoothie

Serves 2	
Carb Level: Moderate	
Per serving:	
Carbohydrate:	19.3 g
Protein:	4.0 g

This is a refreshing drink for an outdoor dinner. Using wine glasses to serve 'dresses up' this non-alcoholic cocktail.

*250ml (8fl oz) unsweetened
    pineapple juice
125ml (4fl oz) plain yogurt
1½ tbsp grated fresh ginger*

*6–8 ice cubes
Ground cinnamon or ground
    nutmeg for garnish*

Put all the ingredients except the garnish in a blender; process on high until smooth and creamy and all the ice particles have disappeared. Add sugar substitute if desired. Serve immediately in chilled wine glasses. Sprinkle a little ground cinnamon or ground nutmeg on top for added spice.

Summer Berries

Use fresh berries when in season for smoothies. 60g (3oz) of fresh strawberries contains 5.25g of carbs and a great flavour punch.

French Entrées

❖ **Indicates Easy Recipe** ❖

Pork and Veal Pâté

Serves 6
Carb Level: Low

Per serving:

Carbohydrate:	2.4 g
Protein:	19.7 g

A French classic, this pâté has a crumbly mixture because it is not weighted during the cooling and setting process.

600g (1lb 4oz) pork shoulder or rump
225g (8oz) veal shoulder
1 small onion, peeled and chopped
225g (8oz) salted pork, finely chopped

⅛ tsp ground cloves
⅛ tsp ground cinnamon
Salt and freshly ground black pepper

1. With a sharp knife, finely chop the pork shoulder and veal to the texture of ground meat.
2. Put the chopped pork shoulder and veal, onions and 375ml (12fl oz) water in a large pot; cook over medium heat until the liquid has evaporated and the meat begins to brown, about 30 minutes.
3. Put the salted pork into a small saucepan; cook uncovered over medium heat, stirring often, until the fat has been rendered and the pork is golden brown, about 30 minutes.
4. Add the pork and rendered fat to the meat mixture along with the remaining ingredients. Transfer to a container with a cover and set aside to cool to room temperature. Cover and refrigerate for at least 2 hours before serving.

The Sophisticated Flavour of Shallots

Shallots can be used in much smaller quantities than onions for their strong flavour, in the same manner as onions. Shallots are used as a staple in French classic sauces and dressings. Two tablespoons of shallots contain 3.4g of carbohydrate. Two tablespoons of onions contains 1.7g of carbohydrate. Consider substituting small amounts of sautéed shallots in place of a larger quantity of onions for a more sophisticated taste.

Crêpes

2 large eggs
250ml (8fl oz) milk
80ml (2½fl oz) water
125g (4oz) flour

⅛ tsp salt
1 tbsp melted butter, plus 1 tsp
    butter for coating

<table>
<tr><td colspan="2">Serves 10</td></tr>
<tr><td colspan="2">Carb Level: Moderate</td></tr>
<tr><td colspan="2">Per serving:</td></tr>
<tr><td>Carbohydrate:</td><td>10.8 g</td></tr>
<tr><td>Protein:</td><td>3.4 g</td></tr>
</table>

An all-time favourite. Versatility is the key: great for breakfast, lunch or dinner at any time of year.

1. Place the eggs, milk, water, flour, salt and 2 tablespoons of melted butter in a blender and process until smooth.
2. Heat a non-stick 150–178mm (6–7in) crêpe pan over medium-high heat. Coat the pan lightly with butter. Lift the pan from the heat and pour in 1 or 2 tablespoons of batter, tilting and rotating the pan to coat the surface. Cook until almost dry on top and lightly browned around the edges. Loosen the edges with a rubber spatula and flip the crêpe over using your fingers or the spatula. Cook the other side for about 15 seconds. Turn the crêpe out onto a paper towel to cool and repeat with the remaining batter. You may need to add more butter to the pan.
3. After cooling, store between layers of waxed paper. If serving immediately, cover the crêpes with foil and keep them warm in a 110°C (200°F) oven.

tips

Crêpes

Crêpes originated in Brittany in the northwest of France. Crêpe is French for 'pancake'. Crêpes can be folded into various shapes for decorative presentation. Roll and slice them for attractive whirligigs for appetizers using the smoked salmon filling, or place the filling in the centre and fold in the edges on four sides for an open-face look. Of course you can always use the traditional rolled style for ease and simplicity.

Crêpe Fillings

Sausage and Cheese Filling

<table>
<tr><td colspan="2">Sausage
and Cheese Filling
Serves 6</td></tr>
<tr><td colspan="2">Carb Level: Low</td></tr>
<tr><td colspan="2">Per serving:</td></tr>
<tr><td>Carbohydrate:</td><td>2.7 g</td></tr>
<tr><td>Protein:</td><td>16.3 g</td></tr>
</table>

454g (1lb) spicy Italian sausage
125g (4oz) ricotta cheese
60g (2oz) grated Parmesan cheese
2 cloves garlic, crushed

Salt and freshly ground black pepper
Fresh chopped parsley (optional)

1. Heat a non-stick sauté pan over medium heat. Add the sausage and cook until lightly browned. Stir throughout the cooking process to break up the sausage into small pieces. Remove with a slotted spoon and transfer to a small mixing bowl. Add the remaining ingredients, mix well, and adjust seasoning as desired.
2. Preheat the oven to 170°C, 325°F, gas mark 3.
3. Spoon about 75–125g (2½–4oz) of filling in a ribbon down the centre of each crêpe and roll up. Arrange in a lightly oiled baking dish. Bake, partially covered, for about 15–18 minutes, until heated through. Garnish with parsley if desired and serve immediately.

Smoked Salmon and Ricotta Cheese Filling

<table>
<tr><td colspan="2">Smoked Salmon and
Ricotta Cheese Filling
Serves 6</td></tr>
<tr><td colspan="2">Carb Level: Low</td></tr>
<tr><td colspan="2">Per serving:</td></tr>
<tr><td>Carbohydrate:</td><td>3.0 g</td></tr>
<tr><td>Protein:</td><td>13.5 g</td></tr>
</table>

2 tbsp chopped fresh dill
90g (3oz) ricotta cheese
225g (8oz) cream cheese, softened at
　room temperature

1 tbsp chopped red onion
225g (8oz) smoked salmon
Salt and freshly ground black pepper

1. Mix together all the ingredients in a bowl.
2. Spoon about 75–125g (2½–4oz) of filling in a ribbon down the centre of each crêpe and roll up. Serve at room temperature. Slice into whirligigs for a great appetizer.

Crêpe Fillings (continued)

Three-Cheese Filling

2 eggs
75g (2¹/₂oz) Gruyère cheese, grated
125g (4oz) ricotta cheese
90g (3oz) goat's cheese
¹/₈ tsp freshly ground nutmeg

Salt and freshly ground black pepper
Chopped fresh herbs for garnish
   (optional)

Three-Cheese Filling Serves 6	
Carb Level: Low	
Per serving:	
Carbohydrate:	2.7 g
Protein:	17.3 g

1. Beat the eggs in a medium-size mixing bowl. Add the remaining ingredients and mix well.
2. Preheat the oven to 170°C, 325°F, gas mark 3.
3. Spoon about 75–125g (2½–4oz) of filling in a ribbon down the centre of each crêpe and roll up. Arrange in a lightly oiled baking dish. Bake, partially covered, for about 18–22 minutes, until the filling is cooked and heated through. Note that there is raw egg in the filling and you will want to actually 'cook' the filling. Garnish with chopped herbs, if desired, and serve immediately.

Ham and Asparagus Filling

185g (6oz) ricotta cheese
60g (2oz) grated Parmesan cheese
1 tsp chopped fresh tarragon
225g (8oz) sliced ham, chopped

680g (1¹/₂lb) asparagus spears, cleaned
   and cooked
Salt and freshly ground black pepper

Ham and Asparagus Filling Serves 6	
Carb Level: Low	
Per serving:	
Carbohydrate:	4.6 g
Protein:	11.0 g

1. Mix together the ricotta, Parmesan, tarragon and ham in a medium-size mixing bowl until thoroughly combined.
2. Preheat the oven to 170°C, 325°F, gas mark 3.
3. Spoon about 75–125g (2½–4oz) of filling in a ribbon down the centre of each crêpe. Top the filling with asparagus spears, with the tips just poking out of the ends. Roll up each crêpe and arrange in a lightly oiled baking dish. Bake, partially covered, for about 15–18 minutes, until heated through. Serve immediately.

Braised Dover Sole
with Béchamel and Vegetables

<table>
<tr><td colspan="2">Serves 4</td></tr>
<tr><td colspan="2">Carb Level: Moderate</td></tr>
<tr><td colspan="2">Per serving:</td></tr>
<tr><td>Carbohydrate:</td><td>17.9 g</td></tr>
<tr><td>Protein:</td><td>19.4 g</td></tr>
</table>

This is a beautiful presentation, worth the effort for an intimate dining setting with close friends.

1 tsp vegetable oil
1½ tsp unsalted butter, softened, divided
1 carrot, cut into strips
2 stalks celery, cut into strips
1 leek, white part only, washed well and cut into strips
Salt and freshly ground white pepper
½ tbsp minced shallots
185g (6oz) Dover sole fillets

250ml (8fl oz) dry white wine
125ml (4fl oz) chicken stock
1 recipe béchamel sauce (see following)
Juice of ½ lemon
½ tbsp chopped fresh flat-leaf parsley for garnish

1. Heat a large non-stick sauté pan over medium heat. Combine the oil and ½ teaspoon of the butter and heat until it starts to foam. Add the carrot, celery and leek. Sauté until just tender, remove from the heat and set aside. Season with salt and pepper.
2. Preheat the oven to 170°C, 325°F, gas mark 3. Using the rest of the butter, lightly brush the bottom of an ovenproof pan large enough to hold all the fish. Sprinkle the shallots on the bottom of the pan. Season both sides of the sole with salt and pepper. Place the fillets on top of the shallots, and add the wine and chicken stock.
3. Place the pan over high heat on the hob, uncovered, until the stock is simmering. Cover the pan with foil and transfer it to the oven for about 15 minutes or until the fillets have cooked through. To check that the fish is done, use a thin-bladed knife to poke into the centre of the thickest part of the fillet. The flesh should be firm and flaky, with no translucence.

(recipe continues on the next page)

Braised Dover Sole
with Béchamel and Vegetables (continued)

4. Using a long, slotted spatula, carefully lift the fillets from the pan and set aside. Strain the pan juices through a fine-mesh sieve into a medium-sized saucepan. Return the fillets to the pan and cover to keep warm. (Move the fish carefully, as the fillets will break apart if handled too roughly.)
5. Add the béchamel sauce to the saucepan and cook over medium heat. Whisk constantly for about 5 minutes or until the sauce has thickened. Whisk in the lemon juice and season with salt and pepper. Fold in the reserved vegetables and bring to a simmer.
6. Place each Dover sole fillet in the centre of a plate and pour the sauce and vegetables around the fish. Garnish with chopped parsley.

Béchamel Sauce

¾ tbsp cornflour
375ml (12fl oz) milk
3 whole cloves
½ small onion
1 bay leaf
Salt and freshly ground white pepper

1. Place the cornflour in a heavy-bottomed saucepan. Whisk in 125ml (4fl oz) of milk until very smooth. Whisk in the remaining milk. Stick the cloves in the onion and add to the saucepan along with the bay leaf.
2. Cook over low heat, uncovered and stirring frequently, for about 12–15 minutes, until the mixture is hot and well infused with the flavours of the onion, clove and bay leaf. The sauce should be fragrant. Increase the heat and simmer, stirring constantly, for about 5 minutes until it thickens. Strain and adjust seasoning to taste.

Mustard-Glazed Monkfish
Wrapped in Bacon

Serves 6

Carb Level: Low

Per serving:

Carbohydrate:	2.1 g
Protein:	17.6 g

You'll consider this a very easy recipe to prepare the second time – and this one is sure to be repeated.

---

12 slices apple-wood smoked or other good-quality bacon
Six 185g (6oz) monkfish fillets
90g (3oz) Dijon mustard

Salt and freshly ground black pepper
1 tbsp tarragon

1. Preheat the oven to 180°C, 350°F, gas mark 4.
2. Place the bacon on a non-stick baking tray and precook for about 8 minutes. The bacon should be almost fully cooked but still pliable. Drain the bacon on paper towels; discard the fat from the baking tray.
3. Make sure the monkfish is trimmed of all membranes and dark spots. Season the monkfish with salt and pepper. Rub each fillet with 2 tablespoons of the mustard to coat it completely.
4. Wrap each fillet with two slices of bacon, making sure the bacon doesn't overlap. Secure the bacon with toothpicks if necessary. Wrap each fillet tightly in cling film, twisting the ends closed, and refrigerate for about 1 hour.
5. Preheat the oven to 190°C, 375°F, gas mark 5.
6. Unwrap the fish and place on an oiled baking tray. Bake for about 20–25 minutes until the fish is almost cooked. Preheat the grill to high. To finish, place the fish under the grill for just about 30 seconds to get the bacon crisp.
7. Drizzle a bit of the natural pan juices over the fish and sprinkle with chopped tarragon. Serve immediately.

tips **Poor Man's Lobster?**

Monkfish has been described as the poor man's lobster, even though it has no resemblance to lobster whatsoever. Cooked properly, it has the texture of shellfish and does not have the 'flakiness' of most fish. Mild in flavour and moderately firm in texture, it is a hearty fish.

Chicken Breasts Chasseur

Four 185g (6oz) chicken breasts
    with skin and bones
Salt and freshly ground black pepper
4 tsp olive oil, divided
1 medium carrot, chopped
90g (3oz) chopped onion

500ml (16fl oz) beef broth
185g (6oz) sliced button mushrooms
2 shallots, crushed
2 tbsp cognac
80ml (2½fl oz) dry white wine
1 tbsp chopped fresh tarragon

Serves 4	
Carb Level: Low	
Per serving:	
Carbohydrate:	8.1 g
Protein:	30.4 g

This recipe forgives timing foul-ups. Keep the chicken covered in a warm oven; reheat the sauce and add the tarragon just before serving.

1. Preheat the oven to 180°C, 350°F, gas mark 4.
2. Season the chicken with salt and pepper. Heat 1 teaspoon of the oil in a large non-stick sauté pan over medium heat. Lay the chicken breasts skin side down in the pan; cook for about 4–5 minutes, or until the skin is golden brown. Transfer the chicken, skin side up, to a non-stick baking pan. Reserve the sauté pan.
3. Bake the chicken uncovered for 20 minutes or until the juices run clear when the chicken is pierced with a knife.
4. While the chicken is baking, remove most of the fat from the sauté pan. Place over medium heat and add the carrot and onion. Cook until the vegetables begin to caramelize. Add the beef stock and raise the heat to high. Bring to the boil, reduce the heat and simmer for 10 minutes uncovered. Strain the stock though a fine-mesh sieve into a small bowl.
5. Warm the remaining teaspoon of oil in the sauté pan over medium heat. Add the mushrooms and shallots, and sauté until the mushrooms are golden. Season with salt and pepper. Remove the pan from the heat and add the cognac. Carefully ignite the cognac with a long match. Allow the flame to burn out, then add the wine. Return the pan to the heat.
6. Bring to the boil over medium heat. Allow to simmer for about 5 minutes, until the liquid is reduced by half. Add the reserved stock and simmer for another 5 minutes or until the sauce has thickened. Stir in the chopped tarragon.
7. Serve the sauce on top of the breasts.

Red Snapper
with Cayenne Tomato Sauce

Serves 1

Carb Level: Low

Per serving:

Carbohydrate:	2.2 g
Protein:	26.9 g

You can also heat the sauce for a nice finishing touch.

1 tsp olive oil
140g (5oz) red snapper fillet with skin on
2 tbsp crème fraîche or sour cream
½ tbsp minced chives
½ tsp sun-dried tomato paste
¼ tsp cayenne pepper
1 tsp lemon juice
Salt and freshly ground black pepper to taste

1. Preheat the oven to 375°F, 190°C, gas mark 5.
2. Add the olive oil to a small ovenproof non-stick sauté pan over medium-high heat. Place the snapper fillet skin side down in the pan and cook until golden brown. Carefully turn the fillet over and place in the oven. Bake the snapper for about 6 minutes or until cooked through. To check it is done, insert a thin-bladed knife into the thickest part of the fillet. The flesh should be flaky, with no apparent translucence.
3. In a small bowl, mix together the crème fraîche, minced chives, tomato paste, cayenne and lemon juice. Season with salt and pepper.
4. Serve the sauce over the snapper fillet.

tips

What Is Clarified Butter?

Clarified butter is also known as ghee in Indian cooking. Clarifying butter separates the milk solids and evaporates the water, leaving a clear golden liquid. Clarified butter has a higher heating point before smoking, and also has a longer shelf life than regular butter. Clarified butter is used to sauté where a high heating point is needed.

Roast Duck with Lemon

3 lemons
Salt
Freshly ground black pepper
2kg (5lb) ready-to-cook duck
1½ tbsp butter

1 tsp sugar
2 tbsp white wine vinegar
500ml (16fl oz) tub chicken stock
3 tbsp dry sherry

Serves 6	
Carb Level: Low	
Per serving:	
Carbohydrate:	5.1 g
Protein:	28.7 g

Meat left over from the duck carcass can be used in a crêpe filling or as a duck salad on a bed of greens.

1. Preheat the oven to 190°C, 375°F, gas mark 5.
2. Cut the rind from two of the lemons as thinly as possible. Juice one lemon and set aside the juice. Separate the other lemon into segments and set aside. Cut the rind into narrow strips and cook in boiling water for 5 minutes. Rinse with cold water and pat dry.
3. Season the inside and outside of the duck with salt and pepper. Place half the lemon rind and half the butter in the cavity, then tie the legs together with a piece of butcher's twine. Place the duck on a rack in a roasting pan just large enough to hold the duck without the skin touching the sides.
4. Roast the duck uncovered for about 1 hour 15 minutes or until the leg meat begins to separate from the bone. (Cover the duck with a tent made of tin foil after about 45 minutes of cooking if the skin appears to be browning too rapidly.) Baste the duck with its natural juices during the roasting process. Let the duck stand for at least 30 minutes before carving.
5. In a medium-size saucepan over medium heat, cook the sugar and vinegar together, stirring often, until a caramel has formed. Add a little chicken stock and stir, scraping the bottom of the saucepan. Add the rest of the stock, the reserved lemon juice and the remaining lemon rind strips. Skim off the fat, add the dry sherry and any natural juices in the roasting pan from the duck; simmer over medium heat until the sauce is thick enough to coat the back of a spoon. Add the reserved lemon segments and the rest of the butter, and simmer for another 5 minutes.
6. To serve, present slices of breast meat on a warmed plate with a drizzle of sauce over the top, or serve full quarters of the duck with the sauce presented on the side. Garnish with lemon slices.

Grilled Lamb Chops
with Provençal Roasted Tomatoes

Serves 4
Carb Level: Low

Per serving:

Carbohydrate:	8.9 g
Protein:	41.0 g

Use ripe, sun-warmed tomatoes for the best flavour. They also work well with grilled steaks or chicken.

For the lamb:

3 cloves garlic, crushed (divided)
2 tbsp olive oil
1½ tsp fresh thyme leaves
4 sprigs fresh rosemary
Freshly ground black pepper
8 baby lamb chops
Salt

1. Place two of the crushed garlic cloves in a mixing bowl. Add the olive oil, thyme, rosemary and pepper; mix with a fork. Coat the lamb chops with the mixture and place them in a single layer in a shallow baking dish. Pour any remaining marinade over the chops. Cover and refrigerate for 4 hours.

Cooking with Wine
tips

Wines are often reduced and used as a flavouring agent for many classical French sauces. 250ml (8fl oz) of white wine reduced by half contains 1.9g of carbohydrates.

(recipe continues on the next page)

Grilled Lamb Chops
with Provençal Roasted Tomatoes (continued)

For the tomatoes:

4 large ripe tomatoes, halved crossways and seeded
1 tsp salt
1 tbsp grated Parmesan cheese
1 tbsp chopped fresh flat-leaf parsley
1 tsp fresh thyme leaves
3 tbsp olive oil
2 cloves garlic, crushed
Salt and freshly ground black pepper
4 sprigs fresh flatleaf parsley for garnish (optional)

1. Sprinkle the tomatoes with salt and put them cut-side down on a wire rack over a pan. Allow them to drain for about 15 minutes. In a small bowl combine the Parmesan, chopped parsley, thyme leaves, olive oil, garlic and salt and pepper; stir to combine.
2. Preheat the grill to high.
3. Place the tomatoes cut-side up into a small oiled baking dish just large enough to hold them. Sprinkle the tomatoes with the cheese and herb mixture. Grill for about 10 minutes or until the tomatoes have softened and the tops are golden brown. Cover with foil to keep warm.
4. Season both sides of the lamb chops with salt and pepper. Grill for 3 minutes on each side for medium-rare (warm, pink centre). Place two tomato halves in the centre of each warm dinner plate and lay two chops over the tomatoes. Garnish with parsley sprigs.

Baked Haddock
with Parsley and Lemon

Serves 2
Carb Level: Low

Per serving:	
Carbohydrate:	4.3 g
Protein:	49.3 g

Use the freshest fish you can get to make this recipe a sure hit.

1 egg beaten with 1 tbsp milk
454g (1lb) haddock fillet
1 tbsp freshly grated Parmesan
  cheese
½ tbsp breadcrumbs
1 tbsp olive oil
2 tbsp butter, divided

1 tbsp minced parsley
1 tsp grated lemon zest

1. Place the beaten egg mixture in a glass bowl and soak the fish in it for about 30 minutes, refrigerated.
2. Mix together the Parmesan and breadcrumbs. Remove the fish from the egg wash, shaking off any excess, and dip it into the breadcrumb mixture, lightly coating the fish.
3. Preheat the oven to 190°C, 375°F, gas mark 5.
4. In a medium-size non-stick sauté pan with an ovenproof handle, heat the oil and 1 tablespoon of the butter together over medium heat until it just starts to foam. Add the fish and lightly brown the fillet on both sides. Place the sauté pan in the oven and bake for about 8–10 minutes or until the fish is cooked through. To check that it is done, insert a thin-bladed knife into the thickest part of the fish. The flesh should be flaky, and there should be no trace of translucence.
5. Remove the fish from the sauté pan and keep it warm while preparing the sauce. Melt the remaining tablespoon of butter in the same sauté pan, scraping the bottom of the pan to loosen any browned bits from the fish. Add the parsley and lemon zest. Cook over medium heat, stirring constantly, until the butter is infused with the lemon flavour, about 1 to 2 minutes.
6. To serve, pour the butter sauce over each fillet and serve immediately.

Halibut with Porcini, Shallots and Tomatoes

180ml (6fl oz) clam juice
250ml (8fl oz) water
1 bay leaf
10 black peppercorns
2 cloves garlic, crushed and peeled
15g (½oz) dried porcini
    mushrooms
80ml (2½fl oz) olive oil
2 large shallots, crushed
125ml (4fl oz) dry white wine

2–3 sprigs fresh tarragon or
    ¼ tsp dried tarragon
Salt and freshly ground black pepper
    taste
225g (8oz) roughly chopped fresh or
    tinned plum tomatoes (drained if
    tinned)
Four 225g (8oz) halibut steaks

Serves 4

Carb Level: Moderate

Per serving:

Carbohydrate:	19.6 g
Protein:	44.5 g

To make this recipe easier to prepare, pre-measure and organize the ingredients before you begin.

1. Combine the clam juice, water, bay leaf, peppercorns and garlic in a medium-size saucepan. Bring to a boil and simmer gently uncovered over medium heat for about 10 minutes. Strain, discard the solids and set the stock aside.

2. Soak the dried porcini mushrooms in 125ml (4fl oz) of the prepared stock. Heat the olive oil in a large sauté pan over medium heat. Add the shallots and cook until tender. Drain and chop the porcini (save and strain the mushroom soaking liquid) and add them to the shallots. Cook for about 1 minute. Add the wine, tarragon, mushroom soaking liquid and the rest of the prepared stock. Bring to the boil and simmer until reduced by half.

3. Season the sauce with salt and pepper and add the tomatoes. Cook over medium heat for 2 to 3 minutes. Add the halibut fillets to the pan, cover and simmer gently for about 5 minutes. Halibut is delicate, so be careful not to overcook it. To check that it is done, insert a thin-bladed knife into the thickest part of the fish. The flesh should be flaky, and there should be no trace of translucence.

4. Use a large slotted spoon to move the fish to a warm platter. Adjust the seasoning of the sauce to taste. Add some fresh squeezed lemon juice if desired. After the fish is removed, the stock may be simmered uncovered over medium heat to concentrate the flavours. To serve, spoon the warm sauce over the fillets.

Lemon Chicken

Serves 4
Carb Level: Low

Per serving:

Carbohydrate:	7.8 g
Protein:	50.0 g

The lemon combined with the richness of skin-on roast chicken is a true treat.

1.8kg (4lb) roasting chicken
Salt and freshly ground black pepper
3 lemons
6 cloves garlic, peeled
½ medium onion, cut in half
Olive oil

1. Preheat the oven to 190°C, 375°F, gas mark 5.
2. Rinse the chicken and pat dry. Salt and pepper the inside cavity of the chicken. Pierce the lemons all over with a fork and place them in the cavity along with the garlic and onion pieces. Truss the chicken by tying the legs together with a piece of butcher's twine and tucking in the wing tips to keep them from overcooking. Rub the chicken with olive oil, and season with salt and freshly ground black pepper. Place the chicken on a rack in a baking dish just large enough to hold the chicken without it touching the sides.
3. Bake for about 1–1½ hours, until the leg meat pulls easily from the bone. Check the chicken occasionally during the cooking process, and baste it with the natural juices from the pan. (Make a tent out of tin foil and place it over the chicken if the skin seems to be browning too rapidly.)
4. When the chicken is ready, discard the stuffing and let the chicken stand covered with a tin-foil tent for about 10–15 minutes. Carve and serve with the natural pan juices.

tips A Twist on the Sauce

Whisk a touch of double cream with a pinch of cayenne pepper in with the natural pan juices to richen the sauce. Don't forget to pick up all the caramelized brown bits at the bottom of the roasting pan for the best flavour. Heat the sauce and simmer it for a few minutes to slightly thicken, and to allow the flavours to blend fully.

Beef Provençal

125g (4oz) bacon, chopped

900g (2lb) boneless chuck or rump roast, cut into 50mm (2in) cubes

Salt and freshly ground black pepper to taste

2 medium onions, peeled and quartered

1 small fennel bulb, trimmed and thinly sliced

1 head garlic, separated into cloves and peeled

6 large strips of orange zest, pith removed

1 bay leaf

Pinch of dried basil

Pinch of dried thyme

Pinch of dried parsley

250ml (8fl oz) red wine (Merlot or Cabernet)

250ml (8fl oz) beef broth

12 whole black olives, stoned (Mediterranean style preferably)

Serves 4

Carb Level: Moderate

Per serving:

Carbohydrate:	13.7 g
Protein:	48.7 g

Great for advance preparation – the flavours improve if allowed to stand refrigerated overnight. Or freeze portions to save for even longer.

1. Using a large sauté pan with a lid, cook the bacon over medium heat until crispy. Remove the bacon with a slotted spoon and set aside. Remove half the bacon fat and reserve it. Season the beef with salt and pepper.
2. Heat the pan over medium-high heat and cook the onions until lightly browned. Add the meat and brown on all sides. Add additional bacon fat as needed. Remove the meat and onions and any accumulated juices, and set aside.
3. Reheat the sauté pan over medium-high heat with a little more of the bacon fat. Add the fennel, garlic cloves, orange zest, bay leaf and dried herbs. Cook until the vegetables are tender. Add the meat and onions, red wine and beef stock. Bring the stew to a simmer and cook covered over very low heat. Braise for about 2 hours or until the meat begins to fall apart. Skim off any fat that rises to the top.
4. Serve the stew in warm bowls garnished with the olives and the crispy bacon.

Trout Grenobloise

Serves 4

Carb Level: Moderate

Per serving:

Carbohydrate:	14.9 g
Protein:	18.2 g

Keep the cream from curdling by using it at room temperature, keeping the pan off the heat and adding the cream slowly.

1 lemon
Four 125g (4z) trout fillets, boned and scaled
Salt and freshly ground black pepper to taste
1 tsp vegetable oil
1 tsp, plus 1 tbsp unsalted butter
1 tbsp capers, well drained
1 tbsp chopped fresh flat-leaf parsley

3 tbsp double cream, room temperature
4 slices lemon for garnish
4 sprigs fresh flatleaf parsley for garnish

1. Peel the lemon, removing all the white pith. Cut the flesh into small dice, discarding any seeds.
2. Season the trout fillets with salt and pepper and keep refrigerated until ready to use.
3. Combine the oil and 1 teaspoon of the butter in a large non-stick sauté pan over medium-high heat. When the pan is hot, place the fillets skin side down in the pan. Cook for about 1–1½ minutes, until golden brown. Carefully turn the fillets over with a long spatula and cook for another 2 minutes or until cooked through.
4. Transfer the fillets to warm plates and keep in a warm spot.
5. Wipe the interior of the sauté pan with a paper towel. Return the pan to medium heat and add the remaining tablespoon of butter. Cook until the butter just begins to brown. Remove the pan from the heat and stir in the capers, parsley and diced lemon. Very slowly add the cream a few drops at a time, and whisk to incorporate. Return the pan to the heat just to warm the sauce through.
6. Spoon the mixture over the trout fillets and garnish with a slice of lemon and a sprig of parsley.

Veal Stew Blanquette

680g (1lb 8oz)) veal stew meat,
    trimmed of all fat and cut into
    25mm (1in) cubes
Salt
1 small onion, quartered with root
    intact
1 stalk celery, cut in half longways
½ leek, white part only, washed well
    and cut in half longways
1 clove garlic, crushed
2 sprigs fresh thyme

2 sprigs fresh flatleaf parsley
1 bay leaf
½ tsp paprika
Freshly ground black pepper
½ tsp unsalted butter
½ tbsp cornflour
375ml (12fl oz) milk
60ml (2fl oz) sour cream
1 tbsp chopped fresh flatleaf parsley
    for garnish

Serves 4	
Carb Level: Moderate	
Per serving:	
Carbohydrate:	12.3 g
Protein:	39.5 g

This French classic usually includes onions, eliminated here to keep the carb count within reason.

1. To blanch the veal, rinse the veal cubes under cold running water. Place enough cold water in a large saucepan to cover the veal by about 25mm (1in), and bring to the boil over high heat. Add the veal for 2 minutes. Remove the pan from the heat and drain well. Rinse the veal under cold running water. Rinse out the saucepan.
2. Return the veal to the saucepan and add cold water to cover by about 25mm (1in). Season with salt. Bring just to a simmer over medium-high heat. Do not allow the mixture to boil. Skim off and discard any fat.
3. Add the onion, celery, leek, garlic, thyme, parsley sprigs, bay leaf, paprika and pepper. Bring to a simmer over medium-high heat. Reduce the heat to medium-low and allow the stew to simmer for 45–60 minutes or until the veal is very tender.
4. Strain the veal mixture though a colander, reserving the cooking liquid. Transfer the veal to a plate.
5. Strain the liquid through a fine-mesh sieve into a large saucepan. Add butter and bring to a simmer over medium heat.
6. Place the cornflour in a small bowl. Gradually whisk in the milk until smooth. Whisk into the cooking liquid and bring to the boil. When the liquid has thickened, add the reserved veal. Cook until heated through. Gently stir in the sour cream.
7. Ladle stew into warm shallow bowls and garnish with the chopped parsley.

Italian Food

❖ **Indicates Easy Recipe** ❖

Open Mushrooms Stuffed
with Basil and Salmon on Rocket Leaves

Serves 2
Carb Level: Low

Per serving:	
Carbohydrate:	7.3 g
Protein:	28.2 g

Baby organic rocket leaves have a mild peppery bite and wonderful texture that complement this dish.

2 large open mushroom caps
3 tsp sunflower oil or light olive oil
Salt and freshly ground black pepper to taste
2 tbsp minced spring onions
2 cloves garlic, crushed
10g (¼oz) fresh basil leaves, cut into strips
2 tbsp cream cheese
225g (salmon, skinned, boned and chopped into medium cubes
300g (10oz) fresh rocket leaves, de-stemmed

1. Preheat the oven to 190°C, 375°F, gas mark 5.
2. Brush the mushrooms with the oil and season with salt and pepper. Place the mushrooms on a foil-covered baking tray, lightly oiled, stem side up. Roast for about 20–30 minutes, until tender when pierced with a fork, but not shrivelled.
3. Mix together the spring onion, garlic, basil and cream cheese in a small bowl. Split the salmon into two equal portions and place each piece on a mushroom cap. Top with the cream cheese mixture. Season with salt and freshly ground black pepper.
4. Bake the stuffed mushroom uncovered for about 20–25 minutes, until the cream cheese is bubbling and starting to brown on top and the salmon is cooked through. Serve each mushroom cap on a bed of rocket leaves.

Green Facts

Rocket is also known as arugula. The tender baby leaves are best, featuring a peppery bite. The larger leaves are somewhat bitter. Fresh rocket contains a fair amount of grit, so the leaves should be rinsed several times before using. Rocket is a good source of iron as well as vitamins A and C.

Veal Cutlets
with Ricotta Cheese and Spinach

*375g (12oz) veal scaloppini
    (pounded veal escalopes)*
*2 eggs beaten with a pinch of salt
    and pepper*
2 tbsp butter
*300g (10oz) frozen chopped
    spinach, thawed, drained and
    moisture squeezed out*
2 cloves garlic, crushed

60g (2oz) ricotta cheese
3 tbsp sour cream
Pinch of freshly grated nutmeg
*Salt and freshly ground black pepper
    to taste*
*½ tbsp freshly grated Parmesan
    cheese, plus extra for garnish*

Serves 2
Carb Level: Low

Per serving:	
Carbohydrate:	9.5 g
Protein:	46.0 g

Ricotta is a rich fresh cheese, with 3.8 carbohydrates per 60g (2oz). It is slightly grainy but smoother and a touch sweeter than cottage cheese.

1. Soak the veal in the beaten egg for 30 minutes.
2. Melt the butter in a large sauté pan over medium-high heat; sauté the spinach and garlic uncovered for about 3–5 minutes. Season with salt and pepper. Remove the spinach from the pan and set aside.
3. Preheat the oven to 190°C, 375°F, gas mark 5.
4. In a large non-stick frying pan, over low heat, add half of the veal slices one at a time, and cook just long enough to set the egg coating on both sides. Remove the slices as they are done and place in a 1.7l (64fl oz) ovenproof casserole dish.
5. Put the ricotta and sour cream in a food processor (or a blender) with a pinch of nutmeg, salt and pepper and the grated Parmesan; blend until smooth. Spread half the cheese mixture over the veal with the back of a spoon. Layer half the spinach on top.
6. Cook the rest of the scaloppini and layer it on top of the spinach in the casserole dish. Layer the other half of the spinach and spread the rest of the cheese on top. Bake for about 30 minutes or until the cheese topping is set. Cut and serve like a lasagna, or scoop with a large spoon. Sprinkle a little Parmesan cheese on top to garnish.

Grilled Scallops
with Apple-Wood Smoked Bacon

Serves 4
Carb Level: Low

Per serving:	
Carbohydrate:	3.4 g
Protein:	19.4 g

This is a delicious appetizer or first-course dish. If serving as an appetizer, use skewers instead of toothpicks.

6 slices apple-wood smoked bacon, cut in half
12 large scallops, patted dry
1 tbsp finely grated lemon zest
1 sprig fresh rosemary, finely minced
75g (3½oz) stoned and chopped black olives
2 plum tomatoes, peeled, seeded and diced
1 tbsp drained capers
1 clove garlic, chopped
1½ tbsp chopped fresh chives
Extra-virgin olive oil

1. Preheat the oven to 180°C, 350°F, gas mark 4.
2. Place the bacon on a non-stick baking tray and precook for about 8 minutes. The bacon should be almost fully cooked but still pliable. Drain the bacon on paper towels; discard the fat from the baking tray. Lay the bacon slices on a clean, flat work surface. Sprinkle the scallops with the lemon zest and rosemary and place one on each piece of bacon. Wrap the bacon around the scallop and secure with a toothpick.
3. Mix the next four ingredients and 1 tablespoon of the chives in a small bowl. Pour in enough olive oil to glaze the mixture together, and mix to combine.
4. Brush the wrapped scallops with the olive oil and brown under a hot grill, or fry in a hot non-stick skillet for 1–2 minutes on each side, until slightly caramelized. Remove the toothpick and serve the scallops with a dollop of the olive relish. Sprinkle with the remaining chives.

Antipasto Platters

tips

Antipasto literally means 'before the food'. These dishes are traditionally served before a hearty pasta course, but can also be a main course all on their own. The platters should include cheeses; marinated, roasted or grilled vegetables; smoked meats; and olives. The platter may also include fish or shellfish.

Veal Osso Buco

4 veal shank cross cuts, about 38mm (1½in) thick (osso buco)
Salt and freshly ground black pepper to taste
Oil for cooking
3 tbsp unsalted butter
1 carrot, sliced
1 stalk celery, sliced
1 onion, sliced
4 cloves garlic, chopped
8 tomatoes, peeled, seeded and chopped
250ml (8fl oz) dry white wine
2 bay leaves
3 sprigs fresh thyme
860ml (32fl oz) beef stock or water
1 tbsp chopped fresh parsley
½ tsp finely grated orange zest
½ tsp finely grated lemon zest

Serves 4	
Carb Level: Moderate	
Per serving:	
Carbohydrate:	19.6 g
Protein:	51.1 g

Time is the key ingredient in making this classic, which is a staple menu item in Italian restaurants.

1. Preheat the oven to 180°C, 350°F, gas mark 4.
2. Trim the meat of any excess fat. Season with salt and pepper. In a covered cookpot, heat a little oil over high heat and brown the veal on both sides, in batches if necessary. Remove the shanks from the cookpot and set aside.
3. Reduce the heat to medium-high and melt the butter in the same pot; cook the carrot, celery and onion for 3 minutes. Add the garlic and mix well. Add the chopped tomatoes and cook for 5 minutes. Add the white wine, bay leaves and thyme sprigs; cook for another 5 minutes. Add the stock and the browned meat; bring to a simmer, season with salt and pepper, and cover. Transfer to the oven and bake for 1½ hours or until the meat is tender (the shank should begin to fall apart somewhat).
4. Use a slotted spoon to transfer the meat to a serving platter, cover and keep warm. Return the cookpot to the hob. Heat the cooking liquid and vegetables, and bring to the boil. Skim off any fat or foam that rises to the top. Cook for 20–25 minutes or until the sauce has thickened and coats the back of the spoon. Stir in the parsley, orange and lemon zest, and season to taste. Simmer for another 5 minutes, then pour over the meat and serve immediately.

Venetian Liver and Onions

Serves 4
Carb Level: Moderate

Per serving:

Carbohydrate:	11.6 g
Protein:	21.2 g

Liver is a great source of protein, vitamin A and iron.

454g (1lb) calf's liver, sliced into medallions
Vegetable oil for cooking
2 medium-size onions, thinly sliced

Salt and freshly ground black pepper to taste

1. Make sure the liver is completely free of veins and remove any of the membrane that may still be attached. (Usually your butcher will do this for you.)
2. Heat 2–3 tablespoons of oil in a large non-stick frying pan on high heat, and add the onion and a large pinch of salt. Reduce to medium heat and cook for 20–30 minutes or until the onions are completely soft and golden brown. Remove the onions from the pan and set aside.
3. Add a little more oil to the pan if necessary, and heat until almost smoking. Fry the liver in small batches, just enough to cover the base of the pan, for about 1–2 minutes or until it has changed colour from pink to brown. (*Hint:* Make sure your pan is very hot, as the liver must fry quickly to ensure that it does not stick or overcook.) Turn the medallions and cook for about 1 minute. Transfer each batch to a warm plate, and season to taste with salt and pepper.
4. Return all the liver to the pan, add the cooked onions, and toss to combine, but do not cook further. Transfer to a warm serving plate and serve immediately.

Rabbit and Herb Stew

1.2kg (2lb 8oz)) rabbit, cut into
   8 pieces
125g (4oz) plain flour, seasoned
   with salt and pepper
125ml (4fl oz) vegetable oil
1 onion, finely chopped
60g (2oz) sliced button mushrooms
½ tsp tomato paste
1 clove garlic, chopped

Salt and freshly ground black pepper
   to taste
500ml (16fl oz) chicken stock
8 ripe tomatoes, peeled, seeded and
   chopped
15g (½oz) chopped fresh herbs (rosemary, marjoram, parsley etc.)

Serves 4	
Carb Level: Moderate	
Per serving:	
Carbohydrate:	16.7 g
Protein:	14.1 g

Many supermarkets carry rabbit in the freezer section. You can prepare this stew ahead and allow the flavours to blend overnight.

1. Coat the rabbit in the flour, shaking off any excess. Heat about 125ml (4fl oz) oil in a large frying pan on high heat. Brown the rabbit on all sides. Remove from the pan with a slotted spoon and drain on paper towels. (Cook the rabbit in batches if necessary to avoid crowding the pan.) Drain excess oil from the pan.
2. Add the onion to the pan and cook over low heat until soft. Increase heat and add the mushrooms. Continue to cook, stirring frequently, for about 5 minutes. Add the tomato paste and garlic, and stir to mix. Transfer to a flameproof casserole dish or a Dutch oven, add the rabbit and season with the salt and pepper.
3. Add the stock (it should be enough to barely cover the rabbit) and simmer gently on the hob for 45 minutes.
4. Add the tomatoes and cook for another 10 minutes. Add the chopped fresh herbs and season to taste. (The meat should be tender and coming off the bone.) Serve the meat on a platter or on individual dishes with the sauce spooned over.

tips Fresh or Dried Herbs?

Fresh herbs have delicate and intense flavours. They should be added to a dish at the end of the cooking process to preserve their flavour. Dried herbs have a stronger, more concentrated flavour, so you'll want to add them early in the preparation of a dish. Crush them before adding them, to extract more of their flavour.

Chicken Cacciatore

Serves 4
Carb Level: Moderate

Per serving:	
Carbohydrate:	17.4 g
Protein:	46.1 g

The vegetables increase the carb count on this recipe to a moderate level.

60ml (2fl oz) olive oil
1.5kg (3lb 8oz) chicken, cut into 8 pieces
Salt and freshly ground black pepper
2 medium onions, thinly sliced into rings
3 cloves garlic, finely chopped
125g (4oz) thinly sliced button mushrooms
1 small green pepper, thinly sliced

60ml (2fl oz) tomato paste
180ml (6fl oz) dry white wine
454g (1lb) tinned plum tomatoes
¼ tsp dried rosemary
¼ tsp dried oregano
Freshly grated Parmesan cheese for garnish

1. Heat the olive oil in a large frying pan on high heat to almost smoking. Season the chicken with salt and pepper, and fry it skin side down for 5 minutes or until lightly browned. Turn over and brown the other side. Remove the chicken pieces with a slotted spoon and set aside.

2. Reduce the heat to medium. Add the onions to the pan and cook for 5 minutes, then add the garlic, mushrooms and green pepper. Cook for another 3–4 minutes or until the onions are golden, stirring frequently. Mix in the tomato paste and white wine and cook for 1–2 minutes, then add the tomatoes, breaking them down with a wooden spoon. Sprinkle in the rosemary and oregano and return the chicken to the pan. Season with salt and pepper, cover and simmer for 30 minutes, stirring occasionally.

3. Check the chicken to ensure it is cooked and tender. If it is still resistant when pierced with a fork, cover and cook for another 10 minutes. The leg meat should easily pull away from the bone. Using a slotted spoon, transfer the chicken pieces to a serving plate; keep warm. If the sauce appears too liquid, allow it to lightly boil uncovered for 5 minutes to slightly thicken. Season to taste, then pour over the chicken. Serve immediately. Garnish with freshly grated Parmesan cheese.

Baked Ocean Perch
with Black Olives and Capers

60ml (2fl oz) olive oil
6 tbsp butter, divided
1 tsp dried oregano
Freshly ground black pepper
*1kg (2lb) ocean perch, cleaned
    with skin on*
*1½ tbsp capers, thoroughly washed
    and drained*

1 tbsp sliced black olives
Salt
2 tbsp lemon juice
*1 tbsp finely chopped fresh flatleaf
    parsley*

Serves 4
Carb Level: Low

Per serving:	
Carbohydrate:	2.1 g
Protein:	16.3 g

Delicate ocean perch is perfectly set in this great trio of Mediterranean flavours.

1. In a large non-stick frying pan heat the oil and 2 tablespoons of the butter over medium heat until it begins to sizzle. Stir in the oregano and a few grindings of black pepper. Add the fish, skin side down. Cook for about 3–4 minutes on each side. With a slotted spatula, carefully transfer the fish to a heated platter.

2. Reduce the heat to low and add the remaining 4 tablespoons of butter to the pan; heat until it turns a light amber brown, but be careful not to burn it. Stir in the capers and olives. Remove the pan from the heat and stir in the lemon juice and parsley. Gently heat and stir to mix; pour over the fish and serve immediately

tips **The Flavour of a Caper**
Capers have an intense, salty taste that lends a burst of flavour to many sauces and condiments. They are usually stored and sold in brine, and should be rinsed in cold running water before use.

Chicken Breast Paillards Layered with Prosciutto and Cheese

Serves 4
Carb Level: Low

Per serving:

Carbohydrate:	7.2 g
Protein:	112.6 g

You can use any left-overs from this dish the next day sliced on top of a salad for an antipasto-style treat.

Four 225g (8oz.) skinless, boneless chicken breasts
Salt and freshly ground black pepper to taste
1½ tbsp plain flour
3 tbsp butter
2 tbsp oil

Eight thin 100 x 50mm (4 x 2in) slices prosciutto
Eight thin 100 x 50mm (4 x 2in)slices imported Bel Paese or fontina cheese
2 tsp freshly grated imported Parmesan cheese
60ml (2fl oz) chicken stock

1. Preheat the oven to 180°C, 350°F, gas mark 4.
2. With a very sharp knife, carefully slice each chicken breast horizontally to make eight thin slices. Lay them 25mm (1in) or so apart between two sheets of wax paper. Beat the chicken slices lightly with the flat side of a cleaver or the bottom of a heavy bottle to flatten them somewhat. Strip off the paper.
3. Season the slices with salt and a few grindings of black pepper, then dip them in flour and shake off the excess. In a heavy, large non-stick frying pan, melt the butter with the oil over moderate heat. Brown the chicken (both sides) to a light golden colour, three or four slices at a time. Do not overcook them.
4. Transfer the chicken paillards to a shallow buttered baking dish large enough to hold them without overcrowding. Place a slice of prosciutto and then a slice of cheese on each. Sprinkle them with the Parmesan, and drizzle the chicken stock over the top. Bake uncovered in the middle of the oven for 10 minutes or until the cheese is melted and lightly browned. Serve immediately.

Tuscan Lamb Chops

*Four 25mm (1in) thick lamb rib
    chops (680g/1lb 8oz total)*
2 tsp olive oil
3 cloves garlic, crushed
*225g (8oz) tin Italian-style stewed
    tomatoes, undrained*

1 tbsp balsamic vinegar
1 tsp finely chopped fresh rosemary

Serves 2	
Carb Level: Moderate	
Per serving:	
Carbohydrate:	12.8 g
Protein:	64.9 g

Classic flavours blend well in this easy, one-pan dinner entrée.

1. Trim any excess fat from the chops. Heat the oil in a large non-stick sauté pan over medium-high heat. Cook the chops for about 6 minutes on each side, turning once. Transfer the chops to a plate; keep warm.
2. Stir the garlic into the drippings in the pan; cook, stirring constantly, for 1 minute. Add the tomatoes, vinegar and rosemary. Bring to the boil; reduce the heat and simmer uncovered for 3 minutes or until it is a fairly thick consistency. Spoon the sauce over the chops and serve immediately.

Veal Scallops with Marsala Wine

Serves 4

Carb Level: Low

Per serving:

Carbohydrate:	5.2 g
Protein:	23.7 g

Marsala wine is fortified with brandy and is commonly used in cooking.

680g (1lb 8oz) veal scallops, sliced 10mm (³⁄₈in) thick
Salt and freshly ground black pepper
1½ tbsp plain flour
2 tbsp butter
3 tbsp olive oil
125ml (4fl oz) dry Marsala wine
125ml (4fl oz) chicken or beef stock, divided
2 tbsp butter, softened

1. Beat the veal scallops until 6mm (¼in) thick. Season with salt and pepper, then dip them in flour and vigorously shake off the excess. In a large non-stick frying pan, melt 2 tablespoons of butter with the olive oil over medium heat. When the foam subsides, add the scallops three or four at a time, and brown them for about 3 minutes on each side. As they are done, transfer them to a plate; keep warm.

2. Pour off most of the fat from the pan, leaving a thin film on the bottom (keeping all the browned meat scraps). Add the Marsala and 60ml (2fl oz) of stock and boil the liquid briskly over high heat for 1–2 minutes to deglaze the pan. Return the veal to the pan, cover and simmer over low heat for 10–15 minutes.

3. Transfer the veal scallops to a heated platter. Add the remaining stock to the skillet with the wine-stock mixture and boil briskly, scraping in the browned bits sticking to the sides of the pan. When the sauce has reduced considerably and has the consistency of a syrupy glaze, add salt and pepper to taste. Remove the pan from the heat, stir in the soft butter and pour the sauce over the scallops. Serve immediately.

Storing Butter

Butter rapidly absorbs flavours. Regular butter can be stored in the refrigerator for up to 1 month if wrapped airtight. Unsalted butter should be stored for no longer than 2 weeks in the refrigerator.

Broiled Marinated Steak-Bistecca

180ml (6fl oz) olive oil
60ml (2fl oz) red wine vinegar
1 tbsp finely chopped fresh flatleaf
   parsley
¼ tsp finely chopped garlic
¼ tsp dried oregano

1.3kg (3lb) 25mm (1in) thick
   T-bone, porterhouse or
   sirloin steak
Salt and freshly ground black pepper
   to taste

Serves 4	
Carb Level: Low	
Per serving:	
Carbohydrate:	1.2 g
Protein:	48.8 g

These steaks also
work well on the grill.

1. In a shallow baking dish large enough to hold the steak comfortably, combine the olive oil, vinegar, parsley, garlic and oregano. Lay the steak in the marinade and turn it to coat both sides completely. Leave the steak to marinate for at least 6 hours in the refrigerator, turning it every so often.
2. Preheat the grill.
3. Remove the steak from the baking dish (discard the marinade). Grill it 75mm (3in) from the heat for about 4 minutes on each side or until it is done to your taste. Remove from the grill and sprinkle with salt and pepper. Let the steak stand for 5 minutes before carving. Slice into 12mm (½ in) strips, cutting slightly on the bias. Transfer the steak to a warmed platter and serve immediately.

(tips) The Lowdown on Olive Oil

The best-quality olive oil is cold-pressed extra-virgin. Cold pressing is a natural, chemical-free process that involves only pressure and no additives. The result is an olive oil with low acidity.

Pork Chops Braised in White Wine

Serves 4

Carb Level: Low

Per serving:

Carbohydrate:	1.4 g
Protein:	29.9 g

Great served with Creamed Spinach (see recipe on page 138).

½ tbsp chopped fresh sage leaves
½ tbsp chopped fresh rosemary leaves
½ tbsp chopped fresh basil leaves
½ tsp finely chopped garlic
½ tsp salt
Freshly ground black pepper
4 tbsp olive oil, divided

Four 25mm (1in) thick centre-cut loin pork chops
2 tbsp butter
180ml (6fl oz) dry white wine, divided
½ tbsp finely chopped fresh Italian flatleaf parsley

1. In a medium-size mixing bowl combine the sage, rosemary, basil, garlic, salt and a few grindings of pepper with 2 tablespoons of the olive oil. Place the chops in the herb mixture, ensuring both sides are evenly coated. In a large, heavy-bottomed frying pan, melt the butter with the remaining 2 tablespoons of olive oil over medium heat. When the foam subsides, add the chops and brown them for 2–3 minutes on each side, turning them carefully with tongs. When the chops are golden brown, remove them from the pan to a platter; keep warm.

2. Pour off all but a thin film of fat from the bottom of the pan, retaining the browned bits on the bottom of the pan. Add 125ml (4fl oz) of the white wine and bring to the boil to deglaze the pan. Return the chops to the pan, cover, and reduce the heat to the barest simmer. Cook the chops for 25–30 minutes, or until they are tender when pierced with the tip of a sharp knife.

3. Transfer the chops to a heated serving platter. Add the remaining wine to the pan. Boil it briskly over high heat, stirring and scraping in any brown bits that cling to the bottom and sides of the pan, until it has reduced to a few tablespoons of syrupy glaze. Remove the skillet from the heat. Adjust seasoning to taste and stir in the parsley. Pour the sauce over the pork chops and serve.

Tomato Sauce

1 medium onion chopped
3 cloves garlic, finely chopped
3 tbsp extra-virgin olive oil
830g (1lb 12oz)) tin crushed
    tomatoes in purée
430g (15oz) tin tomato sauce with
    no added sugar

½ tsp bicarbonate of soda
15g (½oz) fresh chopped herbs,
    including basil, thyme and
    parsley
Salt and freshly ground black pepper
    to taste

Makes 1.25l (40fl oz)	
Carb Level: Low	
Per serving:	
Carbohydrate:	8.1 g
Protein:	1.5 g

A great simple sauce that freezes well. It makes a nice topping for red meats or chicken.

1. In a medium-size frying pan sauté the onion and garlic in the olive oil over medium heat until tender. Add the crushed tomatoes and tomato sauce, stirring to mix. Continue to stir to prevent scorching.
2. Add the bicarbonate of soda and fresh herbs, continuing to stir. Lower the heat to a simmer, and add salt and pepper to taste. Simmer for 15 minutes, stirring frequently.

(tips) The Carb Counts of Tomatoes

Tomato juice 180ml (6oz)	8g
Red, ripe raw tomatoes 185g (6oz)	8g
Tinned tomatoes 185g (6oz)	16g
Tinned tomato sauce 125ml (4fl oz)	9g
Tinned tomato paste 60ml (2fl oz)	12.5g

Mexican Specialities

❖ **Indicates Easy Recipe** ❖

Chickens Stuffed
with Chorizo and Spinach

Serves 4

Carb Level: Moderate

Per serving:

Carbohydrate:	11.6 g
Protein:	90.1 g

You can find annatto, or achiote, paste in specialist Mexican and West Indian stores and deli-catessens.

Two 1.3kg (3lb) chickens
1 pack annatto (also called
    'achiote') paste
125ml (4fl oz) olive oil
½ tsp toasted cumin
½ tsp ground coriander
½ tsp oregano
2½ tbsp chopped garlic, divided
Four large links of hard dried
    Spanish chorizo

1 Spanish onion, diced
375g (12oz). frozen chopped
    spinach, thawed and drained
60ml (2fl oz) chicken stock
½ tbsp sliced green olives, drained
Salt and freshly ground black pepper

1. Rinse the chickens under cold running water and pat dry with paper towels, including the cavities. In a food processor, combine the annatto paste, olive oil, cumin, coriander, oregano and 1 tablespoon of the garlic; purée to a paste. Wearing plastic gloves (the achiote will stain your fingers), rub the paste inside the chicken under the skin and on the outside. Marinate in the refrigerator overnight.
2. Preheat the oven to 190°C, 375°F, gas mark 5.
3. In a large sauté pan over medium-high heat, cook the chorizo and onion for about 5–8 minutes, until it starts to brown. Add the remaining garlic; cook for 2 minutes. Add the spinach and the chicken stock and cook for another 4–5 minutes. Add the green olives and salt and pepper. Allow the filling to cool before stuffing the chickens.
4. Divide the stuffing equally between the cavities of the chickens. Place them in a roasting pan on top of a wire rack. Roast for about 1–1½ hours or until the leg meat starts to pull away from the bone. The internal temperature should reach 100–102°C (160–165°F). Allow the chicken to stand in a warm place under a tin foil tent for about 20 minutes until ready to serve.

Spicy Pork Roast

60ml (2fl oz) olive oil
15g (¹⁄₂oz) chilli powder
15g (¹⁄₂oz) chilli flakes
1 tbsp oregano
¹⁄₂ tbsp seasoned salt
¹⁄₂ tbsp ground cumin
1 tbsp fresh garlic, crushed
15g (¹⁄₂oz) chopped coriander leaves
15g (¹⁄₂oz) chopped parsley leaves
1 tbsp black pepper

175g (6oz) chopped spring onions
175g (6oz) chopped Spanish onions
500ml (16fl oz) chicken or vegetable
   broth
3kg (6lb 9oz) pork loin, cut into
   50–75mm (2–3in) cubes

Serves 12	
Carb Level: Low	
Per serving:	
Carbohydrate:	8.3 g
Protein:	55.2 g

Make a large batch and freeze some for later. It makes a great, filling winter meal.

1. In a large bowl, mix together all the ingredients *except* the stock and pork. Add the pork, mix to ensure the meat is evenly coated, and allow to marinate in the refrigerator for about 4 hours.
2. Preheat the oven to 180°C, 350°F, gas mark 4.
3. Place all the ingredients in a Dutch oven and add the stock. Roast covered for about 3 ½ –4 hours or until the pork is very tender. Adjust seasoning to taste. Be careful not to stir too much, as the meat will start to come apart.

Do Onions Make You Cry?
tips
Refrigerating an onion before chopping it will help to keep your eyes from watering.

Halibut Ceviche with Herbs

Makes 8 appetizer portions

Carb Level: Low

Per serving:

| Carbohydrate: | 9.0 g |
| Protein: | 12.7 g |

The acid from the lime juice actually cooks the fish.

454g (1lb) very fresh halibut
125ml (4fl oz) freshly squeezed lime juice
375ml (12fl oz) spicy tomato juice
1 ripe mango, peeled, seeded and medium diced
8 tsp (or to taste) hot pepper sauce
1 tbsp honey
4 tsp very finely minced green chillies

25g (³/₄oz) finely chopped herbs (mint, parsley, chervil, chives, coriander etc.), plus extra herb leaves for garnish
Salt and freshly ground black pepper to taste
Extra-virgin olive oil for drizzling

1. Using a sharp knife, cut the halibut into thin slices. In a bowl, mix the fish with the lime juice and allow to stand for 10 minutes at room temperature.
2. Remove the fish from the lime juice; discard the juice. Add all the remaining ingredients except the olive oil; mix to combine. Keep refrigerated until ready to serve.
3. When ready to serve, drizzle a little oil around the ceviche and garnish with fresh herb leaves.

 Citrus Juice and Carbohydrates
Note the carbohydrate counts for 60ml (2fl oz) of the following freshly squeezed citrus juices:

Freshly squeezed lemon juice	5.3g
Freshly squeezed lime juice	5.5g
Freshly squeezed orange juice	6.5g

Classic Gazpacho

680g (1lb 8oz) red peppers
454g (1lb) ripe tomatoes
454g (1lb) cucumbers
2 medium cloves garlic, peeled
125g (6oz) chopped sweet onion
60ml (2fl oz) extra-virgin olive oil
60ml (2fl oz) sherry vinegar

2 tbsp good-quality tomato paste
Salt and freshly ground black pepper
   to taste
Fresh coriander leaves and lemon
   wedges for garnish

Serves 6	
Carb Level: Moderate	
Per serving:	
Carbohydrate:	16.4 g
Protein:	2.9 g

A refreshing summer treat when served in a chilled glass mug or bowl.

1. Roast the peppers over an open flame or under the grill, turning often, until the skins are completely charred. Transfer the peppers to a bowl and cover with cling film. Allow to stand for about 15 minutes or until they are cool enough to handle. Rub off all the charred skin carefully. Save any juices that may have accumulated in the bowl. (You can rinse the peppers under running water if desired, but you will loose some of the oils, which enhance the flavour.) Cut around each stem and pull it out. Scoop out the seeds with a spoon, and add the peppers to the work bowl of a food processor.
2. Cut out and discard the stems of the tomatoes. Place the tomatoes in a pot of boiling water for only 30 seconds. Use a slotted spoon to remove the tomatoes from the boiling water and plunge them in a bowl of ice water. (This will stop the cooking process.) Skin and seed the tomatoes. Cut them into quarters and add to the work bowl. Discard the skin and seeds, but save any residual juice.
3. Peel the cucumbers and cut them in half longways. Scoop out the seeds (a teaspoon is a good tool for this task). Cut the cucumbers into chunks and add them to the food processor work bowl. Add the garlic, onion, olive oil, vinegar and tomato paste to the food processor. Add the reserved tomato and pepper juices. Process for at least 2 minutes or until smooth. Season with salt and pepper to taste.
4. Place the gazpacho in a bowl, covered, and refrigerate for 2 to 4 hours. Classic gazpacho calls for straining the soup through a fine-mesh strainer. Serve in cold bowls and garnish with fresh coriander leaves and wedges of fresh lemon.

Fiesta Salsa

Makes 500ml (16fl oz)

Carb Level: Moderate

Per serving:

Carbohydrate:	15.5 g
Protein:	1.7 g

This salsa is also good heated and served over sliced grilled steak or poultry.

4 fresh tomatoes, chopped
2 fresh green chillies, finely chopped
1 large onion, chopped
1 green pepper, seeded, stemmed and chopped
1 tbsp honey

1 tbsp sherry vinegar
2 tsp olive oil
Salt and red pepper to taste
1 tbsp chopped fresh coriander
⅛ tsp oregano

Mix together all the ingredients in a bowl and refrigerate.

 More About Salsas

Traditional salsa contains 3.2g of carbohydrates for a 60ml (4fl oz) serving. Salsa Cruda is 'uncooked salsa' made with fresh tomatoes, garlic, onions and peppers. Salsa verde is 'green salsa' made with tomatillos, green chillies and coriander.

Garlic Prawns with Salsa

Serves 2

Carb Level: Low

Per serving:

Carbohydrate:	9.9 g
Protein:	24.8 g

An easy dish for a large group. If you use frozen prawns, make sure they are properly thawed before cooking.

2 tbsp extra-virgin olive oil
225g (8oz) prawns, peeled and de-veined
Salt and pepper

1 clove garlic, crushed
2 tbsp salsa
½ avocado, sliced
½ yam, grated

1. Add the oil to a medium-size sauté pan over medium-high heat. Season the prawns with salt and pepper; sauté for about 2 minutes. Add the garlic, turn the prawns and cook for another 2 minutes or until done.
2. Place the prawns on warm plates and garnish with the salsa, avocado and yam.

Drunken Chicken

1.75kg (4lb) frying chicken, cut into
    eight pieces
Salt and freshly ground black pepper
    to taste
½ tsp dried oregano
125ml (4fl oz) olive oil
1 large onion, thickly sliced

3 cloves garlic
1 bay leaf
125ml (4fl oz) dry white wine
125ml (4fl oz) tequila
175g (6oz) Spanish olives, drained

Serves 4
Carb Level: Moderate

Per serving:	
Carbohydrate:	11.1 g
Protein:	81.4 g

This is a fun party dish for a group of friends.

1. Preheat the oven to 190°C, 375°F, gas mark 5.
2. Rinse the chicken under cold running water and pat dry with paper towels. Season the chicken with salt and pepper and oregano. Heat the olive oil in a large ovenproof sauté pan over medium-high heat. Brown the chicken pieces on all sides. Cook in batches if necessary to avoid overcrowding the pan.
3. Remove the chicken from the pan and set aside. Reduce the heat and add the onions and garlic; cook for about 5 minutes until tender. Remove from the heat and add the bay leaf, wine, tequila and olives. Return to the heat, bring to a simmer and cook for about 5 minutes, until the alcohol is cooked off. Return the chicken to the pan, cover and cook in the oven for about 45 minutes until tender.

Pompano with Salsa Fresca

Serves 8

Carb Level: Moderate

Per serving:

Carbohydrate:	15.0 g
Protein:	24.0 g

Pompano have small scales that must be removed prior to cooking. Have your fish supplier do this for you.

900g (1lb) diced plum or other ripe tomatoes
175g (6oz) finely chopped Spanish onion
60g (2oz) finely chopped coriander
½ tbsp chopped finger chilli peppers
2 tbsp extra-virgin olive oil
4 tbsp fresh lime juice

2 medium avocados, peeled, seeded and cut into a small dice
Salt and freshly ground black pepper to taste
Eight pompano fillets
Olive oil

1. In a medium-size bowl, mix together the tomatoes, onion, coriander, finger chillies, olive oil, lime juice, avocados and salt and pepper. Allow to stand for about 1 hour at room temperature.
2. Preheat the grill to medium-high.
3. Coat the fish with olive oil, and season with salt and pepper. Place the fish skin side up on a non-stick pan or baking tray. Grill about 100mm (4in) from the heat source, until the skin is crisp and the flesh is opaque and white, about 6–8 minutes. Serve the fish skin side down, with the prepared salsa fresca on top

tips Chipotle Chillies
Chipotles are actually dried smoked jalapeños. Chipotles are hot and intense in flavour, and are available dried or tinned in adobo sauce. Adobo sauce is a vinegar-based sauce with ground chillies and herbs.

Guacamole

4 tomatillos, peeled, rinsed and
    finely chopped
$^1/_4$ medium onion, finely chopped
15g ($^1/_2$oz) coarsely chopped fresh
    coriander
1–2 jalapeño peppers, seeded and
    finely chopped
1 clove garlic, minced

2 small avocados, peeled
    and stoned
1 tomato, diced small
1 tbsp lime juice
Salt and freshly ground black pepper
    to taste

Serves 10
(makes 2fi cups)

Carb Level: Low

Per serving:	
Carbohydrate:	5.3 g
Protein:	1.2 g

Tomatillos are available from specialised vegetable and fruit importers.

In a medium-size bowl, combine all the ingredients. Use the back of a fork to mash all of the ingredients until puréed but still slightly chunky. Best served the same day. Keep the avocado stone in the guacamole to prevent it from browning.

Substitutes for Seasonal Produce

tips

You can substitute tinned tomatoes and chillies if it's the dead of winter and quality vegetables aren't available. During the warm months, always use fresh, quality produce. There's no substitute for the flavour.

Mexican Tomato Salad

Serves 4	
Carb Level: Low	

Per serving:

Carbohydrate:	5.5 g
Protein:	1.6 g

Queso blanco (or queso fresco) is a slightly salty white Mexican cheese.

2 large, round ripe tomatoes, sliced
   6mm ($\frac{1}{4}$ in) thick
1 red onion, thinly sliced
2 serranos or jalapeños,
   thinly sliced
$\frac{1}{2}$ tbsp chopped coriander leaves
30g (1oz) queso blanco, crumbled
$\frac{1}{2}$ tsp oregano
$\frac{1}{2}$ tsp crushed garlic

1 tbsp extra-virgin olive oil
1 tbsp white wine vinegar
Salt and freshly ground black pepper
   to taste

1. Arrange the sliced tomatoes, red onions and chillies on a chilled platter. Sprinkle the coriander and queso blanco over the top.
2. In a small bowl, combine the remaining ingredients. Drizzle the vinaigrette over the salad just before serving.

tips

What Is Yam?

Yam is a large, bulbous root vegetable with a thin brown skin and white crunchy flesh. It has a sweet, nutty flavour that is good both raw and cooked. Fresh yam can be added to salads for a satisfying crunchy texture. Yam contains 3.8g of carbohydrates per 25g ($\frac{1}{2}$oz).

❖ Indicates Easy Recipe ❖

Roasted Pork
with Asian Glaze

Serves 6
Carb Level: Low

Per serving:	
Carbohydrate:	5.3 g
Protein:	26.5 g

You can let the meat marinate for up to 8–10 hours. Serve it with an assortment of Chinese vegetables.

1kg (2lb 3oz) boneless fresh pork butt, loin or shoulder
3 tbsp soy sauce
3 tbsp dry sherry
2 tbsp barbecue sauce
½ tbsp sugar
3 tbsp peanut oil
½ tsp salt
⅛ tsp freshly ground white pepper

1. Cut the pork into strips about 19mm (³/₄in) thick and about 38mm (1½ in) long. Trim off any excess fat. In a medium-size bowl, mix together the remaining ingredients. Add the pork to the marinade, mixing to ensure the meat is evenly coated. Let stand, refrigerated and uncovered, for about 4 hours.
2. Preheat the oven to 200°C, 400°F, gas mark 6.
3. Place the pork in an oiled baking dish and roast uncovered for about 30 minutes, turning several times. Make a tent with tin foil to cover the meat during the last 15–20 minutes of cooking if it appears to be browning too quickly. Let stand for about 5 minutes to allow the juices to absorb, and serve hot. Can be used as a filling or served with a side salad.

Grilled Swordfish
with Wasabi and Spinach

³/₄ tsp wasabi powder
1 tbsp water
¹/₂ tbsp sesame seeds
454g (1lb) fresh baby spinach leaves
2 tbsp soy sauce or tamari, divided
Juice of ¹/₂ lemon
Four 25mm (1in) thick) swordfish
steaks (about 185g/6oz each)

Salt and freshly ground black pepper
to taste
Juice of ¹/₂ lime
2 spring onions, white and green
parts, finely minced

Serves 4
Carb Level: Low

Per serving:

Carbohydrate:	6.2 g
Protein:	38.0 g

You can use frozen spinach as a time-saving step. Wasabi powder is available in specialist Asian shops.

1. Prepare a charcoal grill, or pre-heat a gas grill to very hot.
2. Set a large pot of salted water to boil. In a small bowl, mix the wasabi powder with 1 tablespoon of water and set aside.
3. Toast the sesame seeds, dry, in a small sauté pan over low heat, shaking them occasionally to brown them evenly. This will take about 3–4 minutes.
4. When the water comes to a boil, plunge the spinach into it and cook for only about 1 minute. Transfer the spinach to a bowl of ice water. Drain the spinach and use your hands to squeeze out any remaining water. Chop the spinach, then mix it with 1 tablespoon of the soy sauce, the lemon juice and half of the sesame seeds; set aside.
5. Using a knife or a small spatula, spread the wasabi paste onto the swordfish. Season each side with salt and pepper. Grill the steaks for about 4 minutes on each side or until done. To check that they are done, use a thin-bladed knife to check between the layers of flesh to ensure that no translucence remains and the meat is flaky. To serve, place the fish on top of the spinach. Drizzle with the remaining soy sauce and lime juice. Garnish with the rest of the sesame seeds and the minced spring onions.

Prawns
with Plum Dipping Sauce

Serves 6
Carb Level: Low

Per serving:	
Carbohydrate:	9.1 g
Protein:	15.9 g

Serve the prawns on petite skewers for a fun party dish. You can also substitute strips of boneless sautéed chicken breast for the prawns.

3 ripe plums, stones removed, peeled and cut into pieces
250ml (8fl oz) water
¼ tsp minced fresh ginger
3 tbsp rice vinegar
¾ tsp Chinese five-spice powder
½ tsp chopped jalapeño pepper
2 tbsp olive oil

454g (1lb) prawns, peeled and de-veined
Salt and freshly ground black pepper

1. Place the plums in a blender. Add the water and process at high speed until puréed. Pour the purée into a medium-size saucepan and add the ginger, rice vinegar, five-spice powder and jalapeño. Simmer over low heat uncovered for 20 minutes to reduce and thicken the sauce. Stir frequently to prevent catching. Adjust seasoning to taste.
2. Add the oil to a medium-size sauté pan over medium-high heat. Season the prawns with salt and pepper. Cook the prawns for about 2 minutes on each side, until done. Serve on a warmed platter with the warm dipping sauce.

More about Rice Wine
The most popular types of rice wine used in the West are mirin and sake. Mirin makes a tasty base for Chinese and Japanese sauces.

Red Snapper
with Garlic Ginger Sauce

180ml (6fl oz) vegetable oil
2 whole red snappers, cleaned, scaled
*   and patted dry on paper towels*
2 tbsp peanut oil
½ tbsp minced garlic
½ tsp peeled and minced fresh ginger
1 tbsp soy sauce

1 tsp sesame oil
Chopped coriander for garnish

Serves 2
Carb Level: Low

Per serving:	
Carbohydrate:	4.1 g
Protein:	47.6 g

Cooking whole fish can be a challenge. This recipe is difficult to prepare for large groups.

1. In a large non-stick sauté pan over medium heat, add the vegetable oil to a depth of 6mm (¼in). When the oil is hot, gently place the fish in the pan. (Be cautious of spitting oil.) Cook uncovered and undisturbed for about 8 minutes. Make sure you watch the temperature during the cooking process. The oil should be at a consistent heavy simmer. Monitor the temperature to ensure the oil does not get too hot and bubble over. Using tongs and a spatula, carefully turn the fish over and cook for about 7–8 minutes.
2. While the fish is cooking, heat a medium-size sauté pan over medium heat. Add the peanut oil to the pan. Add the garlic and ginger, and cook until it just starts to turn golden. (Overcooked garlic will leave a bitter taste.) Add the soy sauce and the sesame oil; set aside and keep warm.
3. When the fish are ready, remove them carefully from the oil and drain on paper towels. Serve the fish hot on a platter. Drizzle the sauce over the fish, and garnish with the chopped coriander.

Szechuan Prawns with Chilli Sauce

Serves 4
Carb Level: Low

Per serving:	
Carbohydrate:	8.8 g
Protein:	23.9 g

The assortment of chillies makes this a spicy dish. You can adjust the temperature by using more or less chilli paste.

454g (1lb) medium prawns, peeled and de-veined
Salt and freshly ground black pepper to taste
2 tbsp hoisin sauce
2 tsp tamari
1–2 tsp chilli paste with garlic
½ tsp sesame oil
½ tsp hot chilli oil
2 tbsp ketchup
60ml (2fl oz) rice wine
1 tsp fish sauce
½ tsp honey

750ml (24fl oz) peanut oil
1 tbsp finely chopped fresh root ginger
4 chopped large spring onions
3 dried red chillies
Fresh coriander for garnish (optional)

1. Season the prawns with salt and pepper.
2. In a medium-size bowl combine the hoisin sauce, tamari, chilli paste, sesame oil, chilli oil, ketchup, rice wine, fish sauce and honey; set aside.
3. Heat the peanut oil to 190°C, 375°F in a wok.
4. Immerse half the prawns in the hot oil and cook for about 20 seconds or until just translucent. Using a slotted spoon, transfer the prawns to paper towels; keep warm. Repeat with the remaining prawns.
5. Drain all but 2 tablespoons of the oil from the wok. Over high heat, stir-fry the ginger, spring onions and dried chillies for about 1 minute. Add the reserved prawns and toss well to blend. Add the reserved sauce and stir to coat the prawns. Transfer the prawns to a platter or individual plates and garnish with coriander.

Chinese Broccoli

1 large bunch of broccoli
2 tbsp peanut oil
5 large cloves garlic, finely chopped
1½ tbsp peeled and finely chopped
    fresh root ginger
2 tbsp light soy sauce
1 tbsp rice vinegar

60ml (2fl oz) chicken stock
½ tbsp sugar
1 tsp sesame oil

<table>
<tr><td colspan="2">**Serves 6**</td></tr>
<tr><td colspan="2">**Carb Level: Low**</td></tr>
<tr><td colspan="2">Per serving:</td></tr>
<tr><td>Carbohydrate:</td><td>7.0 g</td></tr>
<tr><td>Protein:</td><td>0.9 g</td></tr>
</table>

Make sure the broccoli does not over-cook – it should be a vibrant green colour when ready to serve.

1. Cut the broccoli into small florets, keeping some of the stem on. Use a vegetable peeler to peel the tough part of the outer skin of the stems.
2. In a large pot of boiling salted water, cook the broccoli for about 2 minutes. Strain through a colander, and run cold water over the broccoli to cool.
3. Heat the peanut oil in a wok or medium-sized sauté pan over medium heat. Cook the garlic and ginger for about 2 minutes, stirring constantly, being careful not to burn them. Add the broccoli, soy sauce, vinegar, chicken stock and sugar; stir to blend. Remove the broccoli from the pan and set on a platter. Turn off the heat and swirl in the sesame oil; pour the sauce over the broccoli.

Add Tofu for a Meal
tips
Using flavoured pressed tofu is a quick entrée addition with stir-fried vegetables. There are a variety of flavours – including five-spice, teriyaki and sesame – available in the Oriental food section of the produce department in most supermarkets.

Coconut Chicken

Serves 4	

Carb Level: Moderate

Per serving:

Carbohydrate:	18.3 g
Protein:	38.0 g

The natural sugars in the coconut milk and carrots bring up the carbohydrate level in this recipe.

4 boneless, skinless chicken breast halves
½ tbsp curry powder
2 tbsp vegetable oil, divided
425g (14oz) sliced asparagus, cut into 25mm (1in) pieces on the bias
185g (6oz) fresh mange touts
1 large carrot, peeled and grated

4 green onions, green and white parts, sliced
425g (14-oz) tin coconut milk

1. Trim, rinse and pat the chicken breasts dry with paper towels. Cut them into 25mm (1in) cubes.
2. In a medium-sized bowl, mix the curry powder with 1 tablespoon of vegetable oil. Toss with the chicken pieces to ensure the meat is evenly coated.
3. In a large sauté pan over high heat, add the remaining tablespoon of oil. Cook the chicken in batches (to avoid overcrowding the pan) until golden brown, stirring frequently to prevent sticking. Return all of the chicken to the pan and add the asparagus, mange touts, carrots and green onions. Cook for about 3 minutes over high heat, stirring constantly, until the vegetables are tender. Add the coconut milk and bring to a simmer. Serve immediately.

tips **Low-Carb Substitutions**

Standard onions contain 3.5grams of carbohydrates per 30g (1oz). Substituting chopped spring onions for onions changes the carb count to 1.8 g – a reduction of almost half.

Grilled Beef Sirloin
with Shiitake Sauce

900g (2lb) beef sirloin, trimmed of
  all fat
Salt and freshly ground black pepper
  to taste
Olive oil
30g (1oz) unsalted butter
½ tbsp very finely chopped fresh root
  ginger
150g (5oz) fresh shiitake mushrooms

250ml (8fl oz) thick whipping
  cream
1215ml (4fl oz) rice wine
2 tbsp tamari
1 tbsp honey
¾ tsp grated orange zest
½–1 tsp Chinese chilli paste
Fresh parsley for garnish

Serves 6
Carb Level: Moderate

Per serving:	
Carbohydrate:	19.9 g
Protein:	30.4 g

You can substitute button mushrooms – which have a tenth of the carbs – for shiitakes, but don't expect the same flavour.

1. Prepare a charcoal grill or preheat a grill to 180°C, 350°F.
2. Season the beef with salt and pepper. Brush the grill with olive oil and grill the beef for about 30–40 minutes, turning about every 10 minutes, until the internal temperature of the meat reads 85°C, 135°F for medium-rare. Let the meat stand in a warm place for at least 10 minutes to allow the juices to reabsorb.
3. Place a large sauté pan over high heat. Add the butter and the ginger and cook, stirring frequently, for about 2 minutes. Add the mushrooms and cook until softened, about 3–4 minutes, stirring frequently. Add the whipping cream, rice wine, tamari, honey, orange zest and chilli paste; bring to the boil, stirring often, and reduce to a simmer until the sauce thickens.
4. Cut the meat into four even steak portions and place on heated plates. Spoon the sauce around the beef, and garnish with chopped parsley.

Chicken Skewers
with Spicy Island Marinade

Serves 4

Carb Level: Moderate

Per serving:

Carbohydrate: 18.7 g

Protein: 36.1 g

This marinade may be made up to three days in advance and refrigerated until ready to use.

Spicy Island Marinade:

30g (1oz) chopped spring onions
60ml (2fl oz) fresh lime juice
½ tbsp chopped fresh parsley
¼ tsp dried thyme
¼ tsp dried crushed
   rosemary
½ tsp chopped garlic
1 fresh jalapeño, seeded and chopped
⅛ tsp (or to taste) hot sauce

Salt and freshly ground black pepper
   to taste

Chicken Skewers:

2 pieces boneless, skinless chicken breast
   (about 454g/1lb total)
8 white mushrooms, stems trimmed
   and brushed clean
4 metal or bamboo skewers
Oil

1. For the marinade, combine all the ingredients in a food processor and mix until finely chopped. Set aside until ready to use.
2. Slice each chicken breast into four equal pieces for a total of eight pieces. Place the chicken in a plastic storage bag with a leak-proof seal. Pour the marinade over the chicken and refrigerate for at least 3 hours.
3. Remove the chicken from the marinade and discard the marinade. Thread a rolled-up strip of chicken on a skewer. Add a mushroom and another strip of chicken. Repeat with the remaining skewers.
4. Prepare a charcoal grill or preheat a gas grill to high heat. Lightly oil the grill rack. Grill the skewers on each side for about 5 minutes or until done. Turn the skewers several times to ensure all sides cook evenly. Transfer the skewers to a warm platter.

What Is Miso?

Miso is a concentrated bean paste that comes in three basic categories: barley, rice and soya bean. Miso is used in sauces, soups, marinades and dressings. It is extremely nutritious – rich in B vitamins and high in protein. Miso is becoming more readily available in the refrigerator sections of supermarkets.

Sea Scallops with Ginger Sauce

$^1/_2$ medium leek

1 tsp unsalted butter

4 tsp olive oil, divided

3 shallots, chopped

125ml (4fl oz) vegetable or chicken stock

60ml (2fl oz) rice wine

$1^1/_2$ tbsp peeled and sliced fresh root ginger

3 sprigs fresh parsley

4 sprigs fresh thyme

250ml (8fl oz) non-fat sour cream

$^1/_2$ tsp chopped fresh root ginger

Salt and freshly ground black pepper to taste

Eight 50mm (2in) sea scallops, trimmed of muscle and cut in half across

Serves 4	
Carb Level: Moderate	
Per serving:	
Carbohydrate:	17.4 g
Protein:	9.5 g

Scallops range in colour from a light beige to a creamy pink; avoid ones that are stark white.

1. Trim the root end and the dark green top from the leek. Cut the white part in half longways, and wash thoroughly. Cut into thin strips.

2. Melt the butter and 1 teaspoon of the oil in a medium-size non-stick sauté pan over medium heat. When the butter is bubbling, add the sliced leeks and cook for about 3 minutes or until tender, stirring frequently. Remove from heat and keep warm.

3. Heat 2 teaspoons of oil over medium heat. Add the shallots and cook for about 2 minutes or until lightly browned. Add the stock, rice wine, sliced ginger, parsley and thyme. Cook for about 5 minutes or until the liquid is reduced by half.

4. Strain the sauce through a sieve into a clean saucepan. Discard the solids. Place the pan over medium heat and whisk in the sour cream. Cook for about 3 minutes, whisking constantly, or until the sauce has reduced slightly. Add the chopped ginger, salt and pepper. Remove from the heat and keep warm.

5. Lightly brush a large non-stick sauté pan with the remaining 1 teaspoon oil and place over high heat. Season the dry scallops with salt and pepper. Cook the scallops in the hot pan uncovered and undisturbed for 1–2 minutes or until a golden brown crust has formed.

6. Using four small warm plates, place the sliced leeks in the centre of the plates. Place the scallops around the leeks and spoon the sauce over the scallops.

Cod with Lemongrass Sauce

<table>
<tr><td colspan="2">Serves 4</td></tr>
<tr><td colspan="2">Carb Level: Moderate</td></tr>
<tr><td colspan="2">Per serving:</td></tr>
<tr><td>Carbohydrate:</td><td>18.5 g</td></tr>
<tr><td>Protein:</td><td>35.5 g</td></tr>
</table>

Cod is an abundant, meaty fish. You can also substitute haddock or red snapper.

Lemongrass Sauce:

2 tbsp extra-virgin olive oil
½ tbsp chopped garlic
½ tbsp chopped fresh ginger
2 tbsp chopped shallots
½ tbsp chopped lemongrass
4 tbsp fresh lemon juice
500ml (16fl oz) chicken stock
4 large tinned artichoke hearts, rinsed, halved longways and cut into very thin slices
2 tbsp butter
Salt and freshly ground black pepper to taste

Cod:

Four 185g (6z) very fresh skinless cod fillets
1 tsp salt
1 tsp coarsely ground black pepper
2 tbsp extra-virgin olive oil
Salt and freshly ground black pepper to taste
1 tbsp chopped chives for garnish

1. For the lemongrass sauce, heat the olive oil in a medium-size sauté pan over medium heat. Add the garlic, ginger, shallot and lemongrass; cook until soft. Add the lemon juice and reduce by half. Add the chicken stock and reduce again by half. Purée the mixture in a blender or food processor. Add the artichokes and cook until heated through. Add the butter and salt and pepper; keep warm.
2. Season the cod with salt and pepper. Heat a large sauté pan over high heat. Add the oil and heat until very hot. Cook the cod for about 4–5 minutes on each side or until done. To check that it is done, insert a thin-bladed knife into the middle of the fish. All translucence should be gone, and the flesh should be flaky. Transfer the fish onto a platter and spoon the sauce over the fillets. Garnish with the chopped chives.

Thai Vinaigrette

2 tbsp hot chilli oil
2 tbsp sesame oil
60ml (2fl oz) rice vinegar
60ml (2fl oz) soy sauce

Whisk all the ingredients together. Shake well before using.

Vinaigrette – One of the Basic Sauces

This is a low-carb diet staple. In its simplest form, a vinaigrette classically contains 3 parts oil to 1 part vinegar seasoned with salt and pepper. This is used as a sauce for meat and fish, greens and vegetables. Variations include spices, mustards, citrus juices, herbs, shallots and a variety of other flavourings.

Serves 4	
Carb Level: Low	
Per serving:	
Carbohydrate:	7.6 g
Protein:	7.6 g

Great over wheat noodles, salads, Chinese vegetables, meat and seafood. It can be refrigerated for up to two weeks.

Thai Beef Salad

Serves 4	
Carb Level: Moderate	

Per serving:	
Carbohydrate:	12.3 g
Protein:	15.3 g

The steak and dressing may be prepared a day in advance. Thai Vinaigrette (page 91) also goes well over this salad.

Dressing:

4 tbsp hot chilli oil
4 tbsp sesame oil
60ml (2fl oz) rice wine vinegar
60ml (2fl oz) soy sauce

Beef and salad:

225g (8oz) fillet mignon, 25–38mm (1–1½ in) thick
Salt and freshly ground black pepper to taste
Oil

225g (8oz) torn lettuce leaves
15g (½ oz) coarsely torn mint leaves, plus whole leaves for garnish
15g (½ oz) chopped coriander leaves, plus whole leaves for garnish
15g (½ oz) purple basil leaves
185g (6oz) thinly sliced red onion
30g (1oz) daikon (white radish), cut into strips
1 tsp finely chopped fresh hot chilli peppers
3 tsp fish sauce

1. For the dressing, combine all the ingredients in a small bowl; set aside.
2. Prepare a charcoal grill or preheat a grill to high heat.
3. Season the beef with salt and pepper. Brush with oil. Cook the fillet mignon for about 3–4 minutes on each side for rare. Allow the beef to stand covered by a tent of tin foil for at least 5 minutes.
4. While the beef is resting, combine the lettuce, mint, coriander, basil, onion, daikon and chillies in a large bowl.
5. Slice the beef into 3mm (⅛ in)-thick slices and toss them with the fish sauce. Add the beef to the bowl of lettuces, add the dressing and toss. Serve on chilled plates and garnish with mint and coriander leaves.

tips

Fresh Ginger

Fresh ginger comes from a plant grown in Jamaica, India, Africa and China. The flavour is peppery and slightly sweet, while the scent is spicy. Fresh unpeeled root ginger can be stored, tightly wrapped, for up to 3 weeks in the refrigerator. The taste of dried ground ginger is very different from fresh root ginger, and is not an appropriate substitute.

Grilled Tuna with Chinese Coleslaw

2 tbsp olive oil

½ tsp Thai chilli sauce or other hot
   sauce

Two 25mm (1in)-thick ahi or yellowtail tuna steaks

Sunflower oil

Chinese Coleslaw:

375g (12oz) very thinly sliced red
   cabbage

375g (12oz) very thinly sliced white
   cabbage

6 spring onions, trimmed and sliced
   longways

185g (6oz) cooked green beans, sliced
   longways

¼ large yellow pepper, cut into thin
   strips

Salt and freshly ground black pepper
   to taste

½ tsp toasted sesame oil

3 tbsp sunflower oil

1 tbsp rice wine vinegar

1 tsp soy sauce

½ tbsp sesame seeds

1 tsp chopped pickled ginger

Small pinch sugar substitute

Serves 2
Carb Level: Moderate

Per serving:	
Carbohydrate:	15.3 g
Protein:	43.6 g

Sushi-grade tuna is worth the extra expense. Ahi and yellowtail are the best tuna available.

1. Mix together the olive oil and the chilli sauce, and rub into both sides of the tuna.
2. For the coleslaw, in a large bowl, combine the red and white cabbage, spring onions, green beans, peppers and salt and, pepper. Whisk together the remaining coleslaw ingredients and pour over the vegetables; mix well to coat.
3. Prepare a charcoal grill or preheat a grill to high heat. Lightly oil the grill. Cook the tuna steaks for about 1–3 minutes on each side. The inside should still be rare. Serve the tuna steaks on top of the ginger coleslaw on a platter or individual plates.

Salads and Dressings

❖ **Indicates Easy Recipe** ❖

Avocado and Cucumber Salad
in Mint Dressing

Serves 4

Carb Level: Moderate

Per serving:

Carbohydrate:	18.5 g
Protein:	6.8 g

Use only the freshest cucumbers for the best taste.

Dressing:

225g (8oz) unpeeled cucumber slices
8 mint leaves
1 tbsp chopped parsley leaves
2 cloves garlic, chopped
90g (3oz) firm tofu
4 tbsp fresh lemon juice
1 tsp honey
Salt and freshly ground black pepper to taste

Salad:

1 head round lettuce, washed, patted dry and cut into strips
2 ripe avocados, stoned, peeled and sliced
1 cucumber, peeled and sliced

1. For the dressing, combine all the ingredients in a blender or food processor and blend to a smooth, creamy consistency. Adjust with a little water if it is too thick.
2. Place the lettuce strips on a serving platter or individual plates. Arrange the avocado and cucumber on top. Drizzle the dressing over the salad, and serve.

More about Avocados

Avocado pears contain about 30 per cent less fat than traditional Hass avocados.

Chicken, Blue Cheese and Apple Salad

225g (8oz) packaged mixed salad greens or baby lettuce
375g (12oz) roasted or grilled chicken breast, sliced
180ml (6fl oz) blue cheese dressing
2 ripe apples, cored and sliced

Freshly ground black pepper to taste (optional)
Blue cheese crumbled for garnish (optional)

Serves 4	
Carb Level: Moderate	
Per serving:	
Carbohydrate:	15.5 g
Protein:	31.1 g

Apples are a great source of vitamins A and C. Slice the apple just before serving to prevent browning.

In a large mixing bowl, combine the salad greens, chicken and dressing; toss gently to coat. Place on a large platter, or divide among four individual salad plates. Arrange the apple slices on top of the salad. Sprinkle with freshly ground black pepper and crumbled blue cheese if desired.

Spinach, Bacon and Goat's Cheese Salad

Serves 2

Carb Level: Moderate

Per serving:

Carbohydrate:	18.8 g
Protein:	22.9 g

Be careful not to use too much dressing. The crisp saltiness of the bacon offsets the tang of the goat's cheese.

Dressing:

60ml (2fl oz) light olive oil
2 tbsp fresh lemon juice
1 tsp Dijon honey mustard
1 tsp chopped fresh dill
Salt and freshly ground black pepper
   to taste

Salad:

375g (12oz) spinach leaves, washed
3 celery stalks, cut into 50mm (2in)
   sticks
6 spring onions, trimmed and
   sliced
60g (2oz) good-quality firm goat's
   cheese, crumbled
4 strips smoky bacon, cooked and
   crumbled
1 tbsp roasted sunflower seeds or
   soya nuts

1. For the dressing, mix together all the dressing ingredients in a food processor or blender; process until smooth in texture. (Like most vinaigrettes, if the dressing stands the oil and vinegar may separate; just stir again before use.)
2. In a mixing bowl combine the spinach, celery, spring onions, goat's cheese and a quarter of the prepared salad dressing. Add additional dressing as desired. Toss to coat evenly. Place the salad on plates or a platter, and sprinkle with the cooked bacon and roasted sunflower seeds or soya nuts.

Carb Facts for Vinegar

60ml (2fl oz) of most vinegars contains 3.5g of carbohydrates. Balsamic, with its developed sugars, contains 3.9g of carbohydrates per 60ml (2fl oz).

Mushroom Custard
with Blood Oranges and Crispy Greens

60g (2oz) butter
4 shallots, chopped
454g (1lb) mushrooms, sliced
1 tbsp chopped fresh parsley leaves
Pinch of fresh grated nutmeg
Salt and freshly ground black pepper
*   to taste*
125ml (4fl oz) double cream
4 eggs, beaten

Juice of 1 lemon
454g (1lb) mixed spring greens or
*   herb salad greens*
2 blood oranges, peeled and seg-
*   mented*
Chopped fresh herbs for garnish

Serves 6
Carb Level: Moderate

Per serving:	
Carbohydrate:	18.2 g
Protein:	8.2 g

Button mushrooms have fewer carbs than others. Beware of using other varieties, as they will substantially increase the carb count.

1. Melt the butter in a saucepan over medium heat and sauté the shallots uncovered until tender. Stir in the mushrooms and cook until the mushrooms are tender and almost dry, stirring frequently. Add the parsley and nutmeg. Season with salt and pepper, and allow to cool.
2. Preheat the oven to 200°C, 400°F, gas mark 6.
3. In a medium-size mixing bowl, beat together the cream, eggs and lemon juice until smooth. Stir in the mushrooms and add a pinch of salt. Spoon the mixture into six greased ramekins, then place them in a deep rectangular casserole dish and fill the pan with boiling water to halfway up the sides of the filled ramekins. Bake for about 25 minutes, until the custard is set. Remove from the oven and set aside to cool.
4. While the mushroom custards are cooling, place the greens on individual chilled salad plates and sprinkle with orange segments. Loosen the edges of the custards from the ramekins with a small thin knife, then turn the custards over on top of the salad. Sprinkle with fresh chopped herbs, and serve while still warm.

Greek Salad

Serves 2	
Carb Level: Moderate	

Per serving:

Carbohydrate:	14.7 g
Protein:	5.3 g

A great picnic treat, this is also very good after marinating overnight.

½ ripe tomato, seeded
½ green pepper, cut into medium
   dice
½ cucumber, peeled, seeded and
   chopped
1 small sweet onion, cut into rings
1 clove garlic, chopped
½ tsp chopped fresh dill
½ tsp dried oregano

90g (3oz) feta cheese, crumbled
1 tbsp chopped fresh parsley
3 tbsp extra-virgin olive oil
1 tbsp red wine vinegar
Salt and freshly ground black pepper
   to taste

Place the first nine ingredients in a mixing bowl. Mix the olive oil and vinegar together in a small bowl. Sprinkle a pinch of salt and pepper in the salad and toss with half of the dressing. Add more dressing as desired. Serve chilled or at room temperature.

tips

Cheese Makes Everything Taste Better

Cheese makes a great topping for salads. Following are the carb and protein counts per 60g (2oz) for the most popular cheeses:

	Carbohydrate	*Protein*
Cheddar	*0.7g*	*14.1g*
Cream cheese	*3.0g*	*8.6g*
Swiss cheese	*1.9g*	*16.1g*
Blue cheese	*1.3g*	*12.1g*

Fennel, Mushroom and Parmesan Salad

*2 small or 1 large very fresh fennel
  bulbs
Salt and freshly ground black pepper
  to taste
3–4 tbsp high-quality extra-virgin
  olive oil*

*6–8 very large button
  mushrooms, brushed clean
½ lemon
60g (2oz) good-quality Parmesan
  cheese, at room temperature*

Serves 4
Carb Level: Moderate

Per serving:	
Carbohydrate:	10.4 g
Protein:	8.6 g

Use the best
Parmesan and olive
oil you can find. Baby
fennel bulbs, if avail-
able, are excellent in
this recipe.

1. Remove any tough or bruised outer leaves from the fennel bulbs. Cut away the feathery tops and root ends. Wash the trimmed bulbs and slice as thinly as possible (a mandolin, available at hardware stores or kitchen shops, is best for this job). Layer the fennel over a platter. Season with salt and fresh pepper and drizzle with 1½ –2 tablespoons of olive oil.
2. Slice the mushrooms as thinly as possible, or shave the mushrooms on the mandolin slicer, producing almost transparent cross sections. Layer the mushrooms over the fennel. Top with a little more salt and pepper, a good squeeze of lemon juice and the rest of the olive oil.
3. With a cheese slicer (or vegetable peeler), grate the Parmesan into shavings. Sprinkle the shavings on top of the fennel and mushrooms. Let stand to marinate a little before serving.

Roasted Beetroot Salad

Serves 4
Carb Level: Moderate

Per serving:	
Carbohydrate:	15.4 g
Protein:	1.8 g

Beetroot is a good source of vitamin A. This colourful salad is great for a brunch buffet.

454g (1lb) unpeeled beetroot, washed
3 tbsp olive oil
1 tbsp chopped shallot
1 tbsp fresh lemon juice
1½ tbsp rice wine vinegar
1 tsp honey
¼ tsp salt

75g (3oz) roughly chopped baby rocket
1 large apple, quartered, cored and cut into strips

1. Preheat the oven to 220°C, 425°F, gas mark 7.
2. Wrap medium-size beetroot in aluminium foil and roast in the middle of the oven until tender, about 1–1½ hours, more for large beetroot. Unwrap the beetroot and let cool.
3. While the beetroot is roasting, make the dressing by stirring together the oil, shallot, lemon juice, vinegar, honey and salt in a large bowl.
4. Slip the skins from the beetroot, trim the green stems and halve any large beetroot. (Wear plastic gloves while peeling and working with beetroot, as it will stain your fingers.) Cut the beetroot into 6mm (¼in)-thick slices and add to the dressing; toss to coat.
5. Arrange the beetroot on a platter and drizzle with any dressing remaining in the bowl. Top with the baby rocket, then the apple. Serve immediately.

tips

Parmesan Cheese
Parmesan is a hard, dry cheese manufactured from skimmed or partially skimmed cow's milk. Parmigiano-Reggiano usually indicates the highest quality of imported Italian cheese, which varies in ageing up to 4 years. There are domestic pre-grated Parmesan-style cheeses on the market, but you should use the best wherever possible, as there is no comparison in taste and flavour. 30g (1oz) of freshly grated Parmesan packs in 41.6g of protein and 1.1g of carbohydrates.

Tomatoes
with Green Goddess Dressing

250ml (8fl oz) mayonnaise
30g (1oz) chopped fresh flat-leaf
    parsley
15g (½oz) chopped fresh chives
1 tbsp chopped spring onion greens
1½ tsp anchovy paste

1 tsp white wine vinegar
¼ tsp chopped garlic
900g (2lb) medium beefsteak
    tomatoes

Serves 4	
Carb Level: Moderate	
Per serving:	
Carbohydrate:	10.7 g
Protein:	3.3 g

A simple and delicious addition to a buffet luncheon.

1. Add all the ingredients *except* the tomatoes to the work bowl of a food processor (or a blender); purée until pale green and smooth. Transfer to a bowl and thin with a little water if desired.
2. Cut the tomatoes into wedges or 6mm (¼in) slices. Place the tomatoes on a platter or individual serving plates, and sprinkle with salt and fresh ground black pepper. Drizzle the dressing over the tomatoes. Serve immediately.

 Dress Up Your Salad

The following garnishes are acceptable low-carb additions to dress up any salad presentation: crumbled crisp bacon, grated cheese, chopped hard-boiled egg and sautéed mushrooms.

Serves 6
Carb Level: Low

Per serving:	
Carbohydrate:	3.0 g
Protein:	1.6 g

Use any of the dressings or vinaigrettes from this chapter to complete this simple salad.

Baby Lettuce and Fresh Herb Salad

300g (10oz) mixed baby lettuce
30g (1oz) fresh flatleaf parsley
   leaves
15g (*1/2oz*) fresh mint leaves
15g (*1/2oz*) fresh tarragon leaves

15g (*1/2oz*) fresh basil leaves, torn
   into small pieces
Salt and freshly ground black pepper
   to taste

Toss together all the ingredients in a large bowl. Add any vinaigrette or dressing and toss again. Serve immediately.

Serves 4
Carb Level: Low

Per serving:	
Carbohydrate:	8.0 g
Protein:	19.8 g

Serve with a platter of fine salamis and roasted sausages and an assortment of grilled vegetables.

Caprese Salad

250ml (8fl oz) extra-virgin olive oil
1 tbsp red wine vinegar
3 tbsp balsamic vinegar
1/8 tsp dried thyme
1/8 tsp dried basil
1/8 tsp dried chervil
1/2 tsp fresh chives

Salt and freshly ground black pepper
   to taste
Cayenne pepper to taste
375g (12oz) ripe plum or beef
   tomatoes
20 fresh basil leaves
375g (12oz) fresh mozzarella, sliced
   into rounds

Combine the first nine ingredients in a food processor or blender; process until smooth. Slice the tomatoes into 6mm (*1/4*in)-thick slices. Overlap the tomato slices, basil leaves and mozzarella rounds in a circular pattern on a platter. Spoon the vinaigrette over the top and sprinkle with salt and pepper.

Pears Wrapped in Prosciutto

6 slices prosciutto
2 ripe pears
Extra-virgin olive oil
Salt and freshly ground black pepper
    to taste

680g (1lb 8oz) mixed salad greens
Salad dressing of your choice
Fresh grated Parmesan cheese

Serves 4	
Carb Level: Moderate	
Per serving:	
Carbohydrate:	14.1 g
Protein:	23.5 g

Prosciutto is available at most delicatessen counters. Use a good-quality Parmesan to enhance the flavours of this delicious salad.

1. Cut each slice of prosciutto in half longways. Cut each pear into six wedges and remove the core.
2. Toss the pear wedges in about 2 tablespoons of olive oil until evenly coated, and season with salt and pepper. Heat a grill pan until very hot, almost smoking. Mark each side of the pear slices with dark brown grill marks on each side, using tongs to turn. This should take only a few minutes on each side. (If it takes longer, the pan needs to be hotter.)
3. Preheat the grill to low. Wrap a piece of prosciutto around the middle of each pear. Place all the wrapped pears on a lightly oiled baking sheet and cook for about 2–3 minutes on each side.
4. Serve hot on a bed of salad greens with your choice of salad dressing (vinaigrettes are best). Top the salad with Parmesan cheese, season with salt and pepper, drizzle with a little extra-virgin olive oil and serve immediately.

tips Dressing Salads

Take care when dressing your salads. It's always easy to add a little more dressing, but harder to remedy an overdressed salad. If you use too much dressing, try adding more greens.

Caesar Salad with Prawns

Serves 2 to 4
Carb Level: Low

Per serving:	
Carbohydrate:	7.9 g
Protein:	29.3 g

Substitute grilled chicken or salmon for the prawns if desired.

Dressing:

1 tbsp fresh lemon juice
1 egg yolk
Pinch of dry mustard
Salt and pepper to taste
Dash of Worcestershire sauce
2 cloves garlic, chopped
12mm (1/2 in) squeeze of anchovy
    paste from a tube (optional)
6 tbsp olive oil

Salad:

4 hearts of romaine lettuce, broken
    into bite-size pieces
1 tbsp freshly grated Parmesan
    cheese
12 large prawns, peeled, de-veined,
    cooked and cooled

1. For the dressing, combine all the ingredients *except* the olive oil in a food processor (or blender). While the processor is on, slowly add the olive oil at a drizzle. Adjust seasoning to taste. (The dressing should be emulsified and will keep for up to a week.)
2. Put the hearts of romaine into a large bowl. Toss the greens with just enough dressing to coat the leaves. Sprinkle with the Parmesan. Dip the prawns into a little dressing and arrange on top of the salad.

Health Hazards of Raw Eggs

This recipe contains raw egg yolk. Raw eggs can contain the bacteria salmonella, which can cause illness, especially in young children, elderly, those with health problems and pregnant women. Bear this in mind before consuming or serving products made with uncooked eggs.

Ham and Cheese Salad

One 6mm (¹/₄ in)-thick slice ham
30g (1oz) Jarlsberg or Swiss cheese
60g (2oz) sliced mushrooms
1¹/₂ tbsp chopped celery
1 tbsp chopped parsley
1 tbsp olive oil
1 tsp white wine vinegar
1 tsp Dijon mustard
1tbsp double cream

1 tbsp freshly grated Parmesan
   cheese
Salt and freshly ground black pepper
   to taste

Serves 2
Carb Level: Low

Per serving:	
Carbohydrate:	4.7 g
Protein:	18.8 g

A hearty entrée salad to be served well chilled either by itself, on top of lettuce or rolled up like a wrap.

1. Slice the ham into strips about 50mm (2in) long. Slice the cheese in the same manner. Put the ham and cheese into a large mixing bowl along with the sliced mushrooms, celery and parsley.
2. Combine the remaining ingredients in a small mixing bowl; whisk together to blend. (You can add sugar substitute to make this more of a 'honey' mustard dressing.) Adjust the salt and pepper to taste. Toss three-quarters of the dressing with the ham and cheese mixture to coat evenly. Add more dressing if desired.

Don't Wash Those Greens (Yet)!

tips

Salad greens should not be washed until just before serving. Loss of vitamins and minerals is increased as soon as the leaves are submerged in water. For best shelf life, store fresh greens wrapped in a damp towel in the crisper section of your refrigerator.

Lobster and Asparagus Salad

Serves 2

Carb Level: Low

Per serving:

Carbohydrate:	10.0 g
Protein:	34.5 g

You can ask your local fish market to cook the lobster and either keep it whole or shell the meat for you.

Dressing:

1 small clove garlic, crushed
2 anchovies, well drained
$^{1}/_{2}$ tbsp snipped fresh chives
$^{1}/_{2}$ tbsp chopped fresh parsley
$^{1}/_{2}$ tsp chopped fresh tarragon
125ml (4fl oz) mayonnaise
1 tsp tarragon vinegar
Salt and freshly ground black pepper
    to taste
1–2 tbsp sour cream (optional)

Salad:

16–20 asparagus spears
2 lobsters, claw and tail meat
    removed, shells discarded
375g (12oz) mixed salad leaves
Fresh herb leaves for garnish

1. To make the dressing, put the garlic, anchovies and herbs in a food processor (or blender); process until smooth. Add the mayonnaise; process to mix. Add the vinegar and salt and pepper to taste. Transfer to a bowl or other container, cover and chill for at least 1 hour. Before serving, stir in a few tablespoons of sour cream, if desired, and adjust the seasoning to taste.

2. Trim off and discard the ends 25–50mm (1–2in) from the asparagus spears, making all the spears the same length. Use a vegetable peeler to peel off any tough outer layer on the stalks if necessary. Start about 38mm (1$^{1}/_{2}$ in) from the tip when peeling. Cook the asparagus in a pan of salted, boiling water for 4–8 minutes, depending on size, or until tender but still somewhat crisp and a vibrant green. Drain and rinse immediately under cold running water, then drain again. Leave to cool.

3. Slice the lobster tail meat into 12mm ($^{1}/_{2}$ in) rounds. Leave the claw meat intact. Arrange the asparagus spears and lobster meat on a bed of salad leaves on a chilled salad plate. Spoon a little of the dressing over the salad, garnish with the fresh herb leaves and serve immediately.

Ranch Dressing

180ml (6fl oz) buttermilk
2 tbsp mayonnaise
2 tbsp sour cream
½ tbsp chopped basil
½ tbsp finely chopped fresh chives
2 tsp cider vinegar

½ tsp dry mustard
½ tsp fresh thyme leaves
1 clove garlic, chopped
¼ tsp sugar

Place all the ingredients in a blender or food processor and process until smooth. Adjust seasoning with salt and pepper to taste.

Makes 250ml (8fl oz)

Carb Level: Low

Per serving:

Carbohydrate:	4.3 g
Protein:	2.1 g

Fresh herbs give this recipe a fresh clean flavour. The dressing will keep for one week covered and refrigerated.

Blue Cheese Dressing

125ml (4fl oz) sour cream
125ml (4fl oz) mayonnaise
2 spring onions, chopped
2–3 tbsp fresh-squeezed lemon juice

60g (2oz) blue cheese, crumbled
Freshly ground black pepper

Combine the sour cream, mayonnaise, spring onions and lemon juice in a bowl; mix well. Stir in the cheese and pepper. (The dressing should be salty enough from the cheese, but add a pinch if desired.) Cover and refrigerate for at least 4 hours before serving. The dressing will keep up to 5 days, covered tightly and refrigerated.

Makes 375ml (12fl oz)

Carb Level: Low

Per serving:

Carbohydrate:	3.0 g
Protein:	1.4 g

Process the ingredients in a food processor for a smooth creamy dressing, or mix by hand for a chunkier, country-style dressing.

Creamy Horseradish Dressing

Makes 500ml (16fl oz)	
Carb Level: Low	
Per serving:	
Carbohydrate:	4.6 g
Protein:	29.9 g

This creamy salad dressing is also a great sauce for roasted salmon or steak.

160ml (5fl oz) mayonnaise
250ml (8fl oz) sour cream
80ml (2½fl oz) light whipping cream
2½ tbsp prepared horseradish

1 tsp Dijon or wholegrain mustard
Salt and freshly ground black pepper
    to taste

Whisk together all the ingredients in a mixing bowl. Adjust seasoning and horseradish to taste.

Balsamic Vinaigrette

Serves 4	
Carb Level: Low	
Per serving:	
Carbohydrate:	1.8 g
Protein:	0.1 g

Add a little extra salt and freshly ground black pepper for a wonderful marinade for grilled vegetables.

80ml (2½fl oz) balsamic vinegar
½ tbsp chopped shallots
½ tsp chopped fresh marjoram or
    ¼ tsp dried
1 tbsp Dijon mustard

Salt and freshly ground pepper to taste
125ml (4fl oz), plus 2 tbsp good-
    quality extra-virgin olive oil

Combine all the ingredients *except* the olive oil in a mixing bowl; whisk to combine. While whisking, slowly add in the olive oil at a drizzle. Adjust seasoning to taste. Whisk before use if separated. This vinaigrette will keep 5 days covered tightly and refrigerated.

Orange Vinaigrette

60ml (2fl oz) champagne vinegar
3 tbsp fresh-squeezed orange juice
2 tsp grated orange rind

Salt and freshly ground black pepper
   to taste
125ml (4fl oz) olive oil

Whisk together the vinegar, orange juice, zest and a good pinch of salt and pepper in a mixing bowl. While whisking, slowly add in the olive oil at a drizzle. Adjust seasoning to taste. The vinaigrette will keep for 1 –2 weeks in the refrigerator. Whisk before use if separated.

Serves 4	
Carb Level: Low	
Per serving:	
Carbohydrate:	2.3 g
Protein:	0.1 g

This goes well with grilled chicken salads or as a sauce to accompany a grilled chicken entrée.

Sherry Vinaigrette

80ml (2½fl oz) light olive oil
80ml (2½fl oz) walnut oil
½ tsp chopped shallots

125ml (4fl oz) sherry wine vinegar
Salt and freshly ground black pepper
   to taste

Mix together the olive oil and walnut oil. Whisk together the shallot, vinegar and salt and pepper in a bowl. While whisking, add the combined oil slowly at a drizzle. Adjust the seasoning to taste. Will keep for 1–2 weeks refrigerated. Whisk before using if separated.

Makes 250ml (8fl oz)	
Carb Level: Low	
Per serving:	
Carbohydrate:	1.9 g
Protein:	0.0 g

Walnut oil must be fresh and properly stored. Taste the oil before adding to ensure that it has not gone bad. Refrigerate after opening.

Soy Sauce Vinaigrette

Serves 4
Carb Level: Low

Per serving:	
Carbohydrate:	2.5 g
Protein:	1.3 g

Mirin is a Japanese sweet wine used for cooking.

¹/₂ tbsp sesame seeds
60ml (2fl oz) rice vinegar
2 tbsp mirin
2 tbsp tamari or soy sauce

1 tsp sesame oil (optional)

1. Toast the sesame seeds dry in a small sauté pan over low heat, shaking the pan occasionally to toast evenly until golden. While the seeds are still warm, crush them using a mortar and pestle (or with the flat part of a chef's knife).
2. Combine all the ingredients in a bowl and whisk to combine. Will keep for 1–2 weeks in the refrigerator; whisk before use if separated.

tips Variations
You can vary this recipe in several ways. Make it a little spicy by adding chilli flakes. Add a teaspoon of freshly grated ginger and use it as a glaze for salmon. Or add two cloves of chopped garlic and use it to season a simple stir-fry.

❖ Indicates Easy Recipe ❖

Caribbean Prawn Stew

Serves 4	
Carb Level: Moderate	
Per serving:	
Carbohydrate:	15.6 g
Protein:	25.4 g

A great dish for a casual get-together with friends for a summer afternoon party.

454g (1lb) prawns, peeled and de-veined
2 tbsp fresh-squeezed lime juice
3/4 tsp ground cumin
Salt and freshly ground black pepper to taste
1 tbsp olive oil
1 onion, finely chopped
1 small green pepper, finely chopped
1 small tomato, diced
3 cloves garlic, chopped
125ml (4fl oz) tomato paste
180ml (6fl oz) dry white wine
180ml (6fl oz) lager
1 bay leaf
1 1/2 tbsp finely chopped fresh coriander

1. In a medium-size bowl, combine the prawns, lime juice, cumin and salt and pepper; stir to mix. Cover and marinate in the refrigerator for about 1 hour.
2. Heat the oil in a large non-stick sauté pan over medium heat. Add the onion, pepper, tomato, garlic and 1/2 teaspoon of the cumin; cook for about 4 minutes or until lightly browned. Turn the heat to high and add the tomato paste; cook for about 1 minute, stirring constantly to keep the tomato paste from burning. Add 125ml (4fl oz) wine, 125ml (4fl oz) lager and the bay leaf. Bring to the boil. Stir in the prawns and reduce the heat to medium-low. Simmer for about 3–5 minutes or until the prawns are cooked through. If the stew seems too dry, add more wine or lager.
3. Remove the bay leaf and season with salt and pepper. Serve in warm bowls garnished with chopped coriander and a sprinkle of the remaining cumin.

Bouillabaisse

900g (2lb) mixed fish (cod, squid,
    salmon, etc.)
454g (1lb) shellfish (prawns,
    mussels, scallops, etc.)
1.5l (48fl oz) water or bottled clam juice
1 medium onion, sliced
1 carrot, sliced
1 stalk celery, chopped
1 bay leaf
Salt and freshly ground black pepper
    to taste

2 tbsp olive oil
2 cloves garlic, finely chopped
2 small leeks, trimmed and finely
    chopped
1 fresh fennel bulb, trimmed and cut
    into strips
4 tomatoes, peeled and chopped
3 strips orange peel, white pith
    removed
Good pinch of saffron threads
3 fresh thyme sprigs

Serves 6	
Carb Level: Moderate	
Per serving:	
Carbohydrate:	16.5 g
Protein:	32.0 g

You can make the vegetable stock a day early, then add the fish and shellfish to cook just before serving.

1. Clean and prepare the fish. Remove the skin and bones and cut the fish into 50mm (2in) pieces, but save any trimmings. (You can have your fish supplier do this step for you.) It is not necessary to peel the shells from the prawns.

2. In a large saucepan, combine the fish trimmings and bones, water (or clam juice), onion, carrot, celery and bay leaf. Bring to just a simmer and season with salt and pepper. Skim off any impurities that rise to the top, and simmer for 30 minutes. Strain the stock into a large bowl, discarding the bones and vegetables; set aside.

3. Add the oil to a large saucepan over medium heat. Cook the garlic, leeks and fennel for about 5 minutes, until tender. Add the tomatoes and cook for an additional 5 minutes. Pour in the reserved fish stock and bring to a simmer. Stir in the orange peel, saffron and thyme; bring to a simmer. Add the mixed fish to the saucepan and simmer for about 8 minutes. Then add the shellfish and cook for 5 minutes. The mussels are cooked when the shells are completely opened. Season with salt and pepper and serve.

Cream of Cauliflower Soup

1 large head cauliflower
30g (1oz) butter
1 medium onion, chopped
500ml (16fl oz) chicken stock
500ml (16fl oz) milk
Salt and freshly ground black pepper
    to taste
Pinch of nutmeg
60ml (2fl oz) crème fraîche or sour
    cream

Cheese diamonds:

1 tbsp grated Parmesan cheese
3 tbsp butter, softened
2 medium-size slices of bread, crusts
    removed

1. Cut the cauliflower into florets. In a large pot of boiling salted water, blanch the cauliflower for 3 minutes. Drain through a colander.
2. Melt the butter in a large saucepan over medium heat. Add the onion and cook until tender. Add the stock, bring to the boil and reduce to a simmer for about 20 minutes. Stir in the milk and add the cauliflower. Season with salt and pepper. Add nutmeg and simmer for 10 minutes. Using a slotted spoon, remove and reserve a third of the cauliflower.
3. In a blender or food processor, blend the soup until smooth. Strain the soup through a fine-mesh sieve into a clean saucepan. Stir in the crème fraîche (or sour cream) and add the reserved cauliflower. Reheat very gently.
4. For the cheese diamonds, preheat the oven to 200°C, 400°F, gas mark 6.
5. Mix the cheese and butter in a small bowl until smooth. Spread this mixture over the bread. (You can use any type of bread.) Cut into small squares or diamonds. Place on a baking tray and bake until golden brown. Serve with soup.

Cauliflower
Cauliflower is frequently used as a substitute for potatoes in low-carb cooking. Look for heads that are white or creamy white, firm and compact.

Chicken and Mushroom Soup

1 bouquet garni:
　1 bay leaf
　⅛ teaspoon thyme
　3 sprigs parsley
2kg (4lb 6oz) chicken, cut into eight
　pieces
2 medium onions, quartered
2 peeled carrots, coarsely chopped
90g (3oz) celery, chopped
1 tbsp butter

125g (4oz) button mushrooms,
　thinly sliced
Salt and freshly ground black pepper
　to taste
2 tsp fresh-squeezed lemon juice
30g (1oz) chopped fresh parsley

Serves 6	
Carb Level: Moderate	
Per serving:	
Carbohydrate:	14.4 g
Protein:	44.7 g

Make a large batch and freeze individual portions to enjoy later, or to give to a friend who is feeling under the weather.

1. To prepare the bouquet garni, wrap the bay leaf, thyme and parsley in cheesecloth and tie with a string to create a little bundle.
2. In a medium-size saucepan, combine the chicken, onions, carrots, celery and bouquet garni. Add water to cover and bring to a simmer. Skim off any impurities that rise to the top. Simmer uncovered until the chicken is tender, about 2 hours.
3. Remove the chicken from the saucepan and pull the meat from the bones. Cut the white meat into a small dice and set aside. (Discard the dark meat, or save it for another use). Strain the stock through a fine-mesh sieve into a bowl; discard the vegetables; set the meat and stock aside.
4. Add the butter to a medium-size saucepan over medium heat. When the butter begins to bubble, add the mushrooms and cook until tender. Season with salt and pepper. Add the reserved chicken stock, bring to a simmer and cook for about 10 minutes. Add the lemon juice and the fresh parsley to finish the soup. Serve in warm bowls and garnish with the diced chicken meat.

Stilton and Cheddar Cheese Soup

<table>
<tr><td>Serves 8</td></tr>
<tr><td>Carb Level: Low</td></tr>
</table>

Per serving:

Carbohydrate:	2.8 g
Protein:	13.5 g

A very rich soup that goes perfectly with a salad for a full winter meal.

2 tbsp butter
60g (2oz) finely chopped onion
60g (2oz) finely chopped, peeled carrot
60g (2oz) cup finely chopped celery
½ tsp finely chopped garlic
750ml (24fl) chicken stock
60g (2oz) crumbled Stilton cheese
60g (2oz) diced Cheddar cheese
⅛ tsp bicarbonate of soda
250ml (8fl oz) double cream

80ml (2½fl oz) dry white wine
Salt and freshly ground black pepper to taste
Dash of cayenne pepper
1 bay leaf
15g (½oz) chopped fresh parsley for garnish

1. Melt the butter in a large saucepan over medium-high heat. Add the onion, carrot, celery, and garlic; sauté for about 8 minutes or until soft.
2. Add the stock, cheeses, bicarbonate of soda, cream, wine, bay leaf, salt, pepper and cayenne pepper. Stir well to combine. Bring to the boil, reduce the heat to low, and simmer for about 10 minutes. Remove the bay leaf. In a food processor or blender, purée the soup until smooth. Add milk to the soup if it is too thick.
3. Serve in warm soup bowls and garnish with fresh parsley.

Tomato Bisque

900g (2lb) ripe tomatoes, chopped
3 green onions, chopped
½ red pepper, seeded and chopped
2 cloves garlic, crushed
500ml (16fl oz) chicken stock
½ tsp sugar

60ml (2fl oz) plain yogurt
1 tbsp chopped fresh basil
Salt and freshly ground black pepper
    to taste
Chopped chives for garnish

1. In a large saucepan, combine the tomatoes, green onions, red pepper, garlic, stock and sugar; bring to the boil, reduce to a simmer and cook for about 15 minutes. Remove from the heat and let cool.
2. In a blender or a food processor, purée the soup until smooth. Strain the soup through a fine-mesh sieve into a bowl. Cover and refrigerate until chilled. Stir in the yogurt, basil and salt and pepper. Serve in chilled bowls garnished with chopped chives.

Serves 6	
Carb Level: Moderate	
Per serving:	
Carbohydrate:	13.8 g
Protein:	3.0 g

This is a wonderful summer soup that is best served chilled. It is a great accompaniment to grilled chicken and a salad.

Greek Chicken Lemon Soup

1l (32fl oz) chicken stock
4 eggs
4 tbsp fresh lemon juice
125ml (4fl oz) whipping cream,
    whipped to soft peaks (optional)

Thin slices of whole lemon, seeded, for
    garnish

1. In a medium-size saucepan, bring the chicken stock to a boil.
2. In a small bowl, beat the eggs with a whisk until they are frothy, then add the lemon juice.
3. Slowly ladle half the hot chicken stock into the egg mixture, whisking constantly. Pour the egg mixture back into the remaining stock, whisking over low heat until the soup thickens. This will take about 4 minutes. Serve in warm bowls garnished with a dollop of whipping cream and a slice of lemon.

Serves 4	
Carb Level: Low	
Per serving:	
Carbohydrate:	6.6 g
Protein:	8.1 g

Leave out the whipped cream if you want a light, creamy soup to accompany a heavier meal.

Texas Chilli

2 tbsp vegetable oil
454g (1lb) beef sirloin, coarse grind
30g (1oz) chopped onion
3 cloves garlic, chopped
1 tbsp chilli powder
¼ tsp crushed dried oregano
¼ tsp paprika
¼ tsp dried cumin seeds
¼ tsp ground cumin

⅛ tsp cayenne pepper
60ml (2fl oz) tomato purée
60g (2oz) diced tomatoes, with juice
125ml (4fl oz) beef stock
1½ tbsp grated Cheddar cheese

1. Heat the oil in a large sauté pan over medium-high heat. Add the beef and cook uncovered until browned. Add the onion, garlic and all the dried seasonings; stir well to mix, and cook until the onions are tender.
2. Transfer to a saucepan with a cover and add the tomato purée, diced tomatoes and stock. Simmer covered for about 1 hour, adding a little water or additional beef stock if the mixture appears too dry: it should be thick and soupy. Serve in warm bowls garnished with grated Cheddar cheese.

Onion Soup with Sherry

125g (4oz) butter
454g (1lb) onions, thinly sliced
30g (1oz) whole wheat flour
125ml (4fl oz) dry sherry
1.5l (48fl oz) chicken stock
90g (3oz) grated Gruyère cheese,
    plus extra for garnish

½ tbsp salt
Freshly ground black pepper
Large pinch of dried thyme
Large pinch of dried mace

Serves 6	
Carb Level: Low	
Per serving:	
Carbohydrate:	7.0 g
Protein:	4.0 g

Heat the butter in a large saucepan over medium heat. Cook the onions for about 6 minutes or until tender. Sprinkle in the flour and stir well. Stir in the sherry and stock, and simmer for about 20 minutes. Add the cheese, salt, pepper, thyme and mace. Simmer for another 5 minutes. Serve in warm bowls garnished with grated cheese.

Beware of chicken stock with too much salt (which will ruin the flavour). Look for homemade frozen stocks at local delis, or make your own.

tips Recognizing Fresh Mussels and Clams
A good rule of thumb to follow when preparing shellfish is to throw away any mussels or clams that remain open when raw, and any that remain closed when cooked.

Vegetable Curry Stew

Serves 8

Carb Level: Moderate

Per serving:

Carbohydrate:	18.1 g
Protein:	3.4 g

Top each portion of the stew with a piece of grilled chicken for a complete entrée.

6 tbsp olive oil
225g (8oz) diced onions
1 red pepper, diced
3 tbsp curry paste
1 tbsp garlic, chopped
1 tbsp peeled and chopped fresh ginger
Salt and freshly ground black pepper to taste
225g (8oz) large-diced pumpkin

2 chayote, peeled, seeded and coarsely chopped
225g (8oz) diced carrots
6 sprigs thyme
125g (4oz) chopped spring onions
Chicken stock or water to cover
1 head cauliflower, cut into florets

1. Put the oil in a large heavy-bottomed braising pot with a cover, over medium-high heat. Cook the onions for about 2 minutes or until tender. Add the pepper and cook for another 2 minutes. Add the curry powder and sauté until fragrant. Add the garlic, ginger and salt and pepper; cook for about 2 minutes.
2. Add the pumpkin, chayote, carrots, thyme and spring onions; cook for about 6 minutes. Add the stock (or water) to cover and bring to a simmer. Add the cauliflower and cover the pot; simmer for about 35 minutes. Add salt and pepper to taste.

tips **Is Your Bought Stock Low-Carb?**

Pre-made stock is available in tetra packs, tinned, frozen or concentrated. Note the 'average' carbohydrate counts for a 250ml (8fl oz) serving of the following stocks:

Chicken stock	*0.9g*
Beef stock	*0.8g*
Vegetable stock	*32.6g*

Aubergine Stew

4 whole aubergines, cut in half
Olive oil
Salt and freshly ground black pepper
   to taste
1 Spanish onion, chopped
4 cloves garlic, chopped

2 round ripe tomatoes, chopped
1 tsp hot pepper sauce
1 tbsp ketchup
1 tbsp chopped fresh parsley for
   garnish

1. Preheat the oven to 200°C, 400°F, gas mark 6.
2. Brush the aubergines with olive oil and season them with salt and pepper. Roast the aubergines in the oven on a non-stick baking tray, turning occasionally until soft, about 45 minutes. Remove from the oven and allow to cool.
3. Use a spoon to scoop out the flesh of the aubergines. Reserve the flesh and discard the skins.
4. Add 2 tablespoons of oil to a large sauté pan over medium heat. Add the onion and garlic; cook until tender, stirring frequently. Add the aubergine flesh, tomatoes, hot pepper sauce and ketchup. Serve at room temperature in individual ramekins and garnish with chopped parsley.

Serves 8	
Carb Level: Moderate	
Per serving:	
Carbohydrate:	18.2 g
Protein:	3.0 g

Serve in preheated ramekins for a great starter course. Use aubergines that are firm, smooth-skinned and even in colour.

Herby Chicken Stew

Serves 6
Carb Level: Low

Per serving:

Carbohydrate:	9.9 g
Protein:	30.1 g

Use any leftover chicken as a great filling for crêpes.

900g (2lb) boneless, skinless chicken, cut into 12mm (½ in) cubes
½ tbsp paprika
Salt and freshly ground black pepper to taste
Vegetable oil
2 onions, sliced
2 large carrots, peeled and cut into 3mm (⅛ in) slices
2 stalks celery, sliced

½ tbsp dried thyme
1 tbsp dried basil
½ tbsp dried oregano
½ tbsp ginger powder
½ tbsp garlic
2 tbsp soy sauce
1l (32fl oz) chicken stock

1. Season the chicken with the paprika and salt and pepper.
2. Heat 3 tablespoons of oil in a large heavy-bottomed pot over high heat; brown the chicken on all sides. (You may need to do this in batches to avoid overcrowding the pan.) Add more oil as needed. As the chicken is browned, remove with a slotted spoon and set aside.
3. In the same pot, add the onions, carrots and celery; cook for about 6 minutes or until lightly brown. Season with salt and pepper. Add the thyme, basil, oregano, ginger, garlic, soy sauce and stock; bring to a simmer. Return the chicken to the pan and simmer until the chicken is cooked through and the liquid is reduced by 20 per cent. Season with salt and pepper.

tips The Benefits of Stew

Stewing not only tenderizes tougher pieces of meat, it allows the flavours of the ingredients to blend and develop in a way that is not attainable in short cooking methods.

Hearty Mushroom Soup

4 tbsp butter
375g (12oz) chopped mushrooms
60g (2oz) chopped onions
2 cloves garlic, chopped
Salt and cayenne pepper to taste
½ tsp dry mustard
1 tsp wild mushroom powder
750ml (24fl oz) chicken stock

2 tbsp Madeira wine
60ml (2fl oz) double cream, at
    room temperature

Serves 4
Carb Level: Low

Per serving:	
Carbohydrate:	5.2 g
Protein:	7.3 g

Grind dried wild mushrooms in a food processor to create the mushroom powder called for in this recipe.

1. Melt the butter in a large saucepan over medium-low heat. Cook the mushrooms, onions and garlic for about 20 minutes or until the mixture seems thick. Add the salt, cayenne, dry mustard and mushroom powder; mix well. Cook for about 5 minutes.
2. Pour in the chicken stock and Madeira; bring to a simmer. Allow the soup to cool slightly and then add the heavy cream very slowly, whisking constantly to ensure the cream does not separate or curdle. Return the pan to the heat and gently reheat, stirring until slightly thick. Serve immediately.

Save Some for Later

When making a batch of your favourite soup or stew, make an extra batch and freeze it to enjoy later. Supermarkets stock plastic freezer containers in 500ml (16fl oz) and 1l (32fl oz) sizes, which are perfect for freezing. Always label the container with the contents and date. Soups and stews can be frozen for up to two months.

Cold Fennel Soup

<table>
<tr><td>Serves 6</td></tr>
<tr><td>Carb Level: Low</td></tr>
</table>

Per serving:

Carbohydrate:	9.4 g
Protein:	2.5 g

Fennel is a great source of vitamin A and contains a fair amount of calcium, phosphorus and potassium.

2 medium fennel bulbs
1 tbsp sunflower oil
1 small onion, chopped
750ml (24fl oz) chicken stock

Salt and freshly ground black pepper
   to taste
160ml (5fl oz) sour cream

1. Cut the green fronds from the fennel bulb and coarsely chop the bulbs and the fronds separately; set aside the chopped fronds.
2. Heat the oil in a large saucepan over medium heat. Add the fennel and the onion. Cover and simmer for about 10 minutes, stirring occasionally.
3. Add the stock and bring to the boil. Reduce the heat and simmer for about 20 minutes or until the fennel is tender.
4. Transfer the soup to a blender or a food processor; process until smooth. Season with salt and pepper. Strain through a fine-mesh sieve into a bowl; chill in the refrigerator.
5. When chilled, whisk in the sour cream and adjust the seasoning to taste. Serve in chilled bowls. Garnish with the reserved fennel fronds.

tips **Food Safety Tip**
When reheating soups, always bring to the boil and allow to simmer for at least 3 minutes. This will effectively eliminate certain forms of bacteria that may have developed.

Lamb Stew with Herbes de Provence

900g (2lb) lamb fillet, shoulder
 or leg
Salt and freshly ground black pepper
 to taste
2 tbsp olive oil
30g (1oz) chopped yellow onion
30g (1oz) chopped carrots
½ tbsp chopped garlic

30g (1oz) peeled, seeded and
 chopped tomatoes
½ tbsp Herbes de Provence
250ml (8fl oz) dry red wine
750ml (24fl oz) beef stock

Serves 4

Carb Level: Moderate

Per serving:

Carbohydrate:	18.5 g
Protein:	32.7 g

Herbes de Provence is the most commonly used herb blend in southern France. It is available readymade.

1. Trim the fat off the lamb and cut the meat into 25mm (1in) cubes. Season the meat with salt and pepper. In a large Dutch oven, heat the oil over medium-high heat. Add the lamb and cook until browned. (You may have to do this in batches to avoid overcrowding the pan.) Use a slotted spoon to remove the lamb and set aside.
2. Using the fat in the pan, add the onions and carrots, and cook for about 3 minutes until tender. Add the garlic and cook for 1 minute. Add the lamb, tomatoes, herbs, ¼ teaspoon of salt, ¼ teaspoon pepper, red wine and stock; bring to a boil. Reduce to a simmer and cook, covered, for about 45 minutes, until the lamb is tender. Serve in warm bowls.

How to Rehydrate Dried Mushrooms

tips

Place the dried mushrooms in a bowl and cover them with boiling water. Allow them to sit for at least 20 minutes and no longer than 40 minutes. The mushrooms should be soft, including the thick stem pieces. Drain the mushrooms, reserving the soaking liquid. Use the rehydrated mushrooms as called for in the recipe. Strain the soaking liquid to remove any grit or sand and add the mushroom liquid to soups, stews or sauces for added flavour.

Red Cabbage Soup

Serves 6

Carb Level: Low

Per serving:

Carbohydrate:	8.7 g
Protein:	2.5 g

Cabbage is a great source of vitamins A and C. This soup is based on the traditional Hungarian speciality soup.

2 tbsp olive oil
185g (6oz) shredded red cabbage
1 medium onion, finely sliced
1 clove garlic, crushed
¼ tsp caraway seeds
404g (14oz) tin tomatoes, drained
1 tbsp red wine vinegar
1l (32fl oz) chicken stock
Salt and freshly ground black pepper
   to taste
60ml (2fl oz), plus 2 tbsp sour
   cream
1 tbsp chopped fresh dill
Fresh dill sprigs for garnish

1. Heat the oil in a large saucepan over medium heat. Add the cabbage and onion; cook covered for about 20 minutes or until the cabbage is soft. Stir in the garlic, caraway seeds, tomatoes, vinegar and stock. Season with salt and pepper, and gently simmer for 30 minutes.
2. In a small bowl, combine the sour cream and chopped dill.
3. Serve the soup in warm bowls and garnish with a dollop of the dilled sour cream and dill sprigs.

tips **Flavouring with a Bouquet Garni**

A bouquet garni is a bunch of herbs – the classic being parsley, thyme and bay leaf – that are either tied together or placed in a cheesecloth bag and used to flavour soups, stews and broths. Tying or bagging the herbs allows for easy removal before the dish is served.

Side dishes

❖ **Indicates Easy Recipe** ❖

Brassica with Chilli Sauce

Serves 6

Carb Level: Moderate

Per serving:

Carbohydrate:	12.1 g
Protein:	6.4 g

Goes well with pork dishes. You can find sweet chilli sauce in most supermarkets.

3 bunches brassica, trimmed, rinsed
    and patted dry
3 tbsp extra-virgin
    olive oil
4 cloves garlic, sliced paper thin

60ml (2fl oz) Chinese sweet chilli
    sauce
Salt and freshly ground black pepper
    to taste

1. Cut the brassica into large florets.
2. Bring a large pot of salted water to the boil. Cook the brassica for about 3 minutes or just until tender and a vibrant green. Drain through a colander and rinse under cool water. Set aside to drain.
3. Heat the olive oil in a large sauté pan over medium heat. Add the garlic and cook until soft, about 2 minutes. Add the brassica and cook, stirring often, until heated through. Toss in the sweet chilli sauce and season with salt and pepper. Serve immediately.

tips **Protein Facts**

Protein-efficient foods contain 100 per cent of the essential amino acids needed by the body. The most complete protein foods are eggs, fish, beef, whole cow's milk and soya beans.

Sicilian-Style Tomatoes

4 firm, medium-size ripe
  tomatoes
Salt
4 anchovy fillets (optional)
2 tbsp olive oil, plus extra for
  drizzling
15g (½oz) finely chopped onions
½ tsp finely chopped garlic
225g (7oz) tin tuna (preferably
  Italian style, packed in olive oil),
  broken into small pieces

1½ tbsp finely chopped fresh flatleaf
  parsley
1 tbsp capers, thoroughly washed and
  drained
6 black olives, finely chopped
½ tbsp freshly grated Parmesan
  cheese
Fresh parsley, finely chopped, for
  garnish

Serves 4
Carb Level: Low

Per serving:	
Carbohydrate:	9.5 g
Protein:	15.7 g

The recipe can easily be doubled or tripled. You can also increase the number of servings by using small tomatoes.

1. Preheat the oven to 190°C, 375°F, gas mark 5.
2. Slice about 6mm (¼in) off the top of each tomato. Using your index finger or a teaspoon, scoop out all the pulp and seeds, leaving a hollow shell. Salt the insides of the tomatoes and turn them upside down over paper towels to drain.
3. Drain the anchovy fillets, if using, and soak them in cold water for 10 minutes. Pat the fillets dry, then finely chop them.
4. Heat the oil in a medium-sized sauté pan over medium heat. Add the onions and the garlic, and cook until soft but not yet beginning to colour. Stir in the anchovy fillets and tuna; cook for about 2 minutes, stirring frequently. Remove the sauté pan from the heat and add the chopped parsley, capers and olives. Spoon the mixture into the hollowed tomatoes and sprinkle them with the Parmesan cheese and a few drops of olive oil.
5. Arrange the stuffed tomatoes in a lightly oiled baking dish. Bake for about 20 to 25 minutes, until they are tender and the cheese is golden brown. Serve them hot or at room temperature and garnish with chopped parsley.

Grilled Courgettes with Balsamic Vinegar

Serves 6
Carb Level: Low

Per serving:

Carbohydrate:	3.4 g
Protein:	1.1 g

This is a wonderful summer side dish to accompany grilled meats.

60ml (2fl oz) extra-virgin olive oil
3 cloves garlic, finely chopped
4 medium courgettes, scrubbed and
    cut in half longways
Salt and freshly ground black pepper
2 tbsp balsamic vinegar

15g ($\frac{1}{2}$oz) coarsely chopped fresh
    herbs (mint, basil, chives,
    parsley, etc.)

1. Heat the oil in a small saucepan over low heat. Add the garlic and cook until just fragrant. Remove from the heat.
2. Prepare a charcoal grill or preheat a grill to high. Make sure the grill grate is clean and lightly oiled to prevent sticking.
3. Brush the courgettes with the garlic oil and season with salt and pepper. Grill the courgettes, skin side down, until they begin to soften, about 3 minutes. Turn and cook the other side until tender; set aside.
4. Cut each piece of courgettes in half at an angle into two or three pieces and place in a bowl. Drizzle the vinegar over the courgettes and add the chopped herbs and the remaining garlic oil. Toss well and season with salt and pepper. Serve warm or at room temperature.

Homemade Pickles

430ml (14fl oz) cider vinegar
1 tsp pickling salt
¼ tsp black peppercorns
¼ tsp whole coriander seeds
2 pickling cucumbers
1 small onion, halved and cut into
    thin slices

8 cloves garlic, crushed and peeled
15g (½oz) fresh dill sprigs, firmly
    packed

Serves 4
Carb Level: Moderate

Per serving:	
Carbohydrate:	19.8 g
Protein:	2.9 g

The longer the cucumbers have a chance to pickle, the better the taste. This is a great picnic dish.

1. Bring the vinegar, salt, peppercorns and coriander to full boil in a medium-size saucepan over high heat. Cool completely.
2. Scrub the cucumbers, but do not peel them. Cut them into 6mm (¼in) rounds or slice them into spears.
3. Sterilize a 1l (32fl oz) jar by boiling it in water for 10 minutes or running it through a full dishwashing cycle. The jar should be hot when the vegetables are added.
4. Layer the cucumbers, onion, garlic and dill in the hot jar. Pour in enough of the vinegar mixture to cover them completely. Screw on the lid and refrigerate for at least 3 days before eating. They will keep for up to 1 month in the refrigerator.

Vegetable Casserole

Serves 6

Carb Level: Moderate

Per serving:

Carbohydrate:	19.5 g
Protein:	14.0 g

This is a great do-ahead recipe – bake partially the day before, then reheat and cook through when ready to serve.

4 tbsp extra-virgin olive oil, divided
1 medium onion, chopped
2 cloves garlic, finely chopped
434g (15oz) tin crushed tomatoes
15g (½oz) chopped fresh basil
Salt and freshly ground black pepper
   to taste
1 medium aubergine, peeled
   and cut longways into 19mm
   (¾in) thick slices

3 medium courgettes, scrubbed and cut
   longways into 12mm (½in) thick
   slices
2 medium-size red peppers, stemmed,
   seeded, and cut into four strips
225g (8oz) fresh mozzarella cheese,
   thinly sliced
30g (1oz) dried breadcrumbs
30g (1oz) freshly grated Parmesan
   cheese

1. Heat 2 tablespoons of the oil in a large sauté pan over medium heat. Add the onion and cook for about 5 minutes or until tender. Add the garlic and tomatoes and bring to a simmer. Simmer on low heat until thickened, about 10 minutes, stirring frequently. Add the basil, salt and pepper; set aside.
2. Prepare a charcoal grill or preheat a grill to high. Make sure the grill grate is clean and lightly oiled to prevent sticking
3. Brush the sliced aubergine and courgettes with the remaining 2 table-spoons of oil, and place them on the grill. Add the red pepper planks to the grill, skin side down. Cook the peppers until the skin is charred, then remove them from the grill and peel off the skin. Return the peppers to the grill, cover and cook for about 8 minutes or until all the vegetables are tender. Remove them from the grill and set aside.
4. Preheat the oven to 180°C, 350°F, gas mark 4.
5. Lightly oil a 2l (64fl oz) shallow baking dish. Spread a thin layer of the reserved tomato sauce in the bottom of the dish. Layer the vegetables, in any order, then the mozzarella and the remaining tomato sauce, ending with a layer of vegetables. Mix together the breadcrumbs and the Parmesan cheese in a small bowl and sprinkle on top.
6. Bake for about 30 minutes or until the juices are bubbling and the top is golden brown. Let stand for at least 5 minutes before serving.

Spinach-Wrapped Courgette Custard

*1 large courgette, trimmed and cut
    into 50mm (2in) pieces*
*4–6 large leaves flatleaf spinach,
    washed thoroughly and stems
    removed*
125ml (4fl oz) double cream
2 eggs
1 egg yolk

*Salt and freshly ground black pepper
    to taste*
Grating of fresh nutmeg
Tiny pinch of curry powder
Tiny pinch of cayenne powder
Butter, softened

Serves 4	
Carb Level: Low	
Per serving:	
Carbohydrate:	2.6 g
Protein:	2.8 g

The flan can be made the day before and gently reheated just before serving.

1. Preheat the oven to 150°C, 300°F, gas mark 2.
2. Bring salted water to the boil in a medium-sized saucepan. Using a steamer insert, steam the courgettes covered until tender. Add the spinach leaves to the steamer when the courgettes are just about done. When the leaves just start to wilt, remove them from the steamer. Spread them out flat on paper towels and pat dry. Remove the courgettes and let cool.
3. Squeeze the courgettes with your hands to remove as much water as possible. Transfer the courgettes to the work bowl of a food processor and process for about 30 seconds. Add the cream, eggs, egg yolk, salt and pepper, nutmeg, curry powder and cayenne; process until very smooth.
4. Lightly butter four 125g (4oz) ramekins. Use the spinach to line each ramekin, positioning the leaves with the ribbed side facing inwards. Leave a little spinach overhanging the edges of the ramekins.
5. Pour the custard into the spinach-lined ramekins. Fold the overhanging spinach leaves over the custard.
6. Place the ramekins in a baking dish. Fill the pan with boiling water two-thirds of the way up the sides of the ramekins. Bake for about 45 minutes or until just set. Remove the ramekins from the water and stand for at least 5 minutes before removing from the ramekins.

Sautéed Brussels Sprouts
with Butter and Pecans

Serves 4
Carb Level: Low

Per serving:	
Carbohydrate:	6.7 g
Protein:	2.6 g

Take care to not overcook Brussels sprouts – they should remain a vibrant green with a bit of crunch.

454g (1lb) fresh Brussels sprouts
3 tbsp unsalted butter
90g (3oz) roughly chopped pecans
60ml (2fl oz) freshly squeezed
    orange juice

Salt and freshly ground black pepper
    to taste

1. Bring salted water to the boil in a medium-size saucepan.
2. Trim the ends of the sprouts and remove any bruised leaves. Boil the sprouts for about 5 to 10 minutes or until cooked through. (The larger the sprouts, the longer it will take.) Drain in a colander.
3. Cut each sprout in half. Heat the butter in a medium-sized sauté pan over high heat. When the butter just starts to foam, add the sprouts, pecans, orange juice and salt and pepper. Stir until heated through and serve immediately.

A Tall Glass of Water

In the midst of counting carbohydrates, making sure vitamin and mineral requirements are in line, and ensuring an overall healthy diet plan, don't overlook the best low carbohydrate beverage available: water! Water is a solvent and carries nutrients throughout your system to ensure that each and every organ can do its job. Some dietary fibres and vitamins are water-soluble, and water is the only way that your system can effectively absorb them.

Classic Coleslaw

500ml (16fl oz) mayonnaise
2 tsp sugar or sugar substitute
¾ tsp dry mustard
4 tbsp white wine vinegar
8 cups shredded red or green
    cabbage

1 carrot, grated
1 onion, cut into small dice
Salt and freshly ground black pepper
    to taste

In a large mixing bowl, whisk together the mayonnaise, sugar, mustard, and vinegar. Add the remaining ingredients, and mix well to coat. Refrigerate for at least 1 hour before serving.

Serves 10
Carb Level: Low
Per serving:

Carbohydrate:	7.1 g
Protein:	1.6 g

Makes a perfect side dish for a picnic or BBQ.

Collard Greens

3 strips lean bacon
900g (2lb) spring greens (about
    2 big bunches)
2 spring onions, sliced

Salt and freshly ground black pepper
    to taste
Squeeze of fresh lemon juice

1. Cut the bacon into 12mm (½ in) pieces. Cook the bacon over medium-low heat in a medium-sized saucepan until the fat is clear and the bacon is crisp.
2. While the bacon is cooking, cut off and discard the stems from the cabbage greens. Roughly chop the greens and wash them thoroughly.
3. Add the greens to the pot with the bacon, along with the spring onions and 250ml (8fl oz) of water. Cover and cook over medium-low heat for about 2 hours, stirring occasionally. Add more water if it seems to be getting too dry. Season with salt and pepper and lemon juice.

Serves 6
Carb Level: Low
Per serving:

Carbohydrate:	5.2 g
Protein:	2.1 g

This American soul-food staple is an excellent source of vitamins A and C as well as calcium and iron.

Grilled Radicchio
with Fontina Cheese

Serves 2

Carb Level: Low

Per serving:

Carbohydrate:	3.0 g
Protein:	24.5 g

Fontina is a great Italian cow's milk cheese that melts easily and has a mild nutty flavour.

1 large head radicchio
Olive oil
Salt and freshly ground black pepper

Two 12mm (¹/₂ in) thick slices
  fontina cheese

1. Prepare a charcoal grill or preheat a grill to high. Make sure the grill grate is clean and lightly oiled to prevent sticking.
2. Trim the stem of the radicchio and cut the head in half lengthwise. Brush the halves with olive oil and season with salt and pepper.
3. Grill the radicchio cut-side down, until it starts to wilt and is slightly charred around the edges. Turn over the radicchio and top each half with a slice of cheese. (The cheese will melt as the other side cooks.) Serve immediately.

Creamed Spinach

Serves 4

Carb Level: Low

Per serving:

Carbohydrate:	3.0 g
Protein:	1.8 g

This popular side dish can be prepared in advance;, then reheated just before serving.

1 tsp unsalted butter
1 tsp chopped garlic
300g (10-oz) frozen spinach, thawed
  and with moisture pressed out
180ml (6fl oz) double cream
2 tsp chopped fresh thyme leaves
A few gratings of nutmeg

Small pinch of cayenne pepper
Salt and freshly ground black pepper
Squeeze of fresh lemon juice

In a medium-size non-reactive saucepan, melt the butter over medium heat. Add the garlic and cook for about 1 minute or until tender. (Be careful not to let it colour.) Add the chopped spinach to the pot along with the double cream, thyme, nutmeg, cayenne and salt and pepper. Cook over low heat uncovered, stirring frequently until the cream has thickened and the spinach is very soft. Season with lemon and serve immediately.

Aubergine Timbale

1 medium aubergine, halved
Olive oil
Salt and freshly ground black pepper
    to taste
125ml (4fl oz) milk

2 eggs
1 egg yolk
Pinch of ground cumin (or to taste)
Butter, softened

Serves 4
Carb Level: Low

Per serving:	
Carbohydrate:	8.6 g
Protein:	4.4 g

This dish is great with grilled meats and lamb dishes, and works well with any entrée with Mediterranean spices and flavours.

1. Preheat the oven to 180°C, 350°F, gas mark 4.
2. Brush the aubergine with olive oil and season with salt and pepper. Roast the aubergine in the oven on a non-stick baking tray, turning occasionally, until soft. This will take about 45 minutes to 1 hour.
3. Allow to cool and use a spoon to scoop out the flesh of the aubergine. Reserve the flesh and discard the skins. In a food processor or blender, process the aubergine until smooth. Discard all but 125ml (4fl oz) of the purée (or freeze the extra purée for the next time you want to make this recipe; the frozen purée will last in an airtight container for 2 weeks). Add the milk, egg, egg yolk, salt and pepper to taste, and the cumin to the aubergine purée; process until smooth.
4. Lightly butter four 125g (4oz) ramekins. Pour the custard into them and place in a baking dish. Fill the dish with boiling water two-thirds of the way up the sides of the ramekins. Bake for about 45 minutes or until just set. Remove and serve on the side with any main dish.

Vegetable Numbers

tips

A 20g (³/₄oz) serving of the following vegetables contains few carbs:

Broccoli	1.8g
Green beans	2.6g
Courgettes	1.3g

Braised Fennel

<table>
<tr><td>

Serves 4

Carb Level: Low

Per serving:	
Carbohydrate:	9.8 g
Protein:	1.8 g

A fennel lover's delight! This dish is relatively easy to prepare and is a perfect pairing with Italian-seasoned entrées.

</td></tr>
</table>

2 large fennel bulbs
2 tbsp olive oil
1 medium onion, chopped
250ml (8fl oz.) chicken stock
1 tsp grated orange zest
½ tsp chopped fresh thyme
2 tbsp Pernod

Salt and freshly ground black pepper
   to taste
1 tsp toasted anise seeds

1. Preheat the oven to 190°C, 375°F, gas mark 5.
2. Cut off and discard the leafy top of the fennel bulbs. Trim off the base of the bulbs and remove any brown outer layers. Cut the bulbs in half longways, and trim and discard the root core. Wash the fennel bulb halves and set aside.
3. Heat the oil in a large ovenproof sauté pan over medium-high heat. Add the onion and cook for about 2 minutes or until tender. Add the fennel bulbs to the pan cut-side down, and cook for about 5 minutes or until they are lightly browned. Add the stock, orange zest, thyme, Pernod and salt and pepper; bring to a simmer. Cover the pan and transfer it to the oven; bake for about 40 minutes or until the fennel bulbs are tender. Transfer to a serving dish and garnish with the toasted anise seeds.

 More Vegetable Numbers
Carb counts per 20g (³/₄oz) serving:

Sweetcorn kernels	*11.4g*
Peas	*7.0g*
Asparagus	*1.9g*

Marinated Beefsteak Tomatoes

3 tbsp aged balsamic vinegar
2 tbsp extra-virgin
  olive oil
Salt and freshly ground black pepper
  to taste
½ tbsp chopped fresh parsley

½ tbsp chopped fresh basil
1 large ripe beefsteak tomato, cut
  into 12mm (½ in) slices

Serves 2	
Carb Level: Low	

Per serving:	
Carbohydrate:	4.4 g
Protein:	0.6 g

Serve these tomatoes with almost any food – use as a garnish for burgers, or serve with anything grilled.

In a medium-size bowl, whisk together the vinegar, olive oil, salt and pepper, parsley and basil. Add the tomato slices and marinate for 1 hour before serving. Best served at room temperature.

Choosing Tomatoes
Commercial tomatoes are grown more for shelf life than for taste. It is better to substitute tinned Italian tomatoes for pulp-like fresh tomatoes. The best tomatoes are those that are freshly grown in your garden or purchased from a farmer's market.

Braised Baby Pak Choi

Serves 4	
Carb Level: Low	

Per serving:

Carbohydrate:	3.2 g
Protein:	1.6 g

Braising is a tasty method for cooking most vegetables.

4 heads baby pak choi
1 clove garlic, peeled and crushed
½ tsp Chinese 5-spice powder
2 spring onions, thinly sliced
Salt and freshly ground black pepper

500ml (16fl oz) chicken stock

1. Rinse the pak choi under cold running water and pat dry with paper towels. Trim off the ends, but leave the heads whole.
2. Place the pak choi in a large non-stick sauté pan with the remaining ingredients. Place the pan over high heat and bring to the boil. Lower the heat to a simmer and cook for about 10 minutes or until the pak choi is tender but still slightly crisp.

tips Different Cooking Methods
Changing the cooking techniques of a recipe indicates a creative cook. Try poaching or steaming instead of sautéing or grilling. Experiment with your food, and enjoy the cooking adventure.

Red Onions Braised with Sherry Vinegar

2 tbsp chicken stock
680g (1lb 8oz) red onions, peeled
    and sliced
1 tsp sugar

Salt and freshly ground black pepper
    to taste
3 tbsp (or to taste) sherry wine
    vinegar

1. Heat the stock in a large saucepan over medium-high heat. Add the onions, sugar and salt and pepper. Cook over low heat covered for about 35 minutes or until the onions are lightly browned.
2. Add the vinegar and cook for another 30 minutes covered over low heat. The onions should be very soft and glazed.

Serves 8
Carb Level: Low

Per serving:	
Carbohydrate:	8.8 g
Protein:	1.0 g

A perfect accompaniment for grilled meats or sausages.

Sautéed Mushrooms with Tarragon

1 tbsp olive oil
300g (10oz) button mushrooms,
    trimmed, cleaned and cut into
    quarters
1/2 tsp chopped garlic

Salt and freshly ground black pepper
    to taste
1/2 tsp coarsely chopped tarragon
Squeeze of fresh lemon

1. Heat the olive oil in a medium-size sauté pan over medium-high heat. Add the mushrooms and cook them for about 5 minutes, stirring often, until they are lightly brown.
2. Lower the heat, add the garlic and cook for 1 minute. Season with salt and pepper. Add the tarragon and a squeeze of lemon juice. Serve immediately.

Serves 2
Carb Level: Low

Per serving:	
Carbohydrate:	7.6 g
Protein:	2.8 g

This is a great side for seafood dishes.

Sautéed Courgettes
with Mustard Dill Sauce

Serves 6
Carb Level: Low

Per serving:

Carbohydrate:	5.9 g
Protein:	3.4 g

Be careful not to overcook the courgettes, as they lose their texture quickly.

3–4 whole courgettes
2 tbsp olive oil
30g (1oz) diced shallots or white onions
500ml (16fl oz) chicken stock
60ml (2fl oz) single cream

2 tbsp grain mustard
2 tbsp Dijon mustard
¼ tsp salt
¼ tsp freshly ground black pepper
2 tbsp chopped fresh dill, divided

1. Wash the courgettes and trim off the ends. Slice the courgettes into 6–12mm (¼–½ in) slices.
2. Heat the oil in a large non-stick sauté pan over medium-high heat. Cook the courgettes for about 1 minute on each side, then remove and drain off any excess oil. Add the remaining ingredients except the dill, cover and reduce the heat to medium-low; cook for about 15 minutes or until the sauce has thickened, then add the courgettes and cook for a further 5–6 minutes until the courgettes are slightly soft.
3. Add 2 tablespoons of the dill and gently fold into the sauce. Serve on a platter and garnish with the remaining chopped dill.

Asparagus
with Orange Herb Butter

225g (8oz) thin asparagus, tough
    ends trimmed off
4 tbsp fresh-squeezed orange juice
3 tbsp cold, unsalted butter, cut into
    small pieces
1 tsp orange zest, finely grated

Salt and freshly ground black pepper
    to taste
1/2 tsp chopped fresh chives

1. In a large pot of salted boiling water, cook the asparagus spears for about 1 minute or until just done. (They should be tender and a vibrant green.) Drain and arrange on a platter; keep warm.
2. Heat the orange juice in a small sauté pan over medium heat until reduced by half. Take the pan off the heat and swirl in the butter a little bit at a time until the sauce thickens. Season the sauce with the orange zest, salt and pepper and chopped chives. Pour the sauce over the asparagus and serve immediately.

Serves 2	
Carb Level: Low	
Per serving:	
Carbohydrate:	4.2 g
Protein:	1.7 g

If you can't find thin asparagus spears, just peel the woody stalks off thicker stalks with a vegetable peeler.

Braised Savoy Cabbage

2 strips lean bacon, cut into 6mm
    (1/4in) pieces
4 spring onions, thinly sliced
375g (12oz) shredded savoy cabbage

125ml (4fl oz) rice wine vinegar
250ml (8fl oz) chicken stock
Salt and freshly ground black pepper
    to taste

1. In a medium-size saucepan, cook the bacon over medium heat until the fat is clear and the bacon is crispy.
2. Add the spring onions and cook, stirring often, until they are soft, about 1–2 minutes. Add the cabbage, vinegar and stock; mix well. Bring to the boil, then reduce the heat to a simmer. Cook uncovered for 15 minutes, stirring occasionally until the cabbage is soft but not falling apart. Serve immediately

Serves 4	
Carb Level: Low	
Per serving:	
Carbohydrate:	9.5 g
Protein:	2.6 g

Makes a great side dish with Chinese entrées – or serve with grilled sausages for a traditional combination.

Wild Mushrooms
in Brandy and Cream Sauce

Serves 2
Carb Level: Moderate

Per serving:	
Carbohydrate:	19.7 g
Protein:	9.6 g

This is a truly elegant dish and a great accompaniment for a simple entrée like grilled fillet mignon.

185g (6oz) raw mixed wild
    mushrooms
1 tbsp unsalted butter
Salt and freshly ground black pepper
    to taste
1 tbsp olive oil
¼ tsp chopped garlic
½ tbsp chopped shallot

2 tbsp brandy
160ml (5fl oz) double cream
Squeeze of fresh lemon juice
Grating of fresh nutmeg
1 tsp chopped mixed mild fresh herbs
    such as parsley, chives and chervil
    (optional)

1. Trim and discard the stems from the mushrooms. Clean them with a damp paper towel or mushroom brush, then quarter them.
2. Heat the butter in a medium-size sauté pan over medium heat. Cook the mushrooms gently, stirring occasionally, for about 15 minutes or until soft. Season with salt and pepper. Remove from the pan and set aside.
3. Heat the oil in a medium-size sauté pan over high heat. Add the mushrooms and cook until slightly browned. Add the garlic and shallot and cook for about 1 minute, stirring constantly. Be careful not to let the garlic and shallot brown.
4. Remove the pan from the heat and add the brandy. Return the pan to the heat and cook until the brandy has almost evaporated. Add the cream and salt and pepper, and reduce over high heat until the sauce has thickened slightly. Add the lemon juice, nutmeg and fresh herbs.

Spiced Carrots

454g (1lb) carrots
250ml (8fl oz) vegetable stock
1 tbsp honey
½ tsp ground cinnamon
¼ tsp ground cumin
⅛ tsp cayenne pepper

125ml (4fl oz) fresh orange juice
Grated zest of 1 orange
Salt and freshly ground black pepper
*   to taste*
Cayenne pepper to taste
1½ tbsp chopped fresh mint

1. Peel and slice the carrots about 6mm (¼in) thick.
2. Bring the stock to the boil in a large sauté pan over medium heat. Add the carrots, honey and spices; stir well. Reduce the heat and simmer until the carrots are just tender, about 6 minutes. (They should remain a little crisp.)
3. Stir in the orange juice and zest, and simmer for an additional 2 minutes. Season with salt, pepper and cayenne. Sprinkle with the chopped mint and serve.

Serves 4

Carb Level: Moderate

Per serving:

| Carbohydrate: | 19.2 g |
| Protein: | 1.8 g |

You can substitute frozen sliced carrots as a time-saving step.

Baked Garlic Tomatoes

45g (1½oz) fresh breadcrumbs
½ bunch flatleaf parsley, stems discarded, leaves chopped
125g (4oz) frozen chopped broccoli, thawed and drained
30g (1oz) freshly grated Parmesan cheese
3 tbsp double cream

20 basil leaves, chopped
4 cloves garlic, chopped
½ tsp sugar
Salt and freshly ground black pepper to taste
8 tomatoes, tops cut off, seeds and juice removed, hollowed out but skin and flesh should stay intact

1. Preheat the oven to 170°C, 325°F, gas mark 3.
2. In a medium-size bowl, mix all the ingredients except the tomatoes. Stuff the tomatoes with this mixture.
3. Place the tomatoes in a baking dish and cook for about 45 minutes or until the tomatoes are soft and the tops are golden brown. Allow to cool for about 5 minutes before serving.

Serves 8

Carb Level: Moderate

Per serving:

| Carbohydrate: | 13.6 g |
| Protein: | 6.5 g |

This is a great stuffed vegetable for a dinner party.

Garlic-Ginger Brussels Sprouts

Serves 3
Carb Level: Moderate

Per serving:	
Carbohydrate:	15.6 g
Protein:	5.6 g

This dish goes well with Chinese entrées.

454g (1lb) Brussels sprouts, ends trimmed
375ml (12fl oz) chicken stock or water, divided
½ tbsp finely chopped garlic
½ tbsp grated fresh root ginger
1 tsp grated lemon zest

¾ tsp fennel seeds
Salt and freshly ground black pepper to taste

1. Cut the stems from the sprouts and remove any bruised leaves. Cut the sprouts in half and then into very thin strips.
2. Bring 250ml (8fl oz) of the stock (or water) to the boil in a large sauté pan. Reduce to a simmer, and add the sprouts, garlic, ginger and lemon zest. Cook uncovered over high heat, stirring often, for about 5 minutes or until the sprouts are tender. Add the reserved stock if they are getting too dry. Stir in the fennel seeds and salt and pepper.

And Even More Vegetable Numbers

Carb counts for a 20g (¾oz) serving of each of the following vegetables:

Cauliflower	1.7g
Fennel	2.1g
Butternut squash	5.5g

Courgettes Stuffed with Mushrooms

5 large courgettes
6 cloves garlic, thinly sliced
375g (12oz) medium-size
   mushrooms, sliced thinly
1 onion, thinly sliced
250ml (8fl oz) water
Salt and freshly ground black pepper
   to taste

1 tbsp chopped fresh tarragon
30g (1oz) peeled, seeded and diced
   tomatoes
15g (½ oz) chervil leaves

Serves 4
Carb Level: Moderate

Per serving:	
Carbohydrate:	15.6 g
Protein:	5.2 g

Courgettes should be brightly coloured and blemish-free when you buy them. Fresh courgettes are available year-round in most supermarkets.

1. Trim the tops and bottoms from the courgettes. Cut four courgettes in half longways and carefully scoop out the pulp and seeds with a small spoon. Be careful not to break the skins. Roughly chop the pulp and seeds and set them aside.
2. In a large pot of boiling salted water, cook the hollowed-out courgettes for about 8 minutes or until tender. Carefully remove from the water and set aside.
3. Cut the remaining courgettes into quarters lengthwise and then into 6mm (¼in) slices.
4. Preheat the oven to 180°C, 350°F, gas mark 4.
5. In a medium-size sauté pan, combine the chopped pulp and seeds, courgette slices, garlic, mushrooms, onion and water. Cook over medium heat, uncovered, for about 35 minutes or until the water has evaporated. Remove from the heat and stir in the tarragon.
6. Stuff the courgette shells with the vegetable mixture. Add salt and pepper to taste. Place the shells in a shallow baking dish and bake for about 15 minutes. Finish cooking them under the grill for an additional 4 minutes or until the stuffing begins to brown.
7. Serve on warm plates and garnish with the diced tomato and chervil leaves.

Turnip Gratin with Onion and Thyme

<table>
<tr><td>Serves 4</td></tr>
<tr><td>Carb Level: Moderate</td></tr>
<tr><td>Per serving:</td></tr>
<tr><td>Carbohydrate: 10.6 g</td></tr>
<tr><td>Protein: 3.5 g</td></tr>
</table>

Smaller turnips are generally more tender and tasty in this recipe.

2 medium or 3 small turnips, peeled and cut into thin discs
1 small onion, peeled and sliced
½ tsp chopped fresh thyme
Salt and freshly ground black pepper to taste
500ml (16fl oz) double cream
2 tbsp butter, plus extra for greasing
Chopped fresh parsley for garnish

1. Preheat the oven to 180°C, 350°F, gas mark 4.
2. Lightly butter a gratin dish. Place half the turnip slices in the dish in an even layer. Layer all of the onion slices on top, sprinkle with the thyme and salt and pepper, and then with the rest of the turnip slices. Pour the cream over the top. Dot the top with butter, and bake for about 45 to 55 minutes, until the gratin is cooked through and brown and bubbling on top. To check that it is done, insert a thin-bladed knife into the centre of the gratin. The blade should go in easily with minimal resistance. Allow to stand for at least 10 minutes before serving. Top with chopped parsley for added colour.

Vegetable Numbers
Carb counts for a 20g (³⁄₄oz) serving of the following vegetables:

Carrots	3.7g
Aubergines	1.7g
Spinach	0.7g

Lunch

❖ **Indicates Easy Recipe** ❖

Grilled Spicy Chicken Salad

Serves 4
Carb Level: Low

Per serving:	
Carbohydrate:	2.7 g
Protein:	39.0 g

Great with the Ranch Dressing (see page 109). Serve on a bed of crispy mixed greens.

1 tsp seasoned salt
¼ tsp each: garlic powder, onion powder, dried thyme, dried oregano, ground black pepper, paprika and cayenne pepper

680g (1lb 8oz) boneless, skinless chicken breasts
440g (15oz) mixed baby greens

1. Mix all the seasoning ingredients in a small bowl to blend. Trim off any excess fat on the chicken breasts, rinse under cold running water and pat dry with a paper towel. Dust each side of the chicken breasts with the seasoning.
2. Prepare a charcoal grill or preheat a grill to high. Make sure the grill grate is clean and lightly oiled to prevent sticking. Cook each side of the chicken for about 5 to 6 minutes, reducing heat or repositioning the chicken on the grill if too much charring is occurring. (Be careful not to overcook chicken, as the colour from the spice mixture will bleed into the meat.) Serve the warm chicken breasts over mixed baby greens with your choice of dressing.

tips   Salt – There Is a Difference

Table salt is a fine-grained, refined salt with additives that allow it to flow freely. Iodized salt is table salt with added iodine. Kosher salt is an additive-free, coarse-grained salt. Sea salt is available in fine-grain and coarse-grain varieties, and is manufactured by evaporating sea water. Rock salt is quite grey, and comes in large crystals. Pickling salt is an additive-free, fine-grain version specifically used in brines.

Hard-Boiled Egg Salad

3 eggs, hard-boiled, peeled, cooled
   and chopped
1 tbsp chopped celery
½ spring onion, sliced
½ tbsp chopped fresh dill
2 tbsp mayonnaise

½ tsp Dijon mustard
Salt and freshly ground black pepper
   to taste

Mix all the ingredients together in a mixing bowl: stir just until combined. Adjust the salt and pepper to taste. Serve chilled.

Serves 2
Carb Level: Low

Per serving:	
Carbohydrate:	1.6 g
Protein:	10.6 g

You can add a little cayenne or Hungarian paprika to add some zip to this traditional recipe.

Pulled Chicken Salad

1 small whole chicken, cooked
   rotisserie style
1 tbsp spring onions, chopped
½ tbsp parsley, chopped
1½ tbsp celery, diced fine

1 tbsp capers, drained (or chopped
   stuffed olives)
1 tbsp mayonnaise
1 tbsp (or more) sour cream
Salt and freshly ground black pepper
2 whole lettuce leaves (optional)

When the chicken is cool enough to handle, pull the meat from the bones and cut it into medium-size pieces. Allow to cool completely. Mix the chopped spring onion, parsley, celery, capers, mayonnaise and sour cream until combined. Add the chicken and toss to coat evenly. Add a pinch of salt and pepper, and adjust the amount of mayonnaise and sour cream to the desired consistency. Serve chilled over a lettuce leaf.

Serves 2
Carb Level: Low

Per serving (without added mayonnaise or sour cream):	
Carbohydrate:	1.4 g
Protein:	73.2 g

Most supermarkets stock rotisserie chickens hot and ready to take home. You can also substitute leftover roast chicken meat.

Curried Chicken Chowder

<table>
<tr><td>

Serves 8

Carb Level: Moderate

Per serving:

Carbohydrate:	16.9 g
Protein:	21.7 g

This can be prepared a day or two ahead – reheat just before serving.

</td><td>

1.3kg (3lb) chicken, cut into 8 pieces
454g (1lb) thinly sliced carrots, divided
150g (5oz) thinly sliced celery, with leaves
1 medium onion, quartered
4 whole cloves
½ tbsp salt (optional)
1 bay leaf

</td><td>

2.5l (80fl oz) water
3 tbsp butter
225g (8oz) fresh mushrooms
½ tbsp finely chopped shallot
¼ tsp salt
¼ tsp (or to taste) curry powder
60ml (2fl oz) dry sherry
250ml (8fl oz) single cream
Avocado slices for garnish

</td></tr>
</table>

1. Rinse the chicken under cold running water and pat dry with paper towels. Place the chicken pieces, 185g (6oz) carrots, celery, onion quarters studded with the cloves, salt and bay leaf in a large saucepan. Add enough water to cover and bring to the boil uncovered. Reduce to a simmer, partially cover and cook on low for about 1 hour. Skim and discard any residue that accumulates on the surface as it cooks.
2. Remove the chicken pieces and allow to cool. Pull the meat from the bones and discard the skin and bones. Cut the meat into 12mm (½ in) cubes; set aside.
3. Strain the chicken stock through a fine-mesh sieve. Reserve the stock and vegetables; discard the cloves and the bay leaf. Let the stock stand for a few minutes, then skim off any fat that accumulates at the top.
4. Put the vegetables and 250ml (8fl oz) stock into a food processor or blender. Blend until smooth in consistency. Heat the remaining stock in a large saucepan to boiling. Stir in the vegetable purée and the remaining carrots. Bring to a boil, then reduce heat to a simmer; cook uncovered for 30 minutes.

(recipe continues on the next page)

Curried Chicken Chowder (continued)

5. In a small frying pan, heat the butter until it foams. Stir the mushrooms and shallot into the butter, and cook for 3 minutes. Stir in the salt and curry powder; cook over low heat for another 3 minutes. Stir the mushroom mixture into the chicken stock; simmer uncovered for 15 minutes.
6. Add the chicken pieces, sherry and cream. Heat until hot and steaming, about 3 minutes, over medium heat – *but do not boil*. Ladle into serving bowls and garnish with the avocado slices.

Chicken Grape Salad

300g (10oz) cooked chicken breast,
   cut into small cubes
150g (5oz) celery, chopped
150g (5oz) seedless green or red
   grapes, halved
250ml (8fl oz) mayonnaise
1 tbsp lemon juice
60g (2oz) flaked almonds

¼ tsp salt
Freshly ground black pepper
   to taste
Mixed greens

Serves 6	
Carb Level: Low	
Per serving:	
Carbohydrate:	5.2 g
Protein:	15.3 g

Serve with a glass of chilled Chardonnay.

Combine all the ingredients except the mixed greens in a medium-size mixing bowl; toss well. Serve chilled over a bed of the mixed greens.

Sautéed Sausage and Peppers

Serves 1
Carb Level: Low

Per serving:

Carbohydrate:	10.0 g
Protein:	18.2 g

It's easy to multiply this recipe from a small dinner for two to a group meal.

2 tbsp olive oil, divided
150g (5oz) salami or Italian sausage
90g (3oz) chopped courgettes
45g (1½oz) chopped onion

90g (3oz) trimmed, seeded and
* chopped red pepper*
Salt and freshly ground black pepper
* to taste*

1. In a small sauté pan, heat 1 tablespoon of the olive oil on medium-high. Place the sausage in the pan: it should sizzle on contact. (If not, remove the sausage immediately and let the pan heat to the proper temperature.) Let the sausage caramelize to a medium golden brown colour, turning as needed. Remove the sausage from the pan, set aside and keep warm.
2. Add the remaining olive oil to the sauté pan, and add the courgettes, onion and red pepper. Sauté uncovered, stirring until the vegetables have softened and start to caramelize a bit; remove from the heat. Sprinkle with salt and pepper, and toss.
3. To serve, cut the sausage links on a bias into thirds and place on a plate. Place the sautéed vegetables on top of the sausage. Serve immediately.

tips

Where to Find Organic Foods
The Web site www.organicfood.co.uk is a good source for organic home and dry goods. The best organic produce can purchased through a farmer's market or through an organic box home-delivery scheme.

Stuffed Tomato with Cottage Cheese

80ml (2½fl oz.) cottage cheese
1 tbsp chopped fresh parsley
½ tsp chopped garlic
Salt and freshly ground black pepper
    to taste

1 medium-size ripe tomato
1 tbsp balsamic vinegar
90g (3oz.) mixed greens

Serves 1
Carb Level: Low

Per serving:	
Carbohydrate:	12.6 g
Protein:	12.6 g

Dice and add any leftover cheeses, cold meats or vegetables, or add fresh herbs and spices to the cottage cheese mixture for a variation.

1. Mix together the cottage cheese, parsley, garlic and salt and pepper (and anything else you would like); set aside.
2. Cut the very top off of the tomato. Scoop out the inside of the tomato with a melon baller or teaspoon. Discard the tomato top and inside pulp. Spoon the cottage cheese filling into the tomato.
3. On a serving dish, drizzle the vinegar over the mixed greens, and sprinkle with salt and pepper. Place the tomato over the top of the greens.

Fruit Facts

tips

   Note the following carb counts for a 45g (1½-oz) serving of the following fresh fruits: fresh mango, 14g; fresh pineapple, 9.6g; fresh apples, 8.4g; fresh raspberries, 7.1g; fresh blueberries, 10.2g; fresh strawberries, 5.2g; fresh pears, 12.5g; fresh red grapes, 13.9g; fresh green grapes, 13.7g.

Teriyaki Beef

Serves 6

Carb Level: Low

Per serving:

Carbohydrate:	9.1 g
Protein:	24.3 g

These skewers also make great appetizers. Prepare them the evening before if you like, then grill just before serving.

Marinade:

60ml (2fl oz) rice wine vinegar
125ml (4fl oz) teriyaki sauce
60ml (2fl oz) vegetable oil
1 tbsp dry white sherry
1 small clove garlic, chopped
25mm (1in piece fresh ginger, crushed

680g (1lb 8oz) boneless beef sirloin, cut into 3mm ($\frac{1}{8}$in) slices
Wooden skewers, soaked in water
1 round lettuce cut into strips
60ml (2fl oz) vinaigrette (see vinaigrette recipes in Chapter 7)
90g (3oz) chopped red onions

1. Combine the marinade ingredients in a shallow casserole dish; mix to combine. Add the beef to the dish and thoroughly coat all the pieces with the marinade. Cover and refrigerate for 1–2 hours or overnight.
2. Prepare a charcoal grill or preheat a grill to high. Make sure the grill grate is clean and lightly oiled to prevent sticking.
3. Thread the marinated meat onto wooden skewers that have been soaked in water. Cook the skewers for 1 or 2 minutes on each side until the desired temperature is achieved.
4. Serve the hot skewers on a bed of lettuce topped with the vinaigrette and garnished with the red onion.

Spinach and Mushroom Rolls

*300g (10oz) frozen chopped
  spinach, thawed, water squeezed
  out and cooked according to
  directions*
4 eggs, separated
*Salt and freshly ground black pepper
  to taste*
30g (1oz) grated Parmesan cheese

Filling:

1 tbsp butter
*300g (10oz) sliced medium-size
  mushrooms*
½ tbsp plain flour
160ml (5fl oz) milk
Pinch of nutmeg
*Salt and freshly ground black pepper
  to taste*

Serves 4	
Carb Level: Low	
Per serving:	
Carbohydrate:	8.5 g
Protein:	14.6 g

You can top the rolls with the Tomato Sauce on page 67.

1. Preheat the oven to 200°C, 400°F, gas mark 6. Line a baking pan with greaseproof paper and then oil lightly.
2. Drain the spinach well and place it in a large bowl. Beat the egg yolks well and thoroughly mix them into the chopped spinach. Season to taste with salt and pepper.
3. Whisk the egg whites in a large grease-free bowl until just holding their shape (soft peaks). Using a metal spoon, quickly fold them into the spinach mixture. Spoon the mixture into the prepared pan, spreading it across completely. Sprinkle the grated Parmesan cheese over the entire surface; bake for 10 minutes.
4. Meanwhile, make the filling. Heat the butter in a small saucepan. Add the sliced mushrooms and cook gently until softened. Stir in the flour; cook, stirring constantly, for 1 minute. Slowly stir in the milk and cook the sauce until thickened. Stir in the nutmeg and season to taste.
5. Remove the spinach roulade from the oven and turn out onto a sheet of greased paper. Quickly spread the mushroom filling over the surface and gently roll up the roulade. Cut into thick slices and serve immediately. Gently reheat the rolls in the oven as necessary.

Crab Cakes with Red Pepper Sauce

Serves 6

Carb Level: Low

Per serving:

Carbohydrate:	9.3 g
Protein:	18.3 g

Cooked crab cakes freeze for up to three weeks. Thaw overnight in a fridge and reheat at 190°C, 375°F, gas mark 5 in the oven until crisp. .

Crab Cakes:

1/8 tsp salt
3/4 tbsp paprika
3/4 tbsp fresh ground black pepper
1/2 tsp (or to taste) onion salt
1/4 tsp cayenne pepper
1/2 tsp fresh thyme leaves
1/8 tsp dried oregano
1/4 tsp white pepper
3/4 tbsp chopped garlic
30g (1oz) breadcrumbs
3/4 tbsp Parmesan cheese
1/2 tbsp chopped fresh parsley
454g (1lb) fresh or frozen crabmeat, picked over for shells
125ml (4fl oz) mayonnaise
1 tbsp chopped spring onions, white part only
1 1/2 tbsp chopped green pepper
2 tbsp diced onion
1 tbsp chopped celery
1/8 tsp Tabasco sauce
1/2 tsp Worcestershire sauce
125ml (4fl oz) corn oil

Red Pepper Sauce:

1 red pepper, roasted in the oven
   until cooked, seeded
1 clove garlic, chopped
125ml (4fl oz) mayonnaise
60ml (2fl oz) sour cream
Salt and freshly ground black pepper to taste

(recipe continues on the next page)

Crab Cakes with Red Pepper Sauce (continued)

1. To prepare the crab cakes, mix together the salt, paprika, black pepper, onion salt, cayenne, thyme, oregano and white pepper, then add the chopped garlic; set aside.
2. Mix together the breadcrumbs, Parmesan cheese and parsley; set aside.
3. In a bowl, blend ¾ teaspoons of the seasoning mix with all the remaining crab cake ingredients *except* the corn oil and the breadcrumb mixture. Form into 38mm (1½ in) balls. Roll them in the breadcrumb mixture and flatten into 12mm (½ in) thick patties.
4. Heat half the oil in a frying pan over medium heat. Sauté the crab cakes in batches until golden brown on each side. Replenish the corn oil as needed. Transfer the cakes to paper towels after cooked to drain; keep warm.
5. To prepare the sauce, in a food processor or blender combine all the ingredients; process until smooth. Serve the crab cakes with the red pepper sauce on the side.

Broccoli Bacon Salad

Serves 12
Carb Level: Low

Per serving:

Carbohydrate:	4.6 g
Protein:	5.6 g

You can substitute frozen chopped broccoli, cooked according to directions, if you are in a hurry.

2 bunches broccoli, chopped, par-
　boiled and drained
8 bacon strips, cooked and crumbled
185g (6oz) grated Cheddar cheese
1 medium-size red onion, chopped
60ml (2fl oz) red wine vinegar
2 tbsp honey

180ml (6fl oz) mayonnaise
1 tbsp fresh lemon juice
½ tsp salt
¼ tsp freshly ground black pepper

In a large bowl, combine the cooled broccoli, bacon, cheese and onion. Prepare the dressing by whisking together all the remaining ingredients. Pour the dressing over the broccoli mixture and toss to combine. Cover and refrigerate until ready to use.

Vegetable Egg Salad

Serves 4
Carb Level: Low

Per serving:

Carbohydrate:	4.5 g
Protein:	8.7 g

Goes great on a bed of fresh greens. This salad holds up well refrigerated for a couple of days.

4 hard-boiled eggs, peeled and
　chopped
60g (2oz) medium-firm tofu,
　drained and diced
90g (3oz) thinly sliced celery
45g (1½oz) chopped onion
½ tbsp chopped fresh parsley

½ tbsp chopped fresh dill
Salt and freshly ground black pepper
　to taste
1 tsp Worcestershire sauce
4 tbsp mayonnaise
90g (3oz) frozen green peas, thawed
　and drained

Combine all the ingredients *except* the peas in a medium-size bowl; mix well. Add the peas and toss gently. Cover and chill before serving.

Curried Chicken Spread

454g (1lb) boneless, skinless chicken
   breasts, cooked and cut into
   medium-size dice
160ml (5fl oz) sour cream
90g (3oz) chopped pineapple (fresh
   or tinned)

¼ tsp curry powder
90g (3oz) chopped celery
Salt and freshly ground black pepper
   to taste

Place the chicken in the work bowl of a food processor. Blend until the cooked chicken meat resembles the consistency of tinned tuna. In a bowl, mix together the chicken and the remaining ingredients.

Serves 2

Carb Level: Low

Per serving:

Carbohydrate:	9.5 g
Protein:	44.8 g

Great as a spread on vegetables or rolled up in lettuce leaves.

Vegetable Cottage Cheese Spread

375g (12oz) cottage cheese
½ tsp dried whole savory
90g (3oz) seeded and diced tomato
60g (2oz) shredded carrot
60g (2oz) unpeeled chopped
   cucumber
60g (2oz) chopped green pepper

45g (1½oz) sliced green onions
1 tbsp red wine vinegar
Salt and freshly ground black pepper
   to taste

Combine the cottage cheese and savory, stirring well. Add the remaining ingredients; toss gently. Serve chilled on a bed of lettuce.

Serves 4

Carb Level: Low

Per serving:

Carbohydrate:	6.3 g
Protein:	12.1 g

Add a variety of different fresh chopped herbs for a different flavour.

Prawn Salad

454g (1lb) small prawns, peeled and
 cooked
1 hard-boiled egg, chopped
3/4 tbsp chopped celery
3/4 tbsp chopped dill pickle
1 tbsp thinly sliced shallot

1 tbsp chopped onion
2 tbsp mayonnaise
1 tsp Dijon mustard
Salt and freshly ground black pepper
 to taste
1/2 tbsp paprika

Combine the prawns, egg, celery, pickle, shallot and onion in a
large bowl. Mix the mayonnaise and mustard together in a small bowl.
Add the mayonnaise mixture to the prawns and toss to coat. Salt and
pepper to taste, and garnish with paprika.

Avocado with Tuna Salad

90g (3oz) tuna, flaked
2 tbsp mayonnaise
1 tsp Dijon mustard
1 hard-boiled egg, chopped
1/2 spring onion, chopped
1/2 tsp chopped fresh dill
Salt and freshly ground black pepper
 to taste

60ml (2fl oz) extra-virgin olive oil
2 tbsp red wine vinegar
90g (3oz) mixed greens
1/2 avocado
3 black olives, quartered, for garnish
1 gherkin, sliced, for garnish

In a mixing bowl, mix together the tuna, mayonnaise, mustard, egg,
spring onion, dill and salt and pepper. In another small bowl, whisk
together the olive oil and vinegar; season with salt and pepper. Toss the
mixed greens with the vinaigrette; place on a plate. Slice the avocado
and fan it across the dressed greens. Top with the tuna salad. Garnish
with the black olives and gherkin.

Serves 6

Carb Level: Low

Per serving:

| Carbohydrate: | 3.1 g |
| Protein: | 17.0 g |

Simple and satisfying. Serve on a bed of baby spinach leaves with a light vinaigrette dressing.

Serves 1

Carb Level: Moderate

Per serving:

| Carbohydrate: | 13.1 g |
| Protein: | 27.6 g |

A great salad lunch dish. You can also serve the tuna salad in lettuce-leaf wraps.

New Orleans Muffuletta Salad

90g (3oz) chopped broccoli florets
90g (3oz) chopped fresh cauliflower
  florets
45g (1½oz) finely chopped celery
185g (6oz) finely chopped pimento-
  stuffed olives, with 60ml (2fl oz)
  liquid from the jar
4 cloves garlic, finely chopped
60ml (2fl oz) extra-virgin olive oil
⅛ tsp freshly ground black pepper

680g (1lb 8oz) chopped iceberg let-
  tuce, rinsed and patted dry
125g (4oz) salami, thinly sliced
125g (4oz) prosciutto, thinly sliced
125g (4oz) provolone, thinly sliced
  and cut into quarters
125ml (4fl oz) vinaigrette salad
  dressing

Serves 4

Carb Level: Low

Per serving:

| Carbohydrate: | 10.0 g |
| Protein: | 21.7 g |

Makes a great lunch salad – a simple stop at the delicatessen and greengrocers is all you need.

1. In a medium-size bowl, combine the broccoli, cauliflower, celery, olives, olive juice, garlic, olive oil and black pepper. Let this mixture, called gardiniere, stand for at least 1 hour.
2. Place the lettuce in a bowl or on a platter. Top the lettuce with the salami, prosciutto and provolone, then spoon some of the gardiniere on top. Serve with your favourite vinaigrette.

More Fruit Please!

How many carbs are in a 45g (1½ oz) serving of the following fresh fruits? Fresh cherries, 12.4g; fresh kiwi fruit, 15.1g; fresh cantaloupe melon, 6.7g; fresh honeydew melon, 7.8g; fresh watermelon, 5.7g; fresh bananas, 26.2g.

Beef Roulade

Serves 4

Carb Level: Moderate

Per serving:

Carbohydrate:	18.2 g
Protein:	64.3 g

You can prepare this in advance and gently reheat before serving. Just be careful not to let the beef dry out or over-cook.

Brown Sauce:

4 tbsp vegetable oil
½ peeled carrot, sliced
½ stalk celery, chopped
½ onion, chopped
1 clove garlic, chopped
2 tbsp plain flour
1l (32fl oz) beef stock
1 bay leaf
2 peppercorns
60ml (2fl oz) tomato purée
30g (1oz) chopped tomatoes

Beef roulade:

2 strips bacon, diced
225g (8oz) ground beef
90g (3oz) chopped onion
1 clove garlic, chopped
2 eggs
3 tbsp French mustard
60ml (2fl oz) milk
150g (5oz) breadcrumbs
½ tbsp chopped fresh parsley
½ tsp salt
½ tsp freshly ground black pepper
4 thinly sliced rounds of beef
4 thin strips sour pickled gherkins
2 tbsp butter
Chopped fresh parsley for garnish

(recipe continues on the next page)

Beef Roulade (continued)

1. To prepare the brown sauce, heat the oil in a large saucepan or covered cookpot over medium-high heat. Add the carrot, celery, onion and garlic; braise until light brown. Add the flour and stir well; cook until the flour turns brown, stirring so that it browns evenly. Add the remaining sauce ingredients; bring to the boil, reduce the heat and let simmer slowly for 1 hour, stirring occasionally. Strain into a bowl; discard the solids.
2. Preheat the oven to 140°C, 325°F, gas mark 3.
3. In a medium-size sauté pan, sauté the bacon, ground beef, onion and garlic until lightly browned; let cool. Transfer the sautéed mixture to a large mixing bowl and add the eggs, mustard, milk, breadcrumbs, parsley, salt and pepper; mix well.
4. Spread the mixture equally on the slices of beef. Place a strip of gherkin on top of the mixture and roll up each beef slice; secure with tooth-picks, or tie with a string. Melt the butter in a sauté pan over medium heat and brown the roulades on all sides. Place the roulades in a baking pan and cover with the hot brown sauce; bake until tender, approximately 1½–2 hours. Sprinkle with a little chopped parsley and serve.

The Importance of Soy Sauce

Soy sauce is a key flavouring agent in Asian cooking. It is manufactured by fermenting boiled soya beans and roasted wheat or barley. It should be used sparingly in recipes, due to its intense salty taste and carbohydrate count. Soy sauce contains 6.1g of carbohydrates per 60ml (2fl oz).

Herb-Stuffed Flank Steak

Serves 4
Carb Level: Moderate

Per serving:	
Carbohydrate:	14.8 g
Protein:	37.4 g

Make sure to cook the stuffed meat completely through, as there is raw egg in the filling.

900g (2lb) beef flank steak
2 tbsp butter
½ large onion, chopped
3 cloves garlic, crushed
90g (3oz) sliced mushrooms
30g (1oz) chopped fresh parsley
45g (1½oz) soft breadcrumbs
¼ tsp dried basil leaves
¼ tsp dried oregano leaves

Salt and freshly ground black pepper
    to taste
125g (4oz) cream cheese
1 egg, slightly beaten
2 tbsp olive oil
250ml (8fl oz) dry red wine

1. Preheat the oven to 180°C, 350°F, gas mark 4.
2. Beat the steak on both sides with a meat mallet to flatten them evenly to about 3mm (⅛in) thickness. In a medium-size sauté pan heat the butter over medium-high heat. When the butter is foaming, add the onion and sauté for about 3 minutes. Add the garlic and sauté for 1 more minute. Add the mushrooms and cook until soft, about 3 minutes. Remove from the heat and add the parsley, breadcrumbs, basil, oregano, salt and pepper, cream cheese and egg; mix well.
3. Spread the mixture on the steak. Roll longways, Swiss roll-style, and tie with string approximately every 50mm (2in). In a large skillet over high heat, brown the meat on all sides in the olive oil. Transfer to a baking dish. Add the wine, cover and bake for 2 hours. Cut into 25mm (1in) thick slices and serve with the pan juices.

Stuffed Cabbage Rolls

1 head Savoy cabbage
1.3kg (3lb) lean ground beef
1 tsp salt
⅛ tsp fresh ground black pepper
1 small onion, chopped
225g (8oz) tin tomato sauce

Sauce:

80ml (2½fl oz) whipping cream
1 tbsp honey
60ml (2fl oz) vinegar
225g (8oz) tin tomato sauce
15g (½oz) chopped parsley

Serves 6	
Carb Level: Moderate	
Per serving:	
Carbohydrate:	16.8 g
Protein:	41.5 g

Great for a casual afternoon lunch.

1. Remove the core from the cabbage head, keeping the head whole. Bring a large pot of salted water to the boil and drop the cabbage in for 4 to 6 minutes. (This will make it easier to separate and remove the leaves.) Pull off 12 whole leaves from the cabbage head.
2. In a medium-size bowl, combine the beef, salt, pepper, onion and tomato sauce; blend well. Place the cabbage leaves in a very large bowl. Bring a large pot of water to the boil, then immediately cover the cabbage with the boiled water. Let stand for 5 minutes. Drain well.
3. Shape the meat mixture into 12 miniature loaf shapes. Place a loaf in the centre of each cabbage leaf; roll up, folding in the sides. Place the rolls, seam side down, in a 255mm (10in) sauté pan or frying pan.
4. Combine all the sauce ingredients. Pour the sauce evenly over the cabbage rolls; bring to the boil, reduce heat to a simmer and cover. Cook, basting often, for about 1–1½ hours.

Layered Taco Salad

Serves 4
Carb Level: Moderate

Per serving:

Carbohydrate:	18.1 g
Protein:	20.0 g

Add cooked chicken or ground beef to make this an even better-tasting salad.

125ml (4fl oz) mayonnaise
250ml (8fl oz) sour cream
¼ tsp chilli powder
¼ tsp onion powder
¼ tsp cumin
¼ tsp garlic powder
½ tsp salt
½ tsp black pepper
⅛ tsp red pepper flakes
680g (1lb 8oz) shredded lettuce

225g (8oz) Cheddar cheese, shredded
225g (8oz) Swiss cheese, shredded
2 ripe tomatoes, finely chopped
100g (3½ oz) tin chopped ripe black olives
½ small bunch green onions, finely chopped

In a medium-size mixing bowl, combine the mayonnaise, sour cream, chilli powder, onion powder, cumin, garlic powder, salt, pepper and red pepper flakes; whisk together until well blended. Spread evenly on a serving platter with sides. Top with the shredded lettuce, then the cheeses, then the tomatoes, black olives and green onions. Cover and refrigerate overnight. Serve with a little salsa on the side.

Mushroom Curry Sauté

2 onions, chopped
30g (1oz) butter
1 tsp tomato paste
$\frac{1}{2}$ tsp ground cinnamon
$\frac{1}{4}$ tsp garam masala or curry
    powder
$\frac{1}{4}$ tsp ground cloves
680g (1lb (8oz) sliced medium-size
    mushrooms
3–4 dashes dry white wine (water
    can be substituted)

160ml (5fl oz) sour cream
250ml (8fl oz) chicken stock
$\frac{1}{8}$ tsp chilli powder
Salt and freshly ground black pepper
    to taste
Fresh coriander leaves for
    garnish

Serves 4

Carb Level: Moderate

Per serving:

Carbohydrate:	12.6 g
Protein:	4.0 g

This is a great way to dress up button mushrooms. Garam masala is available in the spice section of most supermarkets.

1. In a large sauté pan over medium-high heat, sauté the onions in the butter until golden brown. Add the tomato paste, cinnamon, garam masala (*or* curry) and ground cloves; cook, stirring constantly, for 4–5 minutes.
2. Add the mushrooms and a few drops of white wine. Cook, stirring constantly, for 4 to 5 minutes. Gradually add the sour cream, and cook for another 3 to 5 minutes. Add the stock and simmer for 15 minutes. Add the chilli powder and salt and pepper. Garnish with fresh coriander leaves. Can be served hot or at room temperature.

Fresh Mozzarella Salad

Serves 2
Carb Level: Moderate

Per serving:

Carbohydrate:	15.3 g
Protein:	46.4 g

You can always sub-
stitute tomato for the
roasted peppers.

4 large red peppers
375g (12oz) fresh mozzarella cheese
16 large basil leaves
Extra-virgin olive oil

Salt and freshly ground black pepper
* to taste*

1. Roast the peppers directly on the hob over high heat, turning them until they are evenly blackened. Place the peppers in a medium-size bowl and cover with plastic wrap. (This allows them to steam, making it easier to peel them.) Once they are cool enough to handle, rinse them under cold running water and peel off the skins (the skin should come off very easily). Cut off the stems, then slice away the ribs and remove the seeds. Quarter the peppers longways.
2. Slice the mozzarella balls into 6mm (¼in)-thick rounds and arrange the slices on a serving platter, alternating them with the pepper quarters. Place the basil leaves between the mozzarella and peppers. Drizzle with extra-virgin olive oil and sprinkle with salt and pepper, then serve.

Beef Salad
with Horseradish Dressing

225g (8oz) green beans
185g (6oz) peeled baby carrots
375g (12oz) beef sirloin steak, cut
*   25mm (1in) thick*
Salt and freshly ground black pepper
*   to taste*
680g (1lb 8oz) mixed salad greens

250ml (8fl oz) Creamy Horseradish
Dressing (see recipe on page 110)

Serves 4	
Carb Level: Moderate	
Per serving:	
Carbohydrate:	18.6 g
Protein:	20.6 g

Try with Ranch
Dressing (see page
109) for a variation.

1. Wash the green beans and trim the ends. Cut the beans in half cross-ways. In a covered medium-size saucepan, cook the beans in boiling salted water until tender and a vibrant green. Remove and rinse under cold running water. Cook the baby carrots for 10–15 minutes or until tender. Drain and rinse under cold running water, then cover and chill both vegetables for 4–24 hours.
2. Trim the fat from the meat. Sprinkle both sides with salt and pepper. Place the meat on the unheated rack of a grill pan; broil 75–100mm (3–4 in) from the heat until done, turning once. Allow 10–12 minutes per 25mm (1in) of thickness for medium-rare or 12–15 minutes for medium. Stand, covered with a tin-foil tent, for 5 minutes after cooking. Thinly slice across the grain into bite-size strips.
3. Divide the greens among individual plates or place on a large plate. Arrange the green beans, baby carrots and meat slices on top of the salad greens. Spoon the Creamy Horseradish Dressing over the top.

Bacon, Lettuce, Tomato and Cheese Salad

Serves 2

Carb Level: Moderate

Per serving:

Carbohydrate:	19.5 g
Protein:	27.1 g

Everyone's favourite sandwich, without the bread – this is a satisfying lunch treat.

10 smoked bacon slices
⅛ tsp chopped garlic
1 tbsp fresh-squeezed lemon juice
60ml (2fl oz) mayonnaise
½ tbsp snipped chives
1 tbsp water
Salt and pepper to taste

1 small red onion, thinly sliced
225g (8oz) cherry tomatoes, halved
125g (4oz) Monterey jack cheese, shredded
1 head Romaine lettuce, torn into bite-size pieces

In a frying pan, cook the bacon over medium heat until crisp. Drain the bacon on paper towels, then crumble. In a small bowl, whisk together the garlic, lemon juice, mayonnaise, chives, water and salt and pepper. In a large bowl toss together the onion, tomatoes, cheese, lettuce, half the bacon and enough of the prepared dressing to coat. Serve the salad on a platter and top with the remaining bacon.

tips **Variations on an Old Favourite**

BLTs can still be a favourite. Buy ripe organic tomatoes, scoop out the seeds and inner membrane and fill with a mixture of crispy chopped bacon, fine diced tomatoes and chopped lettuce lightly dressed with mayonnaise. Top with crumbled blue cheese if desired and serve on a bed of crisp lettuce – you'll never miss the bread. One medium whole tomato contains about 5g of carbohydrates and is loaded with vitamin C, as well as potassium and other minerals.

Spinach Salad
with Warm Bacon Dressing

454g (1lb) tender young spinach,
  trimmed of coarse stems
6 slices bacon, chopped crossways
  into strips
4 green onions, washed, trimmed
  and thinly sliced
1 clove garlic, peeled and crushed
1 tbsp tomato ketchup

125ml (4fl oz) red wine vinegar
1/4 tsp salt
1/4 tsp black pepper

Serves 4

Carb Level: Moderate

Per serving:

Carbohydrate:	18.2 g
Protein:	9.0 g

You can make this dressing in advance and refrigerate it – reheat it in the microwave, then dress the salad.

1. Wash the spinach well in several changes of cold water, dry very well, then wrap in paper towels and refrigerate.
2. To prepare the dressing, brown the bacon in a large, heavy frying pan over medium heat for 3–5 minutes, until crisp. Remove the bacon with a slotted spoon and set it aside on paper towels to drain.
3. Add the green onions and garlic to the bacon drippings in the pan and sauté over low heat for about 2 minutes, until soft. Mix in the remaining ingredients and bring to the boil. Place the spinach in a large heat-proof salad bowl. Pour the mixture over the spinach, sprinkle in the bacon bits and toss well to mix. Serve immediately.

Hearts of Romaine
with Parmesan Dressing

Serves 1
Carb Level: Low

Per serving:	
Carbohydrate:	8.9 g
Protein:	17.7 g

This simple salad is similar to the Caesar, but quicker to make.

*1 heart of Romaine lettuce, outer
  leaves removed*
2 tsp white wine vinegar
*2 tbsp extra-virgin
  olive oil*

*45g (1½ oz) freshly grated
  Parmesan cheese*
*Salt and freshly ground black pepper
  to taste*

Separate the Romaine leaves. In a large bowl, whisk together the vinegar, oil, half the Parmesan and salt and pepper. Toss the Romaine leaves with the dressing and serve sprinkled with the remaining Parmesan cheese.

CHAPTER 11
Comfort Food

❖ **Indicates Easy Recipe** ❖

Devilled Eggs

Serves 2

Carb Level: Low

Per serving:

Carbohydrate:	1.6 g
Protein:	13.0 g

This is great added to salads or used as a wholefood protein supplement.

4 large eggs
2½ tbsp mayonnaise
1½ tsp Dijon mustard
Hot pepper sauce to taste

Salt and freshly ground white pepper
  to taste
1 tbsp chopped fresh chives

1. Place the eggs in a medium-size saucepan and cover with water. Bring to the boil, reduce to a simmer and cook for 9 minutes. Plunge the eggs into a bowl filled with ice water. Allow the eggs to cool completely.
2. Carefully peel the shells from the eggs. Cut the eggs in half and remove the yolks from the whites. Place the yolks in a bowl and add the mayonnaise, mustard, hot pepper sauce, salt and pepper and chives. With the back of a fork, mash all of the ingredients until blended.
3. Fill the egg whites with the yolk mixture, using a teaspoon or a pastry bag fitted with a star tip. Serve chilled.

Lime-Grilled Catfish

2 tbsp butter
2 tbsp fresh-squeezed lime juice
1 tsp finely grated lime zest
$\frac{1}{4}$ tsp garlic powder
$\frac{1}{4}$ tsp paprika

Salt and freshly ground black pepper
  to taste
Two 185g (6oz) catfish fillets, boned
  and with skin on

Serves 2	
Carb Level: Low	
Per serving:	
Carbohydrate:	1.8 g
Protein:	26.3 g

A favourite recipe from the Southern states of the USA.

1. Melt the butter in a medium-size sauté pan over medium-low heat. Stir in the lime juice, lime zest, garlic powder, paprika and salt and pepper to taste; set aside.
2. Preheat the grill to medium-high.
3. Season the catfish fillets with salt and pepper. Brush each fillet generously with the lime sauce. Place the fish skin side down on an oiled baking tray and grill for about 6–8 minutes or until done. Add any leftover lime marinade to the pan juices, heat, and spoon over the fillets. Serve immediately.

Salmon
with Chive Mustard Butter

Serves 6

Carb Level: Low

Per serving:

Carbohydrate:	1.2 g
Protein:	12.3 g

Sea bass or snapper can be substituted for the salmon.

1½ tbsp stoneground Dijon mustard
1½ tsp finely grated orange zest
3½ tbsp fresh-squeezed lemon juice, divided
½ tsp salt
¼ tsp freshly ground black pepper
8 tbsp unsalted butter, softened

5 tbsp finely chopped fresh chives, divided
1.3kg (3lb) salmon fillets, boned and with skin on

1. In a medium-size bowl, combine the mustard, orange zest, 1½ tbsp lemon juice, salt, pepper, butter and 3 tbsp of chives; mix well to blend.
2. Preheat the oven to 220°C, 425°F, gas mark 7.
3. In a lightly buttered baking dish, place the fillets skin side down. Brush each fillet with the remaining lemon juice and season with salt and pepper. Spread about 2–2½ tablespoons of the butter mixture over each fillet to coat evenly.
4. Bake for about 12 minutes or until done. To check it is done, insert a thin-bladed knife into the thickest part of the fillet. The flesh should flake and separate easily, and there should be no trace of translucence. The fish should be opaque and flaky. Transfer the fish to a warm platter and brush any remaining mustard chive butter over the fish while it is hot. Sprinkle with the remaining chives to garnish. Cut each fillet in half to serve.

Cooking Times for Fish
As a rule of thumb, you can expect fish to take about 12 minutes per 25mm (1in) to cook through in a preheated 220°C, 425°F, gas mark 7 oven.

Baby Back Ribs with Sauerkraut

900g (2lb) sauerkraut, drained and
  rinsed
500g (1lb 2oz) shredded red
  cabbage
1 tbsp, plus ½ tsp paprika
4 cloves garlic, chopped

425g (14½ oz) tin stewed tomatoes
1.3kg (3lb) pork baby back ribs,
  trimmed of fat
Salt and freshly ground black pepper
  to taste

Serves 4	
Carb Level: Moderate	
Per serving:	
Carbohydrate:	19.5 g
Protein:	37.2 g

This is a good dish for a casual family get-together.

1. In a medium-size bowl, combine the sauerkraut, cabbage, 1 teaspoon of paprika, garlic and tomatoes; stir well to mix. Spread this mixture into the bottom of a large oiled baking dish.
2. Preheat the oven to 190°C, 375°F, gas mark 5.
3. Arrange the ribs on top of the sauerkraut mixture, curved side up. Season with salt and pepper and the rest of the paprika. Bake in the oven, covered with tin foil, for about 1½ hours or until the meat is tender. Uncover the pan, turn the ribs over and bake uncovered for another 20 minutes.
4. To serve, cut the ribs apart from the bones and serve over the sauerkraut.

tips Sauerkraut

Although it is thought of as a German creation, sauerkraut was eaten by Chinese labourers on the Great Wall of China over 2,000 years ago. Chinese sauerkraut was made from shredded cabbage fermented in rice wine. Eventually it found its way to Europe. Quality sauerkraut can be purchased in jars or tins at the supermarket, while fresh sauerkraut is available in delicatessens and in plastic bags in the refrigerated foods section of supermarkets. All sauerkraut should be rinsed before being used. Sauerkraut is an excellent source of vitamin C and some B vitamins. A 20g (½oz) serving contains 3.4g of carbohydrates.

Fried Chicken

<table>
<tr><td>Serves 4</td></tr>
<tr><td>Carb Level: Moderate</td></tr>
<tr><td>Per serving:</td></tr>
<tr><td>Carbohydrate: 17.4 g</td></tr>
<tr><td>Protein: 47.9 g</td></tr>
</table>

This is especially good eaten cold the day after being made. Also a great picnic dish.

375ml (12fl oz) buttermilk
1.3kg (3lb) whole chicken, cut into
    eight serving pieces
60g (2oz) plain flour
3/4 tsp salt
1/4 tsp black pepper
1/2 tsp paprika
1/4 tsp garlic powder

Large pinch of grated nutmeg
Oil for deep-frying
Fresh parsley sprigs for garnish

1. Pour the buttermilk into a large non-metallic bowl. Add the chicken pieces to the buttermilk and turn to coat. Cover and refrigerate, turning occasionally, for 2–3 hours.
2. In a large bowl, combine the flour with the salt, pepper, paprika, garlic powder and nutmeg. Remove the chicken pieces from the buttermilk and shake off any excess liquid. Allow to drain. Toss the chicken pieces in a large plastic food storage bag with the flour mixture to ensure the pieces are evenly coated.
3. Pour 19mm (3/4in) of oil into a deep frying pan and heat to 180°C, 350°F. Use a deep-fry thermometer to get an accurate reading.
4. Fry the chicken in batches to avoid overcrowding the pan. Cook for about 10–15 minutes, turning occasionally so the pieces cook to an even crispy golden brown. Drain the chicken on paper towels. Transfer to a large platter and garnish with fresh parsley sprigs.

Crustless Salmon Potpie

900g (2lb) salmon fillets
5 tbsp vegetable oil, divided
Salt and freshly ground black pepper
    to taste
300g (10oz) cleaned and thinly
    sliced leeks, white parts only
275g (9oz) thinly sliced fennel bulbs
5 tbsp butter
2½ tbsp plain flour

657ml (20fl oz) milk
6 tbsp fresh-squeezed lemon juice
Salt and freshly ground black pepper
    to taste
1 tbsp chopped fresh dill for garnish

Serves 8
Carb Level: Moderate

Per serving:	
Carbohydrate:	10.2 g
Protein:	21.1 g

A great hearty winter dish. Use quality centre-cut fillets for the best results.

1. Preheat the oven to 220°C, 425°F, gas mark 7.
2. Brush the salmon fillets with 1 tablespoon of oil and season with salt and pepper. Lightly oil a baking tray. Bake the salmon for about 8–12 minutes or until the centres are just cooked. Remove from the pan and let cool. Remove the skin and cut into 25mm (1in) pieces. (The salmon may flake apart.)
3. Heat the remaining oil in a large sauté pan over medium heat. Add the leeks and fennel, and cook for about 5 minutes or until tender. Remove from the heat and add to the salmon pieces.
4. Melt the butter in a medium-size saucepan over medium heat. Add the flour and cook, stirring, for a few minutes until well blended. Gradually pour in the milk, whisking constantly until slightly thickened. Add the lemon juice a little at a time according to taste. Season with salt and pepper. Add the salmon and vegetables, and heat to just bubbling. Serve in warm bowls and garnish with chopped dill.

Where to Buy Fresh Fish
tips
If you don't have a reliable fresh fish provider, try a reputable local sushi restaurant. They may be willing to sell you a piece of salmon. Use the freshest, highest-quality fish you can find.

Spicy Chicken Wings

Serves 10
Carb Level: Moderate
Per serving:
Carbohydrate: 18.2 g
Protein: 10.9 g

Serve with blue cheese dressing and celery stalks.

250ml (8fl oz) white wine vinegar
2 tsp pepper sauce, preferably
* Tabasco*
2 tbsp honey
2 tbsp soy sauce
1 tbsp dried thyme leaves
1 tsp cayenne pepper
2 tbsp garlic powder
2 tsp salt

900g (2lb) chicken wings, split at
* joints into two pieces, wing tips*
* removed*
1 bunch green onions, cleaned and
* chopped*

1. Combine the vinegar, pepper sauce, honey, soy sauce, thyme, cayenne, garlic powder and salt in a large resealable plastic bag. Add the chicken wings and toss well to coat. Refrigerate overnight.
2. Preheat the oven to 190°C, 375°F, gas mark 5.
3. Line a baking tray with tin foil and brush it lightly with oil. Drain the chicken, reserving the marinade. Arrange the chicken on the baking tray. Place the marinade in a medium-size saucepan over medium-high heat and cook for about 6 minutes or until reduced by half. Brush the wings generously on all sides with the reduced marinade.
4. Bake the wings for about 20 minutes, then turn and bake for 10 more minutes. Serve on a platter garnished with the chopped green onion.

Baked Pork Chops with
Caramelized Onions and Smoked Cheddar

Eight 225g (8oz) lean centre-cut pork chops 25mm (1-in) thick, trimmed of excess fat
Salt and freshly ground black pepper to taste
4 tbsp vegetable oil, plus more if needed
1.3kg (3lb) sliced onions
½ tsp sugar
2 tsp chopped garlic
1.25l (40fl oz) beef broth
90g (3oz) grated smoked Cheddar with the rind
1½ tbsp chopped fresh flatleaf parsley for garnish

Serves 8
Carb Level: Moderate

Per serving:	
Carbohydrate:	16.9 g
Protein:	39.7 g

The flavour improves when this dish is allowed to stand refrigerated overnight; gently reheat just before serving.

1. Preheat the oven to 180°C, 350°F, gas mark 4.
2. Season both sides of the pork chops with salt and pepper. Heat 2 tablespoons of oil in a large sauté pan over high heat. Cook the pork chops in batches, making sure not to overcrowd the pan. Cook for about 4 minutes on each side or until golden brown. You may need to add more oil with the remaining chops. Place the browned chops in a large baking dish.
3. Add the remaining oil to the sauté pan, set on medium heat. Add the onions and cook them slowly until they start to brown. Sprinkle them with sugar and continue to cook, stirring, until the onions are well browned. Add the garlic and cook for 1 minute more. Arrange the onions on top of the chops and add the beef broth. The chops should be just covered with liquid. Cover the dish with foil and bake for about 45–60 minutes or until tender.
4. To finish the dish, remove the cover and sprinkle the cheese over the chops. Bake uncovered for about 7 minutes more, until the cheese is melted and golden brown. Garnish with fresh parsley.

Stuffed Bell Peppers

Serves 5
Carb Level: Moderate

Per serving:	
Carbohydrate:	18.0 g
Protein:	52.5 g

Increase the cooking times if you use the large peppers, to account for the density of the filling.

10 medium or 5 large green
  peppers
275g (9oz) chopped onions
60g (2oz) chopped carrots
1.3kg (3oz) ground sirloin beef
1 tbsp chopped fresh parsley
½ tbsp finely chopped garlic
½ tsp dried thyme
½ tsp dried basil
1 tsp salt
½ tsp freshly ground black pepper
⅛ tsp cayenne pepper
1 tbsp Worcestershire sauce
825g (1lb 12oz) tinned chopped
  tomatoes
100g (3½ oz) grated Parmesan
  cheese

1. Preheat the oven to 180°C, 350°F, gas mark 4.
2. Slice off the tops of the green peppers and remove the seeds and membranes.
3. In a medium-size bowl, combine the onions, carrots, ground meat, parsley, garlic, thyme, basil, salt, pepper, cayenne, Worcestershire sauce and tomatoes.
4. Stuff each pepper to the top with the ground beef filling. Place the peppers upright in a lightly oiled baking dish. Bake for about 55–60 minutes or until the beef is cooked through and the peppers are tender. When the peppers are cooked, top them with the cheese and place them back into the oven until the cheese is melted.

Beware of Additives

There are many web sites that offer comfort foods. Make sure you research the products before purchasing online. Many preheat-packaged products contain commercial thickeners that are high in carbohydrate.

Pot Roast with Vegetable Sauce

2 tbsp olive oil
1.8kg (4lb) boneless beef sirloin steak
Salt and freshly ground black pepper
*   to taste*
185g (6oz) thinly sliced onions
185g (6oz) chopped celery
185g (6oz) chopped carrots
1½ tsp fresh thyme leaves or ½ tsp
*   dried*
Large pinch of ground allspice
Large pinch ground cloves

3 fresh flatleaf parsley sprigs, plus extra,
*   chopped, for garnish*
2 bay leaves, broken in half
3 large garlic cloves, peeled and
*   crushed*
825g (1lb 12oz) tinned Italian toma-
*   toes, drained and coarsely chopped*
750ml (24fl oz) beef stock
500ml (16fl oz) dry white wine
Sugar (optional)
2 tsp unsalted butter

Serves 8	
Carb Level: Moderate	
Per serving:	
Carbohydrate:	11.1 g
Protein:	47.0 g

Serve with a fresh green vegetable or another favourite for a change of pace from the standard potatoes and carrots.

1. Preheat the oven to 180°C, 350°F, gas mark 4.
2. Heat the oil in a Dutch oven over medium-high heat. Pat the roast dry and season with salt and pepper. Cook the roast on each side for about 5 minutes or until brown. Remove and set the roast aside.
3. In the same pan, add the onions, celery and carrots; cook for 5 minutes, stirring, or until the vegetables are tender. Add the thyme, allspice, cloves, parsley sprigs, bay leaves, garlic, tomatoes, stock and wine; stir to mix well. Return the roast to the pan and bring the liquid to a simmer. Transfer the contents of the pan to the oven and cook covered for 2½–3 hours or until the meat begins to fall apart. Baste and turn the roast every 30 minutes during the cooking process.
4. When the roast is done, remove the meat from the pan. Strain the vegetables from the liquid and discard the bay leaves. In a food processor, purée the vegetables until smooth. Add the puréed vegetables back to the liquid. Add a little sugar if it is too acidic.
5. Over medium-high heat, reduce the sauce by a third until it coats the back of a spoon. Season with salt and pepper, and swirl in the butter.
6. To serve, cut the roast into thin slices, spoon the sauce over the top, and garnish with parsley. Serve additional sauce in a bowl.

Classic Meat Loaf

Serves 6
Carb Level: Moderate

Per serving:	
Carbohydrate:	15.8 g
Protein:	44.5 g

Serve with Tomato Sauce (see recipe on page 67). Also good the next day sliced and eaten cold.

4 tbsp butter
185g (6oz) chopped mushrooms
90g (3oz) chopped onion
900g (2lb) ground beef
225g (8oz) ground pork
225g (8oz) ground veal
15g (oz) chopped fresh parsley
Salt and freshly ground black pepper
   to taste

125ml (4fl oz) double cream
100g (3½oz) breadcrumbs
100g (3½oz) grated Gruyère cheese,
   divided

1. Preheat the oven to 180°C, 350°F, gas mark 4.
2. Melt the butter in a medium-size sauté pan over medium-high heat. When the butter starts to foam, add the mushrooms and onion; cook for about 5 minutes or until tender.
3. Transfer the sautéed vegetables to a large bowl. Add the ground meat, parsley, salt and pepper, cream, breadcrumbs and three-quarters of the cheese; mix well, then press the mixture into a loaf pan. Sprinkle the top with the remaining cheese and bake for about 1 hour or until done.

Mashed Cauliflower?

You can use cauliflower as a satisfying potato substitute. Steam cauliflower florets until soft. Purée in a food processor until smooth. Add butter, cream or sour cream and salt and pepper until the desired taste and consistency are achieved. Serve hot, garnished with grated cheese if desired. A 45g (1½ oz) serving of cauliflower has 2.6g of carbohydrates.

Chicken Potpie Stew

454g (1lb) boneless, skinless chicken breasts
500ml (16fl oz) (or more as needed) chicken stock
1 medium onion, diced
2 carrots, diced
2 stalks celery, diced
1½ tbsp arrowroot

125ml (4fl oz) evaporated skimmed milk
1 tbsp chopped fresh parsley
½ tbsp chopped fresh tarragon
Salt and freshly ground black pepper to taste

Serves 4
Carb Level: Moderate

Per serving:	
Carbohydrate:	17.8 g
Protein:	25.2 g

A great recipe for a group, easily prepared a day ahead and gently reheated just before serving.

1. Rinse the chicken under cold running water and pat dry on paper towels. Trim the chicken of any fat, then cut into medium dice. Place the chicken in a medium-size saucepan and add the stock, which should just cover the chicken. Bring the liquid to a gentle simmer until the chicken is just cooked. Remove the chicken with a slotted spoon and reserve.

2. Add the onion, carrots and celery to the stock, and simmer until the vegetables are tender. Dilute the arrowroot in evaporated milk and add to the stock and vegetables. Stirring constantly, bring the stock to a full simmer to activate the arrowroot. Remove the pan from the heat and stir in the parsley, tarragon and salt and pepper. Return the chicken to the sauce and simmer until heated through. Serve in warm bowls.

tips Chilli, Chilli, Chilli

Modernize your chilli – eliminate the beans and reduce the tinned tomatoes. Add some ground red chillies and spices such as cumin, paprika, cayenne and oregano to develop the flavour. Add a tablespoon of cornflour if you require a thicker consistency. Garnish the bowls with sour cream, chopped coriander and grated cheeses.

Chapter 12
Breakfast

❖ Indicates Easy Recipe ❖

Strawberry Jam

Serves 10

Carb Level: Low

Per serving:

Carbohydrate:	3.7 g
Protein:	3.3 g

This jam can accompany any breakfast dish.

1 punnet fresh ripe strawberries
Juice of ½ lemon
60ml (2fl oz) water

40g (1¼ oz) envelope unflavoured gelatin
2½ tsp sugar substitute or less to taste

1. Wash, stem and quarter the berries. In a medium-size non-reactive saucepan over medium heat, simmer the berries with the lemon juice covered for about 3 minutes or until the berries are soft and start to release their juices.
2. In a small bowl, pour the water over the gelatin and allow to soften for 1 minute. Add this to the berries and remove from the heat. Mix in the sugar substitute to taste and store covered in the refrigerator. Serve when completely chilled.

Hollandaise Sauce

Serves 6

Carb Level: Low

Per serving:

Carbohydrate:	0.6 g
Protein:	1.6 g

This is a classic match with any egg dish. Add tarragon for a variation of flavours.

60g (2oz) butter
3 egg yolks
2 tbsp fresh-squeezed lemon juice
Dash of cayenne pepper

Salt and freshly ground black pepper to taste

Melt the butter in a small saucepan over low heat. In a blender, mix the egg yolks, lemon juice and cayenne. With the motor running, add the melted butter in a slow stream. Blend for about 30 seconds or until thick. Keep over a bowl of very hot water, stirring occasionally until ready to serve. Add salt and pepper to taste.

Cream Cheese and Spring Onion Scramble

3 tbsp unsalted butter
45g (1¹/₂oz) spring onions, chopped
1 tbsp shallots, chopped
10 large eggs
125g (4oz) cream cheese, cut into
*   bits and softened*

Salt and freshly ground black pepper
*   to taste*
¹/₂ tbsp snipped fresh dill
Chopped chives or spring onions
*   tops, thinly sliced for garnish*

Serves 4	
Carb Level: Low	
Per serving:	
Carbohydrate:	3.3 g
Protein:	15.1 g

This is a simple recipe that kids also enjoy.

1. Melt the butter in a medium-size non-stick sauté pan over medium heat. When the butter starts to foam, add the spring onions and shallots; cook for about 2 minutes or until the spring onions are tender.
2. In a bowl, whisk together the eggs, cream cheese, salt and pepper and dill. Pour the mixture into the sauté pan and cook over low heat, stirring until cooked. Transfer to a plate and garnish with chopped chives or spring onions.

Does Colour Matter?

Is there a difference between brown-shelled eggs and white-shelled eggs? The shell colour does not affect the nutritional value, cooking characteristics or quality. Egg shell colour is determined by the breed of the chicken.

Steak and Eggs

Serves 4	
Carb Level: Low	

Per serving:

Carbohydrate:	1.2 g
Protein:	33.2 g

If you don't own a cast-iron frying pan, use the heaviest ovenproof sauté pan you have.

1 tbsp vegetable oil
*454g (1lb) sirloin steak (about
    25mm/1in thick)*
Salt and cayenne pepper
2 tbsp butter

8 large eggs
½ tsp snipped chives

1. Preheat the oven to 180°C, 350°F, gas mark 4.
2. Preheat a large cast-iron frying pan over medium heat until hot, about 5 minutes. Raise the heat to high and add the oil. Season the steak with salt and cayenne pepper. Place the steak in the pan and cook on each side for about 4 minutes or until golden brown. Transfer the steak to the oven and cook for about 5 minutes for medium-rare.
3. Let the steak stand in a tin-foil tent for 10 minutes.
4. Heat 2 non-stick sauté pans over medium-low heat. Melt 1 tablespoon of butter in each pan. Break 4 eggs into each sauté pan. Season the eggs lightly with the chives, salt and cayenne pepper. Cook until the whites are just set. Divide the eggs among four warm plates.
5. Cut the steak into slices and serve with the eggs.

tips **Food Safety Tip**
Salmonella bacteria does not come from the shell or cracks in the shell, but from the yolk itself. You can have a perfectly clean, crack-free egg that contains salmonella.

Homemade
Breakfast Sausage Patties

454g (1lb) lean ground pork
30g (1oz) breadcrumbs
2 tbsp cream
2 tbsp pure maple syrup
2 tsp grated orange zest
2 tsp finely chopped fresh parsley
$^1/_8$ tsp dried sage
$^1/_4$ tsp red pepper flakes

$^1/_4$ tsp salt
$^1/_4$ tsp freshly ground black pepper
$1^1/_2$ tbsp vegetable oil

Serves 6
Carb Level: Low

Per serving:

Carbohydrate:	5.4 g
Protein:	20.2 g

You can omit the maple syrup and add your own blend of herbs or spices.

1. In a medium-size bowl, use your hands to mix together all the ingredients until completely bended. Divide into 12 equal portions.
2. Place a non-stick sauté pan over medium heat. Wearing plastic gloves, gently form each patty about 12mm ($^1/_2$ in) thick and 50mm (2in) in diameter. Working in batches, cook the patties on each side for about 5 minutes or until they are golden brown. (Make sure they are cooked all the way through.) Serve immediately.

Sausage Fact

Nutritional information: 125g (4oz) of breakfast sausage equals 1.2g of carbohydrates and 13.3g of protein.

Corned Beef Hash

Serves 4
Carb Level: Low

Per serving:

Carbohydrate:	6.1 g
Protein:	26.3 g

Serve a poached egg on top of the hash for an amazing breakfast.

2 tbsp unsalted butter
1 large mild onion, cut into 12mm (½ in) dice
1 red pepper, seeded, trimmed, and cut into 12mm (½ in) dice
680g (1lb 8oz) unsliced cooked lean corned beef, cut into 6mm (¼-in) dice
80ml (2½fl oz) milk

30g (1oz) finely chopped fresh parsley
1 tbsp finely chopped fresh chives
Salt and freshly ground black pepper to taste
4 tbsp vegetable oil, divided

1. Melt the butter in a large non-stick sauté pan over medium heat. Add the onion and pepper and cook for about 5 minutes or until tender. Transfer the vegetables to a large bowl and set aside.
2. Add the corned beef, milk, parsley, chives and salt and pepper to the vegetables; toss well to mix.
3. Heat 2 tablespoons of the oil in the sauté pan over medium heat. Add the hash mixture, pressing it down with the back of a spatula to form an even compact cake. Reduce the heat to medium-low and cook for about 15 minutes, shaking the pan occasionally, or until the bottom is golden brown and crusty. Transfer the patty to a heatproof plate.
4. Heat the remaining 2 tablespoons of oil in the same pan and slide the hash cake, browned side up, back into the pan. Cook the second side for about 10 minutes or until golden brown and crusty. Transfer onto the same heatproof plate and cut into wedges.

Scrambled Eggs
with Smoked Salmon and Onions

2 tbsp butter
½ sweet onion, finely chopped
12 eggs, lightly beaten
185g (6oz) lox, thinly sliced and cut
    into 25mm (1in) long, 6mm
    (¼in) wide strips

Freshly ground black pepper
    to taste
½ tbsp finely chopped fresh chives for
    garnish

Serves 6
Carb Level: Low

Per serving:	
Carbohydrate:	2.0 g
Protein:	17.8 g

This is an easy breakfast dish to prepare for guests.

1. Melt the butter in a non-stick sauté pan over medium-low heat. Add the onion and cook for about 4 minutes until slightly brown.
2. Add the eggs and raise the heat. Stir occasionally while the eggs cook. While the eggs are still fairly loose, add the smoked salmon and pepper. Continue stirring until the eggs are cooked to your liking.
3. Serve on warm plates and garnish with chopped chives.

Taking Medication?

Some medications will reduce your body's ability to absorb and use certain vitamins and minerals. Periodically review your diet plan and medications with your doctor to see if a supplement is needed. Always review your overall plan with your doctor whenever you implement a change in either diet, medication, supplements or exercise plans.

Herby Omelette

Serves 1
Carb Level: Low

Per serving:

Carbohydrate:	2.4 g
Protein:	19.2 g

Adding grated cheese when you add the herbs lends even more flavour.

3 eggs
Salt and freshly ground black pepper
   to taste
1 tbsp butter

$1/2$ tsp each finely chopped: fresh flatleaf parsley, fresh chives, fresh
   chervil, fresh tarragon

1. In a medium-size bowl, whisk together the eggs, salt and pepper until they are frothy.
2. Melt the butter in a small non-stick sauté pan over medium heat. Add the eggs, and as they begin to set, use a spatula to carefully lift the edges and gently push them toward the centre, tilting the pan slightly to allow the liquid egg on top to flow underneath. Continue to cook the eggs until they are almost set but still slightly moist on top.
3. Sprinkle the herbs over the surface of the eggs. Carefully slide the omelette from the pan to a warm plate, and when halfway out, flip the pan over to fold the omelette in half. Serve immediately.

Ethnic Variations

Many combinations of herbs will work with this recipe. Try coriander with a touch of chopped jalapeños for a Mexican flair and top with homemade salsa – or try basil with a touch of oregano for an Italian flavour and top with Tomato Sauce (see recipe on page 67).

Denver Scramble

2 tbsp unsalted butter
½ onion, cut into 12mm (½ in) dice
½ green pepper, seeded and cut into 12mm (½ in) squares
½ red pepper, seeded and cut into 12mm (½ in) squares
185g (6oz) lean bacon, cut into 12mm (½ in) dice
8 eggs, lightly beaten

Salt and freshly ground white pepper to taste
60g (2oz) Cheddar cheese, shredded
½ tbsp finely chopped fresh parsley

Serves 4	
Carb Level: Low	
Per serving:	
Carbohydrate:	5.0 g
Protein:	25.3 g

Cleaning up is easy with this recipe, since everything is done in one pan.

1. Melt the butter in a medium-size non-stick sauté pan over medium heat. Add the onion and peppers, and cook for about 3 minutes or until tender. Add the bacon and cook for 1 more minute.
2. Add the eggs to the pan and season with salt and pepper. Cook at medium-low heat, stirring frequently. Stir in the cheese and continue cooking until done to your liking.
3. Serve on warm plates and garnish with parsley.

Juice Alert

Note the high carb counts for just 250ml (8fl oz) of fresh-squeezed juices:

Orange juice	25.8g
Grapefruit juice	22.7g
Cranberry juice	36.4g
Lemonade	26.9g

Courgette Frittata

680g (1lb 8oz) small courgettes	2 tbsp unsalted butter
10 eggs	2 tbsp olive oil
30g (1oz) freshly grated Parmesan cheese, divided	
Salt and freshly ground black pepper to taste	

Serves 6

Carb Level: Low

Per serving:

Carbohydrate:	4.5 g
Protein:	13.5 g

Goes well with Tomato Sauce (see page 67).

1. Preheat the oven to 180°C, 350°F, gas mark 4.
2. Trim the courgettes and cut them crossways into very thin slices. In a medium-size bowl, beat the eggs until light and frothy. Add the courgettes, half the cheese and the salt and pepper.
3. Melt the butter and add the oil to a medium-size non-stick ovenproof sauté pan over medium heat. Add the egg mixture. Sprinkle with the remaining cheese. Place it in the oven and bake until set but still slightly moist, about 20 minutes.
4. Serve the frittata directly from the pan or slide it onto a plate. Cut into wedges and serve immediately.

tips **Egg Facts**
One whole large egg equals 0.6g of carbohydrates and 6.3g of protein. The breakdown: one large egg yolk equals 0.3g of carbohydrates and 2.8g of protein; one large egg white equals 0.3g of carbohydrates and 2.8g of protein.

Corn and Egg Pudding

Butter, for greasing
2 whole eggs
2 egg yolks
454g (1lb) fresh sweetcorn kernels
125ml (4fl oz) double cream
125g (4oz) smoked ham, chopped

125g (4oz) Gruyère cheese,
    shredded
¼ tsp sweet paprika

Serves 6
Carb Level: Moderate

Per serving:	
Carbohydrate:	13.2 g
Protein:	11.2 g

You can substitute tinned creamed corn if fresh is not available.

1. Preheat the oven to 190°C, 375°F, gas mark 5. Butter a small baking dish.
2. In a bowl, whisk together the eggs and the yolks until blended. Stir in the corn and cream until well mixed. Stir in the ham, cheese and paprika.
3. Pour the mixture into the prepared baking dish. Bake for about 30 minutes or until lightly golden. Scoop out onto warm plates and serve immediately.

Milk It for All It's Worth

Note the following carb counts for 250ml (8fl oz) of milk:

Low-fat soya milk	4.3g
Low-fat cow's milk	11.7g
Whole cow's milk	11.4g

Crabmeat Omelette

Serves 1
Carb Level: Low

Per serving:

Carbohydrate:	1.9 g
Protein:	24.8 g

For a richer dish, top the omelette with Hollandaise or Tomato Sauce (see recipes on pages 192 and 67).

3 eggs
¼ tsp salt
Pinch freshly ground white pepper
1½ tbsp unsalted butter, divided
60g (2oz) flaked cooked
   crabmeat
¼ tsp grated lemon zest

Fresh dill sprigs or chopped parsley
   for garnish

1. In a medium-size bowl, whisk together the eggs, salt and pepper until frothy.
2. Melt ½ tablespoon of the butter in a small non-stick sauté pan over low heat. Add the crabmeat and cook until just heated through. Stir in the lemon zest. Cover to keep warm, and set aside.
3. Melt the remaining butter in another small non-stick sauté pan over medium heat. Add the eggs. As they begin to set, use a spatula to carefully lift the edges and gently push them towards the centre, tilting the pan slightly to allow the liquid egg on top to flow underneath. Continue to cook the eggs until they are almost set.
4. Sprinkle the crabmeat over half the omelette. When sliding the omelette out of the pan, start with the crab-covered side towards the plate. When the omelette is halfway out, flip the pan over to fold the omelette in half. Garnish with dill or parsley.

Desserts

❖ **Indicates Easy Recipe** ❖

Glazed Bananas

Serves 6

Carb Level: Moderate

Per serving:

Carbohydrate:	19.8 g
Protein:	1.5 g

The banana slices can be prepared in advance and baked just before serving.

60g (2oz) crumbs of sugar-free
    butter biscuits
2 tsp vegetable oil
1 tsp butter, melted
1 large egg white
2 tbsp honey

1 tsp fresh-squeezed lemon juice
3 large ripe, but firm, bananas
Lemon wedges for garnish
Mint sprigs for garnish

1. Preheat the oven to 230°C, 450F°, gas mark 8. Line a baking tray with aluminium foil. Set a baking rack on top and coat it with non-stick cooking spray.
2. In a shallow dish, combine the biscuit crumbs, oil and butter. Mix with your fingertips until well blended; set aside.
3. In a medium-size bowl, whisk together the egg white, honey and lemon juice; set aside.
4. Peel the bananas and trim the pointed tips. Cut the bananas crossways into 19mm(¾in) pieces. Dip each banana piece into the egg-white mixture, then transfer them to the crumb mixture. Roll the banana pieces in the crumbs, trying to lightly but evenly coat them. (It helps to use dinner forks to transfer the bananas during the coating process.) Place the bananas on the prepared baking rack.
5. Bake the bananas until crisp, golden and heated through, about 8–12 minutes. Arrange the hot bananas on dessert plates, garnish with lemon wedges and mint sprigs, and serve with Vanilla Ice Cream (see recipe on page 211).

tips **Avoid Temptation**
Clean your pantry, kitchen shelves and cabinets of high-carb products that you will not be using. Donate unopened usable items to your local homeless shelter. Call the shelter before delivering the food, to find out the procedure for donations.

Orange Cups with Lemon Cream

4 large oranges
Grated zest of 1 lemon
80ml (2½fl oz) light whipping
cream

125ml (4fl oz) vanilla yogurt
Strips of lemon and orange peel for
garnish

<table>
<tr><td colspan="2" align="center">**Serves 6**</td></tr>
<tr><td colspan="2" align="center">**Carb Level: Moderate**</td></tr>
<tr><td colspan="2">Per serving:</td></tr>
<tr><td>Carbohydrate:</td><td>11.6 g</td></tr>
<tr><td>Protein:</td><td>2.2 g</td></tr>
</table>

This dish must be served the same day it's prepared, or the filling will start to separate.

1. With a sharp knife, cut each orange in half across. Remove the flesh with the help of a grapefruit spoon and chop finely, then place in a bowl. Set the peels aside.
2. Mix the lemon zest with the chopped orange flesh. In a separate bowl, whip the cream until it is stiff. With a rubber spatula, fold the yogurt into the whipped cream. Add the cream mixture to the chopped oranges, and stir gently to mix. Very thinly slice the bottom off each orange shell so the shells sit level on a plate.
3. Fill all the shells with the orange mixture, then place on a serving plate. Refrigerate the filled shells until ready to serve. To serve, decorate with lemon and orange peels strips.

Desserts on the Web

There are a number of new Web sites offering low-carb sweets.
Try the following sites to purchase sugar-free desserts and products: www.low-carb-mem.co.uk *and* www.low-carbdiet.co.uk

Warm Berry Compote

Serves 6	

Carb Level: Moderate

Per serving:

Carbohydrate:	12.9 g
Protein:	0.7 g

A great recipe in winter when you want the taste of fresh berries. Frozen berries are put to perfect use in this cooked berry recipe.

680g (1lb 8oz) assorted frozen
   berries, no sugar added, thawed

¼ tsp (or to taste) sugar substitute
90g (3oz) butter

1. Simmer the berries with about 2 tablespoons of water in a non-reactive medium-size saucepan for about 5 minutes. Add a pinch of sugar substitute, check for taste and add more sugar substitute as desired. Add the butter and stir in to combine.
2. Remove the pan from the heat, stir once more, and divide the compote among six small bowls. Top with Vanilla Ice Cream (see recipe on page 211) or whipped double cream.

Champagne Summer Berries

Serves 4

Carb Level: Moderate

Per serving:

Carbohydrate:	16.5 g
Protein:	0.9 g

Add the sugar substitute pinch by pinch until you determine the natural sweetness of the berries.

185g (6oz) strawberries, hulled and
   cut in half
185g (6oz) raspberries
90g (3oz) redcurrants
90g (3oz) blueberries
Sugar substitute to taste

60ml (2fl oz) fresh lemon juice
250g (8fl oz) chilled champagne
Mint sprigs for garnish

1. Mix all the berries in a glass bowl and sprinkle them with a pinch of sugar substitute and half the lemon juice; set aside for 10 minutes.
2. To serve, spoon the fruit into glass dishes. At the table, pour the chilled champagne over the fruit and decorate with mint sprigs.

Chocolate Grand Marnier Mousse

*125g (4oz) unsweetened chocolate,
   roughly chopped
4 eggs, separated
60ml (2fl oz) Grand Marnier*

*60ml (2fl oz) brandy
60ml (2fl oz) double cream,
   whipped
Pinch of salt*

Serves 6
Carb Level: Low

Per serving:

Carbohydrate:	10.0 g
Protein:	6.5 g

This dessert is very rich, so servings should be kept small.

1. Melt the chocolate by placing it in a bowl over a saucepan of simmering water until it melts (do not let the water touch the bowl filled with chocolate). Put the egg yolks into another bowl and pour the melted chocolate over them; whisk to blend thoroughly. Add the Grand Marnier, brandy and cream; mix thoroughly.
2. In a separate bowl, beat the egg whites with the salt until medium peaks form. With a rubber spatula, fold this mixture in thirds very slowly and carefully, into the chocolate cream so that it is completely combined but still light and fluffy.
3. Spoon the mousse into individual ramekins and refrigerate for 2 hours before serving.

tips **Elegant End**
End a meal with a perfectly ripe pear, cored, sliced and fanned on an attractive plate, served with 60g (2oz) of a fine cheese such as a French Muenster or Stilton (8.3g carbohydrates).

Chocolate Meringue Biscuits

Serves 12
Carb Level: Moderate

Per serving:	
Carbohydrate:	13.3 g
Protein:	1.1 g

You can make smaller biscuits by using a teaspoon measure of batter instead of a tablespoon.

3 large eggs, separated
⅛ tsp cream of tartar
185g (6oz) granulated sugar

1½ tbsp unsweetened cocoa powder,
*   plus extra for garnish*

1. Preheat the oven to 120°C, 250°F, gas mark ½. Cover two baking trays with baking paper.
2. Place the egg whites and cream of tartar in a medium-size bowl or the bowl of an electric mixer; mix on medium-high speed until soft peaks form. Gradually beat in the granulated sugar (1 tablespoon at a time) until the whites are stiff and shiny.
3. Sift the cocoa over the egg whites and gently fold in until just blended. Drop tablespoons of the batter 25mm (1in) apart on the prepared baking sheets. Bake for 1 hour, until the biscuits are dry. Carefully peel the biscuits from the paper and cool on a wire rack. When cool, sprinkle the biscuits with a little more cocoa powder. Store covered at room temperature.

tips **A Sophisticated Dessert**

Tradition dictates that dessert, or the ending course of a formal meal, includes a sweet, carbohydrate-heavy dessert. Consider ending the meal by focusing on a sophisticated cheese course for the final course with a very simple dessert, such as a small platter of little biscuits, for those who want something sweet.

Chocolate Fudge

250ml (8fl oz) double cream
225g (8oz) unsweetened chocolate,
*   chopped*

403g (14oz) granulated sugar
*   substitute*
2 tbsp unsalted butter
1 tbsp vanilla extract

Line a baking tray with greaseproof or baking paper. Spray with non-stick coating. Place a medium-size saucepan over medium heat and add the cream. Bring to a boil, add the chocolate and stir until completely melted. Remove the pan from the heat and add the sugar substitute, butter and vanilla extract. Mix until smooth and thoroughly combined. Transfer to the prepared baking tray. Spread evenly over the entire sheet. Refrigerate until cool and stiff, about 2 hours. To serve, cut the fudge into squares.

Serves 40	
Carb Level: Low	
Per serving:	
Carbohydrate:	2.0 g
Protein:	0.8 g

The quality of the chocolate is vital; quality Belgian or Swiss chocolate is widely available.

Egg Custard

3 large eggs
3/4 tbsp sugar substitute
1/4 tsp salt
500ml (16fl oz) milk
1/4 tsp vanilla extract

1/8 tsp grated nutmeg
1/8 tsp ground cinnamon
Fresh raspberries for garnish
*   (optional)*

Preheat the oven to 180°C, 350°F, gas mark 4. Beat the eggs in a large mixing bowl until frothy and blended. Add the sugar substitute and salt; mix to combine. Add the milk, vanilla, nutmeg and cinnamon; mix well to combine. Divide the mixture into six ramekins or custard cups. Set the filled cups in a large baking dish and add enough boiling water to fill the dish with 25mm (1in) of water. Bake until the custard is set (doesn't jiggle if shaken with a pair of tongs), about 30 minutes. Serve warm, room temperature or chilled, with a garnish of fresh raspberries.

Serves 6	
Carb Level: Low	
Per serving:	
Carbohydrate:	4.9 g
Protein:	5.8 g

Try orange extract instead of the vanilla extract, and add a touch of grated orange zest for orange custard.

Refrigerator Pumpkin Pie
with Macadamia Nut Crust

Serves 8

Carb Level: Moderate

Per serving:

Carbohydrate:	10.8 g
Protein:	3.4 g

A delicious dessert to make in advance, this recipe requires a few mixing bowls but is worth the effort.

275g (9oz) finely chopped macadamia nuts
2½ tbsp sugar substitute
2 tbsp butter, softened, plus extra for greasing
1 packet gelatin
60ml (2fl oz) water

1 tsp mixed cinnamon, ginger, nutmeg and allspice
425g (15oz) tin pumpkin purée
2 tsp grated orange zest
375ml (12fl oz) double cream
2 tsp vanilla extract

1. Heat the oven to 200°C, 400°F, gas mark 6. Grease the bottom and sides of a 230mm (9in) loose-base flan case.
2. In a medium-size bowl, combine the macadamia nuts, ½ tablespoon sugar substitute and butter; mix well. Press the mixture onto the bottom and 25mm (1in) up the sides of the prepared pan. Bake for 10 minutes, until golden brown. Cool on a wire rack.
3. In a small bowl, sprinkle the gelatin over the water; leave for 5 minutes until the gelatin softens. Heat a small frying pan over medium heat and toast the pumpkin pie spice for 1 to 2 minutes, until fragrant, stirring frequently. Reduce the heat to low, stir in the gelatin mixture, and cook for 1–2 minutes until the gelatin melts. Remove from the heat and cool to room temperature.
4. Place the pumpkin purée in a large bowl and mash with a fork to loosen. Mix in the orange zest. In another large bowl, using an electric mixer on high speed, beat the cream with the remaining sugar substitute and the vanilla until soft peaks form. With a rubber spatula, slowly fold in the gelatin mixture (if too stiff, heat on the stove until melted but not hot). In three parts, gently fold the whipped cream mixture into the pumpkin purée. Pour the filling into the cooled pie shell and smooth the top. Refrigerate for at least 3 hours before serving.

Vanilla Ice Cream

250ml (8fl oz) double cream
4 egg yolks
250ml (8fl oz) whole milk
225g (8oz) sugar substitute

¼ tsp salt
2 tsp vanilla extract
3 egg whites

Serves 12
Carb Level: Low

Per serving:	
Carbohydrate:	6.9 g
Protein:	5.7 g

You don't have to have an ice-cream maker for this recipe!

1. Oil a 125 x 230mm (5 x 9in) metal bread loaf pan. Line the pan with two layers of cling film, leaving at least a 100mm (4in) overhang on the long sides. Freeze the pan for 30 minutes.
2. Using an electric mixer, whip the cream until it thickens, but is still somewhat loose (before soft peaks form). Beat in the egg yolks, whole milk, sweetener, salt and vanilla until the mixture is not quite as thick as regular whipped cream.
3. In a separate bowl, beat the egg whites until they hold soft peaks. Fold the egg whites into the whipped mixture until uniformly blended. (If you have an ice-cream machine, add the mixture to the prepared machine following the manufacturer's instructions.) Pour the mixture into the chilled pan, cover with foil and freeze for 12–24 hours until it is solid.
4. Place your food processor bowl and blade in the freezer. Dip the metal loaf pan into hot water for 5 seconds to help remove the plastic-wrapped ice cream. Firmly pull up on the cling film and remove the ice cream loaf. Peel off the cling film. Cut the loaf into thick slices with a large knife, slicing off only the amount desired to be served. Cut each slice into four chunks, immediately put these chunks into the chilled food processor bowl, and begin to process in 5-second blends, adding as little milk or cream as needed to make the ice cream smooth. Scrape down the sides of the bowl as necessary. Serve immediately when the ice cream is smooth in texture, or freeze to hold for several minutes if serving as an accompaniment to another dessert.

Blancmange

Serves 6
Carb Level: Low

Per serving:

Carbohydrate:	5.1 g
Protein:	2.6 g

A lovely, elegant, and classic French dessert.

Cooking spray, for greasing
1 envelope gelatin
500ml (16fl oz) double cream
1 tbsp sugar substitute

½ tsp almond extract
1 vanilla pod
90g (3oz) fresh berries
        (any kind) for garnish

1. Lightly spray six ramekins or custard cups with cooking spray. In a small bowl, sprinkle the gelatin over 3 tablespoons cold water; let stand for 5 minutes until softened.
2. Combine the cream, 125ml (4fl oz) water, the sweetener, almond extract and vanilla pod in a medium-size saucepan; bring to a boil over medium heat. Remove from heat, add the gelatin mixture and stir until melted.
3. Pour the mixture into the prepared cups. Cover the surface with cling film to prevent skin from forming. Refrigerate for at least 3 hours. When ready to serve, score a small sharp knife along the sides of the ramekin to separate the custard from the dish. Turn out onto serving platters or individual plates, and serve with a few fresh berries.

Little Nibbles

Consider serving a small platter of sweet nibbles instead of full servings of a rich, carbohydrate-laden dessert. Chocolate-covered roasted coffee beans are elegant treats, while candied ginger pieces, chocolate-covered nuts and nut meringues are also nice finishes.

No-Crust Cheesecake

1 tbsp butter, for greasing
900g (2lb) cream cheese, at room
    temperature
225g (8oz) sugar substitute
4 large eggs, at room
    temperature

¼ tsp orange extract
¼ tsp lemon extract
2 tbsp double cream
1 tsp pure vanilla extract

Serves 12

Carb Level: Moderate

Per serving:

Carbohydrate:	13.4 g
Protein:	7.9 g

You can vary the taste by substituting different extracts for the citrus extracts, but always add the vanilla extract.

1. Preheat the oven to 180°C, 350°F, gas mark 4. Grease the bottom and sides of a 230mm (9in) loose-base flan case and set aside.
2. Using an electric mixer, beat the cream cheese on medium speed until it's very smooth. Slowly beat in the sweetener 1 tablespoon at a time. Then, add the eggs one by one, beating the mixture well after each addition. Add the remaining ingredients, scrape down the bowl and stir to combine.
3. Pour the cheesecake batter into the prepared flan case and smooth the top with a rubber spatula. Bake for 10 minutes. Turn down the heat to 140°C, 275°F, gas mark 1, and bake for approximately 1 hour, or until the edges are lightly brown (the cheesecake may be cracked on top). Turn off the oven.
4. Remove the cheesecake from the oven, run a thin-bladed knife around the edge of the flan case and return the case to the oven to cool slowly. If the centre of the cheesecake still looks a little undercooked, it will become firm in the oven as it slowly cooks.
5. Cover the cooled cheesecake with cling film and refrigerate overnight, or up to 3 days. To serve, run a knife around the edges again and remove from the sides of the flan case.

Mocha Mousse

Serves 6

Carb Level: Moderate

Per serving:

Carbohydrate:	12.6 g
Protein:	5.0 g

Don't overmix the mousse when adding the chocolate to the egg whites.

125g (4oz) chocolate, cut into small chunks
4 large eggs, separated
1 tsp vanilla extract

2 tsp brewed strong black coffee or instant espresso, cooled
Pinch of salt

1. Put the chocolate in a stainless steel bowl and place the bowl over the top of a saucepot of simmering water; stir until fully melted. Remove from heat and let the chocolate stand for 5 minutes.
2. In a small bowl, beat the egg yolks with the vanilla extract and cooled coffee; stir into the melted chocolate, whisking well. Beat the egg whites with the salt until they form stiff peaks. Using a rubber spatula, gently fold half of the chocolate mixture into the egg whites. Fold in the remaining mixture. Fold to just blend; the mixture may appear streaky.
3. Pour into six ramekins, small dessert bowls or glasses, cover and chill for at least 4 hours or overnight.

tips

What's the Best Way to Crack an Egg?

Hit the egg firmly, but not forcefully, against a hard, flat surface. This way there is less chance that bits of shell will be in the eggs.

Rhubarb and Strawberry Cream

680g (1lb 8oz) diced rhubarb
1½ tbsp sugar substitute
Pinch of salt

1 punnet strawberries, cut into small
pieces, plus extra for garnish
500ml (16fl oz) double cream

Serves 8
Carb Level: Low

Per serving:	
Carbohydrate:	8.3 g
Protein:	2.0 g

The season for fresh rhubarb is short, so you have to be ready for it to make this delicious dessert.

1. Put the diced rhubarb into a medium-size non-reactive saucepan and stew it gently uncovered. You may need to add 1 tablespoon of water. Add 1 tablespoon of sugar substitute and salt. Cook until the rhubarb is very tender and can be mashed easily with a fork. Add additional water tablespoon by tablespoon to prevent the rhubarb from scorching. Add the strawberries and cook just until combined with the rhubarb mixture, about 4 minutes. Allow to cool.
2. Whip the cream until stiff peaks have formed. Mix in the remaining sugar substitute. Using a rubber spatula, gently fold the whipped cream into the rhubarb mixture. Spoon the mousse into individual ramekins, cover with cling film, and chill thoroughly before serving. Serve with a garnish of fresh strawberries.

A Simple Finish When Berries Are in Season
Combine 15g (½oz) sliced strawberries (3.5g of carbohydrates), 1 teaspoon honey (5.8g of carbohydrates), and 50ml (2fl oz) cup vanilla yogurt (2.6g of carbohydrates) for an easy and delicious treat.

❖ **Indicates Easy Recipe** ❖

Seared Salmon Carpaccio

Serves 4
Carb Level: Low

Per serving:

Carbohydrate:	6.5 g
Protein:	26.2 g

An elegant starter course for a summer dinner party. Keep the salmon chilled until you serve it.

454g (1lb) sushi-grade salmon fillet
Salt and freshly ground black pepper to taste
4 tbsp, plus 1 tsp extra-virgin olive oil
2 tbsp, plus 1 tsp fresh-squeezed lime juice

60g (2oz) stemmed baby organic rocket leaves
125g (4oz) domestic mushrooms, trimmed and thinly sliced
1 tbsp finely chopped chives

1. Season the salmon with the salt and black pepper. Heat a heavy-bottomed, non-stick sauté pan over high heat until almost smoking. Quickly sear the top side of the salmon, only about 1 minute, then sear the other side for about 1 minute. Immediately transfer the salmon to a plate and refrigerate for 1 hour. Using a sharp knife, slice the salmon as thinly as possible. (The slices should be so thin that you should be able to see through them.) Cut enough salmon to cover the bases of four small chilled salad plates. Cover with cling film and refrigerate.
2. In a small bowl, whisk together 3 tablespoons of the olive oil, 1 tablespoon of the lime juice, and season with salt and pepper. Toss the rocket and the mushrooms in a separate bowl and drizzle with the vinaigrette.
3. Uncover the plates of salmon and drizzle each plate with the remaining lime juice and olive oil. Sprinkle the salmon with the chives. Garnish the centre of each plate with the rocket and mushrooms, and serve at once.

tips

The Perfect Addition to Brunch
Smoked salmon is actually a carbohydrate-free food, deliciously rich. Traditional pairings are sour cream (1.2g of carbohydrates per 30g/1oz), cucumber slices (1.5g of carbohydrates per 60g/2oz)), fresh dill (0.3g of carbohydrates per 1/2 teaspoon) and capers, a carbohydrate-free item.

Smoked Salmon Rillette

454g (1lb) smoked salmon
Salt and freshly ground white pepper
*   to taste*
1 tbsp unsalted butter, softened
2 tbsp mayonnaise
Grated zest of 1 lemon

Juice of ½ lemon, or more
*   to taste*
1 tbsp chopped dill
1 tbsp finely chopped fresh chives

In a food processor or blender, purée the smoked salmon, salt and pepper until smooth. Transfer to a mixing bowl and add the butter; mix until thoroughly blended. Add the mayonnaise, lemon zest, lemon juice, dill and chives. Add the salt and pepper and more lemon juice if desired. Cover and refrigerate for at least 2 hours.

Serves 8
Carb Level: Low

Per serving:	
Carbohydrate:	0.3 g
Protein:	10.5 g

Rillettes refer to 'potted meat'. Try this recipe as a filling for crêpes.

Spinach and Ricotta Filling

185g (6oz) frozen chopped spinach,
*   thawed and drained*
1 tbsp unsalted butter
Pinch of freshly grated nutmeg

Salt and freshly ground black pepper
*   to taste*
125g (4oz) ricotta cheese
1 large egg

1. In a medium-size sauté pan over medium heat, cook the spinach with the butter, nutmeg, salt and pepper. Drain well and cool.
2. Squeeze any water out of the spinach until very dry. Mix the spinach with the ricotta and egg. Adjust the seasoning as needed.

Serves 2
Carb Level: Low

Per serving:	
Carbohydrate:	8.1 g
Protein:	20.3 g

A very versatile and traditional filling – use for stuffed chicken breasts or as a filling for crêpes.

Grilled Lobster
with Lemon and Tarragon

Serves 2
Carb Level: Low

Per serving:

Carbohydrate:	2.6 g
Protein:	28.7 g

This elegant dish is well suited for an anniversary meal.

60g (2oz) butter
2 tbsp fresh lemon juice
1½ tsp grated lemon zest
2 tbsp chopped chives
1 tbsp chopped fresh tarragon
Salt and freshly ground black pepper
    to taste

2 frozen uncooked lobster tails,
    thawed

1. Prepare a charcoal grill, or preheat a grill to high heat.
2. In a small saucepan over low heat, melt the butter and add the lemon juice, lemon zest, chives, tarragon, salt and pepper; set aside and keep warm.
3. Use heavy kitchen scissors to split the lobster tails by cutting the length of the underside. Brush the cut side of the tails with 1 tablespoon of the butter sauce.
4. Grill the lobsters cut-side down for about 4 minutes. Turn and grill for another 4 minutes. Turn them again to the cut side and grill until the lobster meat is just opaque but still juicy, about 2 minutes. Transfer to plates. Brush the lobster with the butter sauce and serve the remaining sauce in a small ramekin on the side.

tips **Serving Lobster Graciously**
Provide your guests with a clean towel and small bowl of warm water with a floating lemon slice for use as a finger bowl. Another alternative is to remove the meat from the shell before serving. Use kitchen scissors to split the shell. Brush the meat with the seasoned butter before serving.

Spring Lamb Chops

1 tsp olive oil
Four 125g (4oz) lamb chops,
*   trimmed of all fat*
Salt and freshly ground black pepper
*   to taste*
60g (2oz) cubed button mushrooms
1 small onion, thinly sliced
1 small carrot, thinly sliced

1 small courgettes, thinly sliced
1 stalk celery, thinly sliced
250ml (8fl oz) chicken stock
1 sprig fresh thyme
2 tbsp chopped fresh parsley

Serves 4	
Carb Level: Low	
Per serving:	
Carbohydrate:	8.9 g
Protein:	20.7 g

A colourful and delicious blend of spring vegetables is perfect as a side dish to these tender chops.

1. Heat the oil in a large non-stick sauté pan over medium heat. Season the lamb chops with salt and pepper. Cook the lamb chops for about 2 minutes on each side or until brown. Transfer to a warm plate and keep warm.
2. Return the pan to medium heat and add the mushrooms, onion, carrot, courgettes and celery. Cook, stirring frequently, for about 7 minutes or until tender. Add the stock, thyme and parsley. Raise the heat to medium-high and bring to a boil. Reduce the heat to medium and simmer covered for 7 minutes. Add the reserved chops and simmer for an additional 3 minutes.
3. Serve on warm plates and spoon the vegetables and the sauce over the chops.

Weekend Guest Tip

Many weekend guests are early risers. As a courtesy, prepare a coffee percolator the evening before so your guests just plug it in. It is also a nice touch to leave out coffee mugs and sugar/sugar substitute for easy access. Don't forget to have fresh milk or cream in the refrigerator.

Roast Pheasant with Cabbage

<table>
<tr><td>Serves 8</td></tr>
<tr><td>Carb Level: Low</td></tr>
</table>

Per Serving:

Carbohydrate:	8.2g
Protein:	54.8g

Pheasants are available in the frozen foods section of many supermarkets. Thaw according to package directions.

Two 1.3kg (3lb) pheasants, trimmed
  of all fat and excess skin
Salt and freshly ground black pepper
  to taste
2 tbsp olive oil
2 shallots, sliced
90g (3oz) celery, chopped
375ml (12fl oz) chicken stock

2 tbsp brandy
1 head red cabbage, cored and
  shredded
1 tbsp butter

1. Preheat the oven to 230°C, 450°F, gas mark 8.
2. Wash the pheasants inside and out. Pat them dry and season with salt and pepper inside and out.
3. Heat the oil in a large roasting pan over medium-high heat on the stove. Add the pheasants breast side down. Cook for about 4 minutes or until golden brown. Continue to do this on all sides of the pheasant. Transfer the pheasants to the oven, breast side up, and roast for 15 minutes.
4. Add the shallots and the celery to the pheasants. Reduce the oven temperature to 190°C, 375°F, gas mark 5. Roast for about 45 minutes or until the inside of the breast registers 85°C, 170°F. (Use an instant-read thermometer to take the internal temperature.) Transfer the pheasants to a warm platter and cover with foil to keep warm.
5. Bring a large pot of salted water to a boil.
6. Drain the liquid from the roasting pan through a fine-mesh sieve into a medium-size bowl. Skim off any fat that comes to the top of the liquid. Discard the vegetables.

(recipe continues on the next page)

Roast Pheasant with Cabbage (continued)

7. Place the roasting pan over high heat on the stove and add the stock and brandy. Bring to a boil, scraping up any browned bits from the bottom of the pan. Reduce the heat to medium and simmer for about 5 minutes. Strain through a fine-mesh sieve into a clean saucepan. Add the reserved liquid from the roasting pan, and bring to a simmer.
8. Add the cabbage to the boiling water. Cover and cook for about 4 minutes. Drain the cabbage well and shake off any excess water. Return the cabbage to the pot and add the butter. Season with salt and pepper; mix well to combine.
9. Slice the breasts on an angle and remove the legs from the thighs on each bird. On warm plates, place the cabbage on the bottom in a mound and arrange the sliced breasts, legs, and thighs on top. Drizzle the sauce over the pheasant.

Grilled Red Snapper
with Basil Aioli

Vegetable oil, for oiling
Four 185g (6oz) red snapper fillets
Salt and freshly ground black pepper
   to taste
15g (½oz) chopped fresh parsley
15g (½oz) chopped fresh basil
1 tbsp mayonnaise
3 tbsp olive oil
60ml (2fl oz) chilli sauce

Serves 4	
Carb Level: Low	
Per serving:	
Carbohydrate:	0.5 g
Protein:	4.9 g

If snapper isn't available, you can substitute salmon.

1. Prepare a charcoal grill or preheat a grill to high heat. Make sure the grill grate is clean and lightly oiled to prevent sticking.
2. Season each fillet with salt and pepper. In a food processor or blender, combine the parsley, basil, mayonnaise and olive oil; blend until smooth. Brush each fillet with the basil aioli.
3. Place the brushed fillets on the grill. Grill on each side for about 4 minutes or until done. Serve immediately with the chilli sauce on the side.

White Wine-Poached Salmon

Serves 4
Carb Level: Low

Per serving:	
Carbohydrate:	9.6 g
Protein:	30.7 g

You can also serve this recipe chilled.

Four 185g (6oz) centre-cut fillets of
  fresh Atlantic salmon, with bones
  and skin removed
Salt and freshly ground black pepper
  to taste
60ml (2fl oz) dry white wine
2 bay leaves
2 tbsp chopped fresh dill
2 tbsp lemon juice
1 tbsp extra-virgin olive oil

1 tbsp nonfat plain yogurt
2 medium cucumbers, peeled and
  halved longways, seeded and cut
  into 6mm (¼in) slices
4 sprigs fresh dill

1. Season the fillets with salt and pepper. Place the fish in a non-stick sauté pan large enough to hold the fillets. Add the wine, bay leaves, chopped dill and enough water to come 3mm (⅛in) up the side of the fish. Cover with a lid. Bring to a simmer and poach over medium heat for about 5 minutes. Turn off the heat and allow the fish to finish cooking, covered, for 6 minutes. Using a slotted spatula, gently remove the fillets from the pan to a warm plate; keep warm.
2. Whisk together the lemon juice and olive oil in a small bowl. Add the yogurt and cucumbers; toss well to combine. Season to taste with salt and pepper. Place the salmon fillets on a warm plate, and spoon the cucumber garnish on top of each fillet. Garnish with fresh dill sprigs.

Chutney-Glazed Smoked Ham

*3.2kg (7lb) raw smoked ham with
    bone in
90g (3oz) peach or mango chutney*

*3 tbsp Dijon mustard
½ tsp ground ginger
Rosemary sprigs for garnish*

1. Preheat the oven to 170°C, 325°F, gas mark 3.
2. Remove the skin and all but 6mm (¼in) of the fat from the ham. Score the fat into 25mm (1in) diamonds. Place the ham on a rack in a medium-size roasting pan and roast uncovered for 1½ hours. Alternatively, boil the ham for 1½ hours.
3. Mix the chutney, mustard and ginger in a small bowl. Brush this glaze all over the ham. Bake the ham for another 30 minutes or until the internal temperature registers 60°C, 140°F. Transfer the ham to a warm platter, and brush with any remaining glaze. Allow the ham to stand for about 15 minutes. Slice and serve garnished with the rosemary sprigs.

Serves 12	
Carb Level: Low	
Per serving:	
Carbohydrate:	9.4 g
Protein:	0.3 g

You can use spiral-cut ham for this recipe to make the slicing step easier.

Pesto-Baked Chicken

Serves 4

Carb Level: Low

Per serving:

Carbohydrate:	2.6 g
Protein:	36.2 g

Double or triple this recipe as needed for a group dinner or buffet luncheon.

4 medium boneless, skinless chicken
    breast halves
1 tbsp olive oil
185g (6oz) finely chopped courgettes
    and/or yellow summer squash

2 tbsp prepared pesto
1 tbsp finely grated Parmesan cheese

Rinse the chicken under cold running water and pat dry with paper towels. Heat the oil in a large non-stick sauté pan over medium heat. Cook the chicken breast side down for 4 minutes or until golden brown. Turn the chicken and add the vegetables. Cook, stirring the squash, for about 5 minutes or until the chicken is cooked through and the courgettes are tender. Transfer to warm plates and spoon the pesto over the breasts. Sprinkle with the grated cheese.

Making Your Own Pesto

You can prepare your own pesto by blending 60g (2oz) fresh basil leaves, washed, dried, and stemmed; 30g (1oz) grated Parmesan cheese; 2 tablespoons toasted pine nuts; and approximately 60ml (2fl oz) extra-virgin olive oil in a food processor until smooth. Add more oil as needed to adjust the consistency, and season with salt and freshly ground black pepper.

Pork Roast

1.8kg (4lb) loin of pork with bone in
2 tbsp extra-virgin olive oil
4 garlic cloves, sliced
2 sprigs fresh rosemary
1 bay leaf

250ml (8fl oz) dry white wine
Salt and freshly ground black pepper
*   to taste*

Serves 6
Carb Level: Low

Per serving:	
Carbohydrate:	1.5 g
Protein:	39.1 g

The pork will continue to cook after you remove it from the oven, adding an additional 2–4°C, 5–8°F to the internal temperature.

1. Place the pork roast in a large plastic bag with a seal. Mix the oil, garlic, rosemary, bay leaf, wine, salt and pepper in a small bowl until combined, then add to the pork. Massage the bag to ensure the pork is evenly coated with the marinade. Marinate for several hours in the refrigerator, turning occasionally.
2. Preheat the oven to 230°C, 450°F, gas mark 8.
3. Place the loin in a roasting pan and set it on a rack in the oven. Season with more salt and pepper and baste it with the marinade. Roast for about 20 minutes or until browned. Turn the heat down to 150°C, 300°F, gas mark 2, and roast for another 45 minutes–1 hour or until the internal temperature is 75°C, 150°F. Baste with the pan liquids while roasting.
4. Allow the pork to stand for at least 15 minutes before slicing. Serve slices on warm plates.

Roasted Sweet Onions

Serves 8
Carb Level: Low

Per serving:	
Carbohydrate:	6.2 g
Protein:	0.8 g

This goes well as a side dish with any grilled meat or fish.

4 sweet onions, peeled and cut in half crossways
3 tbsp olive oil
2 tbsp balsamic vinegar

Salt and freshly ground black pepper to taste
2 strips bacon, cut into eight pieces

1. Prepare a charcoal grill or preheat a grill to high. Make sure the grill grate is clean and lightly oiled to prevent sticking.
2. Place each onion half cut side up in a 255mm (10in) square of foil. Drizzle the onions with the oil and vinegar, and season with salt and pepper. Turn the onions cut side down. Place a piece of bacon on top of each onion. Fold the foil into packets.
3. Grill the onions for about 25 minutes or until they are tender and slightly charred. Allow the onions to cool in their packets for 15 minutes.
4. Remove the onions, discarding the bacon but reserving the juices. Serve warm or at room temperature, and drizzle the juices over the top.

tips **Balsamic Vinegar**
This prized Italian specialty is manufactured from white Trebbiano grape juice. The rich burgundy colour and sweetness are developed during an ageing process in barrels of different woods in graduating sizes. Aged balsamic can be as expensive as a fine wine, and is well worth the investment. You need only a small amount of a quality balsamic to add punch to a dressing or sauce. If your balsamic is not the best quality, you can develop the flavour by bringing it to a low boil and allowing it to simmer until reduced by a quarter to a third; the concentration will improve the taste.

Pork Crown Roast

4kg (9lb) crown roast of pork
5½ tbsp olive oil, divided
Salt and freshly ground black pepper
Grated zest of 1 orange
4 large cloves garlic, chopped
2 tbsp chopped fresh rosemary
180ml (6fl oz.) dry white wine

125ml (4fl oz.) fresh apple cider
250ml (8fl oz.) chicken stock
1 tbsp unsalted butter, at room temperature
1 tbsp plain flour

Serves 12–14
Carb Level: Low

Per serving:	
Carbohydrate:	2.3 g
Protein:	43.7 g

This is the perfect centrepiece for a family get-together.

1. Preheat the oven to 220°C, 425°F, gas mark 7.
2. Brush the roast with 4 tablespoons of olive oil, and season well with salt and pepper. In a small bowl, mix together the orange zest, garlic, rosemary and the remaining oil. Spread this mixture evenly over the meat, inside and out. Place the roast on a rack in a large roasting pan. Roast for 15 minutes and reduce the heat to 190°C, 375°F, gas mark 5. Continue roasting for 45 minutes, rotating the roasting pan to ensure even cooking. Cook until the roast is browned and the internal temperature reads 75°C, 150°F, about 1½ hours.
3. Remove the roast from the oven and place on a cutting board. Make a tent of tin foil over it and allow to stand for at least 20 minutes. Deglaze the roasting pan over medium heat by adding the white wine and scraping the bottom of the pan to loosen any browned bits; stir to incorporate them into the wine. Simmer until the wine reduces by half. Add the apple cider and stock. Season with salt and pepper and return the liquid to a boil.
4. In a small bowl, combine the butter with the flour; mix until well combined. Add this to the roasting pan, whisking, until the sauce has thickened, about 5 minutes. Strain through a fine-mesh sieve into a bowl. Remove any fat that accumulates at the top. Carve the roast at the table and pass the sauce around.

Cod Cakes

Serves 4
Carb Level: Low

Per serving:	
Carbohydrate:	9.7 g
Protein:	28.3 g

Serve the cakes with Thai sauce or vinaigrette instead of tartare sauce, and a side of stir-fried vegetables for a totally different variation.

*580g (1lb 4oz) cod, cleaned and
   boned*
4 spring onions, chopped
2 tbsp finely chopped fresh tarragon
1 egg, lightly beaten
3 dashes (or to taste) Tabasco sauce
*Salt and freshly ground black pepper
   to taste*

30g (1oz) breadcrumbs
3 tbsp olive oil, divided
Tartare sauce for garnish

1. Cut the fish into large chunks and blend in a food processor until coarsely chopped, or chop by hand using a very sharp knife. Transfer to a medium-size bowl and add the spring onions, tarragon, egg and Tabasco; mix well. Season with salt and pepper, then form eight equal patties. Dredge them in the breadcrumbs and shake off any excess.
2. Heat a tablespoon of oil in a large non-stick sauté pan over medium-low heat. Cook the patties on each side for about 4 minutes or until they are golden brown. Turn them over and cook for about 5 minutes or until brown and cooked all the way through; add more oil as needed. Transfer to a warm plate and serve with tartare sauce on the side.

tips
Snacks for Weekend Guests
When entertaining weekend guests, prepare a simple fruit platter and cheese and salami tray, and leave them in the refrigerator for your guests to nibble on at their leisure.

Grilled Mushrooms and Peppers

250ml (8fl oz) olive oil
60ml (2fl oz) balsamic vinegar
Salt and freshly ground black pepper
to taste
12 large open mushrooms, stems
removed

6 large red, yellow or green peppers,
halved longways, stemmed and
seeded
Mixed salad greens

Serves 16	
Carb Level: Low	

Per serving:	
Carbohydrate:	6.1 g
Protein:	2.0 g

Easy to prepare in advance. Add your favourite grilled sausages for a delicious grilled main dish.

1. Prepare a charcoal grill or preheat a grill to high heat. Make sure the grill grate is clean and lightly oiled to prevent sticking.
2. In a medium-size bowl, whisk together the oil and vinegar, and season with salt and pepper. Brush the mushrooms and peppers with some of the dressing. Grill the mushrooms and peppers on each side until tender and slightly charred. Transfer to a large bowl and allow to cool for about 15 minutes.
3. Cut the mushroom and peppers into 12mm (½ in)-wide strips and return to the bowl. Mix in the remaining dressing and season with salt and pepper. Serve on a bed of mixed salad greens.

Coriander-Crusted Flank Steak

2 tbsp fresh-squeezed lemon juice
2 tbsp soy sauce
2 tbsp olive oil
1½ tbsp ground coriander
2 cloves garlic, chopped
680g (1lb 8oz) beef flank steak, trimmed
60ml (2fl oz) red wine

1 tbsp black pepper
2 tbsp chopped fresh coriander
Fresh coriander sprigs

1. Combine the lemon juice, soy sauce, oil, coriander and garlic in a large plastic bag with a seal. Squeeze the bag to mix the marinade ingredients. Add the steak and again squeeze the bag to be sure that the meat is evenly coated on both sides. Cover and refrigerate overnight, turning occasionally.
2. Prepare a charcoal grill or preheat a grill to high heat. Make sure the grill grate is clean and lightly oiled to prevent sticking
3. Remove the steak from the marinade. Transfer the marinade to a small saucepan and add the red wine. Season the steaks with pepper on both sides. Grill the steaks on each side for about 5–6 minutes or until done. Transfer the meat to a platter and cover with a tin-foil tent; allow to stand for about 15 minutes.
4. Heat the marinade to a boil and then reduce the heat to a simmer and cook until the sauce is slightly reduced. Strain the sauce through a fine-mesh sieve into a bowl. Slice the steak thinly across the grain and arrange on a platter. Drizzle the sauce over the steak. Sprinkle with chopped coriander and garnish with coriander sprigs.

Boneless Chicken Thighs with Mango Chutney

6 boneless chicken thighs
Salt and freshly ground black pepper
    to taste

60g (2oz) low-carb mango chutney
185g (6oz) goat's cheese
2 tbsp olive oil

Serves 6
Carb Level: Low

Per serving:	
Carbohydrate:	7.8 g
Protein:	30.3 g

Traditional Indian-style mango chutney varies from mild to extra-hot.

1. Loosen the skin on the chicken thighs. Season with salt and pepper. Evenly divide the chutney among the thighs; press the relish onto the thighs, under the skin. Press the goat cheese over the relish, evenly dividing it among the thighs. Stretch the skin over the stuffing and secure with a toothpick.

2. Preheat the oven to 190°C, 375°F, gas mark 5.

3. Heat the oil in a large oven proof sauté pan over medium-high heat. Add the chicken thighs to the pan, skin side down, for about 5 minutes or until the skin is golden brown and crispy. Turn the thighs over and place the pan in the oven for about 20–25 minutes or until done.

Food Safety on the Web

A great up-to-date Web site is www.foodstandards.gov.uk, *which has the latest information and technical details on foods and proper preparation.*

Sautéed Ham
with Cider Sauce

375ml (12fl oz) apple cider
3 tbsp cider vinegar
1 tsp mustard seeds
1 tsp Dijon mustard
1 tbsp olive oil
454g (1lb) fully cooked ham steak
   (12mm/½ in thick) with bone in

1 small onion, finely chopped
2 tbsp butter
1 tbsp chopped fresh
   flatleaf parsley

Serves 2

Carb Level: Moderate

Per serving:

Carbohydrate: 16.3 g
Protein: 46.3 g

Try different fully cooked ham steaks from the meat counter of your supermarket to find which one you like best.

1. In a small bowl, mix together the cider, vinegar, mustard seeds and mustard.
2. Heat the oil in a large sauté pan over high heat and sauté the ham until it is golden and heated through, about 4 minutes on each side. Transfer the ham to a platter and keep warm.
3. In the same sauté pan, cook the onions over medium heat until golden. Stir in the cider mixture. Simmer uncovered for about 5 minutes or until slightly thickened. Add the butter and parsley to the sauce and mix well. Pour the sauce over the ham and serve.

Barbecued Beef

1 slice bacon, cut into 25mm (1in) pieces
60g (2oz) chopped onion
125ml (4fl oz) ketchup
80ml (2½fl oz) apple cider vinegar
1 tsp Dijon mustard
Dash of BBQ cooking sauce
1 tsp Worcestershire sauce
⅛ tsp salt

⅛ tsp freshly ground black pepper
½–¾ tbsp sugar substitute
375g (12oz) roast beef, thinly sliced

Serves 4

Carb Level: Moderate

Per serving:
Carbohydrate:	15.2 g
Protein:	14.7 g

This is a great way to use leftover roast beef or roast pork.

1. In a medium-size saucepan over medium heat, cook the bacon until it just starts to crisp. Add the onion and cook for about 3 minutes, stirring, or until the bacon is crispy and the onion is tender.
2. Add the ketchup, apple cider vinegar, mustard, BBQ cooking sauce, Worcestershire sauce, salt and pepper to the bacon mixture. Reduce the heat and simmer for about 15 minutes. Stir in ¾ tablespoon sugar substitute; add more substitute and adjust seasoning to taste.Add the sliced roast beef and simmer for 10 minutes.

Sautéed Swordfish
in White Wine Sauce

Serves 4
Carb Level: Moderate

Per serving:	
Carbohydrate:	12.2 g
Protein:	38.5 g

If swordfish is not available, you can substitute snapper or halibut and reduce the cooking time accordingly.

Four 220g (7oz) swordfish steaks about 25mm (1in) thick
Salt and freshly ground white pepper to taste
2 tbsp vegetable oil
60ml (2fl oz) dry white wine
2 tbsp fresh-squeezed lemon juice
30g (1oz) unsalted butter
1 tbsp freshly chopped parsley leaves

5 spring onions, finely sliced on the bias, white parts only
1 tbsp capers, drained and rinsed
1 large ripe tomato, peeled, seeded, and cut into 6mm (¼in) dice

1. Season the swordfish with salt and pepper on both sides. Heat the oil in a large sauté pan over medium-high heat. Cook the fish on one side for about 6 minutes or until lightly browned. Turn the fillet over, reduce the heat to medium, and cook for about 4 more minutes or until browned. Cover and cook until the fish is done, about 5 minutes. To check it is done, insert a thin-bladed knife in the thickest part of the fish. The flesh should be flaky, and no translucence should be apparent. Transfer the fish to a platter, and cover to keep warm.
2. Pour off any oil remaining in the pan and add the wine and lemon juice. Raise the heat to high and scrape the bottom of the pan to loosen any browned bits. Simmer until the sauce reduces by half. Stir in the butter a piece at a time. Add the parsley, spring onions, capers and tomato, and season with salt and pepper. Pour the sauce over the fish and serve immediately.

Grilled Mediterranean Grouper

Vinaigrette:

250ml (8fl oz) extra-virgin olive oil
2 tbsp tarragon vinegar
90g (3oz) tomatoes, peeled, seeded
 and diced
60g (2oz) pitted and halved calamata
 olives
1 medium shallot, thinly sliced
½ tsp chopped garlic
Salt and freshly ground black pepper
 to taste

Fennel:

2 medium fennel bulbs, trimmed
2 tbsp extra-virgin olive oil
Salt and freshly ground white pepper
 to taste

Grouper:

Four 185g (6oz) grouper fillets
2 tbsp vegetable oil
Salt and freshly ground white pepper
 to taste
2 tbsp chopped fresh chives for garnish

Serves 4	
Carb Level: Low	

Per serving:

Carbohydrate:	10.0 g
Protein:	15.9 g

You can substitute salmon if fresh grouper is not available.

1. To prepare the vinaigrette: Combine the olive oil, vinegar, tomatoes, olives, shallot, garlic, salt and pepper in a medium-size bowl; set aside.
2. Prepare a charcoal grill or preheat a grill to medium-high heat. Make sure the grill grate is clean and lightly oiled to prevent sticking.
3. To prepare the fennel, cut the fennel bulbs in half longways. Slice each half longways into 6mm (¼in)-thick slices. Try to keep each slice attached at the root end. Brush the fennel with olive oil and season with salt and pepper.
4. Grill the fennel for about 5 minutes on each side until tender and slightly charred; set aside and keep warm.
5. Before preparing the grouper, clean and lightly oil the grill.
6. Brush the fillets with the oil and season with salt and pepper. Grill the fish for about 4 minutes on one side, then turn the fillet and cook for an additional 2 minutes or until done. To check it is done, insert a thin-bladed knife in the thickest part of the fish. The flesh should be flaky, and no translucence should be apparent.
7. Serve the fennel under the fish and spoon the vinaigrette over the fish. Garnish with fresh chives and serve immediately.

Cauliflower Vichyssoise

Serves 4
Carb Level: Moderate

Per serving:	
Carbohydrate:	14.2 g
Protein:	2.7 g

This satisfying soup can be served hot or cold.

1 tbsp vegetable oil
2 medium leeks, white parts only, sliced
1 medium onion, diced
1 large head cauliflower, cut into florets

1l (32fl oz.) chicken stock
Salt and freshly ground white pepper to taste
60ml (2fl oz) extra-virgin olive oil
1 tbsp finely chopped chives for garnish

1. Heat the oil in a large soup pot over medium heat. Cook the leeks and onion for 3–4 minutes, stirring until tender. Be careful not to overcook the leeks and onion; they should retain their original colour.
2. Add the cauliflower and stock and bring to the boil. Reduce the heat and simmer covered for about 20 minutes or until the cauliflower florets are tender.
3. Transfer the soup to a blender and purée until smooth. Return the soup to the pot to warm; season with salt and pepper.
4. Serve the soup in warm soup bowls and garnish with a drizzle of extra-virgin olive oil and a sprinkling of fresh chives.

Are You Losing Vitamins?

Vitamins are destroyed by heat, water, air and fat. Different cooking methods will dictate the amount of vitamins retained or lost. For example, vitamin C is an oxygen-sensitive and water-soluble vitamin. Cooking 60g (2oz) of cabbage in 1l (32fl oz) of water loses 90 per cent of natural vitamin C. Cooking 225g (8oz) of cabbage in 60ml (2fl oz) of water retains about 50 per cent of natural vitamin C.

Beef Sirloin with Endives

1½ tsp butter, divided
2½ tsp vegetable oil, divided
8 endives, washed, cored and cut in half
*   longways*
Salt and freshly ground black pepper
*   to taste*
2 shallots, chopped

125ml (4fl oz) dry white wine
60ml (2fl oz) veal or chicken stock
Four 150g (5oz) beef sirloin fillets
185g 6oz) button mushrooms, sliced
1 clove garlic, chopped
2 tbsp chopped fresh flatleaf parsley

Serves 4	
Carb Level: Moderate	
Per serving:	
Carbohydrate:	17.3 g
Protein:	26.2 g

The endives add a nice change of pace to a traditional dinner with mushrooms.

1. Heat 1 teaspoon of the butter and 1 teaspoon of the oil in a large non-stick sauté pan over medium-low heat. Add the endives to the pan in a single layer. Season with salt and pepper. Cook covered for 15 minutes. Turn the endives over, cover and cook for another 10 minutes. Transfer the endives to a plate and keep warm.

2. In the same sauté pan, add the shallots and the remaining ½ teaspoon of butter, and increase the heat to medium. Cook for about 4 minutes or until the shallots are softened. Add the wine and bring it to the boil for 5 minutes or until the wine is reduced by half. Add the stock and bring to the boil. Reduce to a simmer and cook until the liquid is reduced by a third. Season with salt and pepper. Remove from the heat and keep warm.

3. Season the beef with salt and pepper. Heat the remaining oil in a medium sauté pan over high heat. Add the beef and cook for about 3 minutes or until brown. Brown the other side. (The beef should be medium-rare at this point; cook longer if preferred.) Transfer the meat to a plate and keep warm.

5. Return the pan to medium heat. Add the mushrooms and season with salt and pepper. Cook for about 5 minutes or until the mushrooms are tender. Add the garlic and sauté for 30 seconds more. Toss in the parsley and stir to mix.

6. Place each sirloin in the centre of a warm dinner plate. Arrange the endive around each sirloin. Spoon the sauce over the beef and then top with the mushrooms.

Fish Stew

Serves 4

Carb Level: Moderate

Per serving:

Carbohydrate:	20.0 g
Protein:	42.8 g

Fish stock can be purchased in powder, liquid or cube form.

375g (12oz) bass or grouper fillets
375g (12oz) medium prawns, peeled and de-veined
225g (8oz) fresh mussels
1½ fennel bulbs
1 tbsp olive oil
1 medium onion, thinly sliced
2 medium leeks, thinly sliced
3 cloves garlic, chopped

1.5l (48fl oz) fish stock
4 very ripe plum tomatoes, peeled, seeded, cored and chopped
2 sprigs fresh thyme
2 pinches saffron threads
Salt and freshly ground black pepper to taste
1 tablespoon chopped fresh tarragon for garnish

1. Cut the fish into medium-size chunks and place in a bowl. Add the prawns and refrigerate.
2. Wash the mussels very well in a few changes of cold water. Scrub off any grit stuck to the mussels and remove the beards. (Your fishmonger will clean the mussels if you ask.) Place the mussels in a medium-size saucepan and add enough cold water to cover by about 25mm (1in). Bring to the boil covered over medium-high heat. Steam the mussels until they open. Discard any that remain closed. Remove the mussels from the pan and lift the meat from the shells; discard the shells. Return the mussels to the saucepan. Reserve the cooking liquid.
3. To prepare the fennel, remove any discoloured outer layers from the bulb. Trim the root end and feathery top. Cut the bulb in half longways and then cut across into very thin slices.
4. Heat the oil in a large saucepan over medium heat. Add the fennel, onions and leeks. Cook slowly, uncovered and stirring often, for about 8 minutes or until tender. Stir in the garlic and cook for another 2–3 minutes until soft. Add the fish stock, tomatoes, thyme and saffron. Season with salt and pepper. Cover and simmer for about 10 minutes.
5. Add the fish and prawns to the stew. Cover and cook over medium heat for about 8 minutes or until the fish and prawns are cooked. Add the mussels with their cooking liquid to the stew. Adjust seasoning to taste.
6. Ladle the stew into warm soup bowls with equal amounts of fish in each. Garnish with chopped tarragon.

Venison Medallions
with Cranberry Dijon Chutney

90g (3oz) fresh cranberries
1 tsp honey
1 tbsp Dijon mustard
2 tsp butter, divided
Salt and freshly ground black pepper
    to taste
Eight 75g (2½ oz) venison
    medallions

2 small shallots, chopped
125g (4oz) quartered mushrooms
250ml (8fl oz) dry red wine
60ml (2fl oz) cider vinegar
125ml (4fl oz) chicken stock
1 tbsp redcurrant jelly

Serves 4	
Carb Level: Moderate	
Per serving:	
Carbohydrate:	14.1 g
Protein:	24.7 g

Venison should never be overcooked, or it will become very dry and tough.

1. In a small non-stick sauté pan, combine the cranberries, honey, mustard and 1 teaspoon of the butter. Season with salt and pepper. Cook over low heat for about 3–5 minutes until the cranberries just start to pop. Remove from the heat and set aside.
2. Season the venison with salt and pepper. Melt the remaining butter in a large non-stick sauté pan over high heat until very hot. Add the venison and cook for about 2 minutes or until golden brown. Turn over and cook for another 2 minutes. The meat should be medium-rare at this point. Transfer to a warm platter and keep warm.
3. Return the sauté pan to medium heat. Add the shallots and cook for about 2 minutes or until tender. Stir in the mushrooms and cook until softened. Add the wine, stock and vinegar, and scrape the bottom of the pan with a wooden spoon to loosen any browned bits. Raise the heat to high and cook for about 10 minutes or until the liquid is reduced to about 125ml (4fl oz). Stir in the jelly and adjust the seasoning to taste.
4. Spoon a small amount of the cranberry sauce on top of each venison medallion. Ladle the sauce on top and around the venison.

Roasted Aubergine Napoleon
with Marinated Goat's Cheese

Serves 6

Carb Level: Moderate

Per serving:

Carbohydrate:	12.7 g
Protein:	9.0 g

An attractive and tasty starter course. Everything can be prepared beforehand and assembled just before serving.

2 cloves garlic, chopped
1 tbsp fresh thyme leaves
3 tsp olive oil, divided
125g (4oz) fresh goat cheese
1 large aubergine
Salt and freshly ground black pepper
*   to taste*
300g (10oz) fresh spinach, washed
*   and stems removed*
2 small red peppers, roasted, peeled,
*   seeded and diced*

3 very ripe plum tomatoes, peeled,
*   seeded, cored and diced*
3 tbsp coarsely chopped fresh basil
Juice of 1 lemon

1. Mix half the chopped garlic, thyme, black pepper and 1 teaspoon oil in a large bowl. Crumble the goat's cheese into the bowl, and lightly toss to ensure the cheese is evenly coated with the marinade. Cover and allow to stand at room temperature.

2. Trim the stem ends from the aubergine. Cut the aubergine across into 3mm (1/8 in) slices. Lay the slices on a baking tray and sprinkle them with salt. Allow them to stand for about 10 minutes. The salt will help extract some of the bitterness from the aubergine.

3. Preheat the oven to 230°C, 450°F, gas mark 8.

4. Using a paper towel, blot away the liquid released from the aubergine and brush off the salt. Pat the skin very dry. Brush both sides of the aubergine with the remaining oil. Roast for about 5 minutes or until the slices begin to slightly colour. Remove from the oven.

(recipe continues on the next page)

Roasted Aubergine Napoleon
with Marinated Goat's Cheese (continued)

5. Heat the remaining oil in a large non-stick sauté pan over medium heat. Add the remaining chopped garlic and cook for about 1 minute or until it just starts to colour. Add the spinach to the pan and season with salt and pepper. Cover and cook over medium heat for about 2 minutes, until all the spinach has wilted. Remove from the heat and drain off the excess water. Mix the spinach with the red peppers in a medium-size bowl.
6. Mix the tomatoes, basil, lemon juice, salt and pepper in a small bowl.
7. To assemble, place a slice of the aubergine on each serving plate, spoon the spinach and pepper mixture in the centre of the aubergine, and top with another layer of aubergine; add the marinated goat's cheese for the next layer, and top with the tomato vinaigrette.

Fried Green Tomatoes

250ml (8fl oz) extra-virgin olive oil
2 large or 3 small green tomatoes
Yellow cornmeal, for coating

Salt and freshly ground black pepper
*   to taste*

1. Heat the oil in a medium-size sauté pan over medium heat.
2. Cut the tomatoes into 6mm (1/4in) slices. Season both sides with salt and pepper. Coat them well on both sides with cornmeal.
3. Fry them in the oil until golden brown, turning them only once. Drain them of excess oil on paper towels. Serve immediately.

Serves 4

Carb Level: Moderate

Per serving:

Carbohydrate:	18.1 g
Protein:	2.6 g

This is a great accompaniment to an end-of-summer BBQ dinner or lunch.

Baked Cod with Tomatoes, Capers and Sautéed Spinach

Serves 4
Carb Level: Moderate

Per serving:

Carbohydrate:	14.3 g
Protein:	46.2 g

You can substitute any firm fish for the cod, such as grouper or haddock.

1 tsp butter, divided
2 tsp olive oil, divided
2 large very ripe tomatoes, peeled, seeded, cored and diced
250ml (8fl oz) fish stock
3 tbsp capers, well drained
Salt and freshly ground black pepper to taste
30g (1oz) fresh breadcrumbs
1 tbsp chopped fresh chives
1 tbsp chopped fresh flatleaf parsley
Four 150g (5oz) cod fillets
454g (1lb) fresh spinach, washed and stems removed

1. Preheat the oven to 230°C, 450°F, gas mark 8. Using ½ teaspoon butter, lightly coat a casserole dish large enough to hold the fish in a single layer.
2. Heat 1 teaspoon of oil in a medium sauté pan over medium-high heat. Add the tomatoes and cook for about 2 minutes. Add the stock and capers; bring to the boil. Reduce the heat to low and simmer for about 10 minutes. Season with salt and pepper and cover to keep warm.
3. In a small bowl, combine the breadcrumbs, chives, parsley and remaining oil; mix well.
4. Season the cod on both sides with salt and pepper. Lay the fillets in the buttered casserole. Top each fillet with an equal amount of the bread crumb mixture. Bake for about 8 minutes or until the cod is almost done. Turn the grill on and grill the fish for about 1 minute or until the tops are golden brown and the fish is done. To check that the fish is done, insert a thin-bladed knife into the thickest part of the fish. The flesh should be white and flaky, and no translucence should be apparent. Remove the fish from the grill and keep warm.
5. Melt the remaining butter in a large non-stick sauté pan over high heat. Add the spinach to the pan and season with salt and pepper. Cover and cook for about 2 minutes or until the spinach has wilted.
6. Place a small pile of spinach in the centre of a warm dinner plate. Place a cod fillet on top of the spinach and pour the sauce around the fish.

Artichoke, Cucumber and Tomato Salad

2 cucumbers, peeled
2 tsp lemon juice
1 tbsp olive oil
Salt and freshly ground black pepper
    to taste
4 very ripe plum tomatoes, peeled,
    seeded, cored and chopped

185g (6oz) baby lettuce salad,
    washed and dried
90g (3oz) quartered tinned arti-
    choke hearts, drained

Serves 4	
Carb Level: Moderate	
Per serving:	
Carbohydrate:	19.5 g
Protein:	5.3 g

This tasty salad has a wonderful blend of textures and flavours. It goes very well with grilled meats.

1. Split the cucumbers in half and use a spoon to scoop out the seeds. Slice the cucumbers into 3mm ($^1/_8$ in) slices. Drain the cucumbers and pat dry, then transfer to a medium-size bowl.
2. In a small bowl, whisk together the lemon juice, olive oil, salt and pepper; add the tomatoes and stir well to combine.
3. Add a quarter of the prepared vinaigrette to the cucumbers and toss well to coat.
4. Place the lettuce in a large bowl. Add the remaining vinaigrette and toss to coat. Place a mound of greens on a chilled plate and top with the marinated cucumbers. Arrange the artichokes around the plate.

tips

Flowers on Your Food?

Spring and summer brunches are always more festive when decorated with fresh flowers and greens. The following common flowers are 'food safe': calendula, chamomile, chives, day lilies, impatiens, lemon balm, lilac, nasturtiums, pansies, roses, violets. Be careful not to use any flowers that may have been exposed to pesticides.

Roasted Rabbit with Garlic

Serves 4
Carb Level: Low

Per serving:

Carbohydrate:	9.9 g
Protein:	24.7 g

Rabbits are available in the frozen foods section in many supermarkets. Thaw according to package directions.

16 large cloves garlic, unpeeled
1 tsp vegetable oil
Two 300g (10oz) rabbit saddles, well tied with butcher's twine to form two small tight roasts
Salt and freshly ground black pepper to taste

125ml (4fl oz) dry white wine
125ml (4fl oz) chicken stock
125ml (4fl oz) water
1 tsp fresh thyme leaves
1 tsp Dijon mustard
½ tsp unsalted butter
½ tsp honey

1. Preheat the oven to 190°C, 375°F, gas mark 5.
2. Place the garlic in a small saucepan and add cold water to cover by 25mm (1 in). Bring to a simmer over medium-high heat and cook for about 5 minutes. Remove from the heat and drain well; set aside.
3. Heat the oil on medium in a large non-stick sauté pan large enough to hold the rabbit uncrowded in a single layer. Season the rabbit with salt and pepper, and place in the hot pan. Brown all sides, add the unpeeled garlic and place in the oven. Roast for about 15 minutes or until the internal temperature of the meat reads 75°C, 160°F. Remove the rabbit from the oven and transfer to a warm plate; cover to keep warm.
4. Place the sauté pan with the unpeeled garlic in it over medium heat. Stir in the wine, stock, water and thyme. Increase the heat and bring to the boil. Reduce the heat to medium and simmer for about 6 minutes or until the liquid is reduced by half. Remove the garlic cloves from the pan with a slotted spoon, and set aside. Strain the sauce through a fine-mesh sieve into a small saucepan. Whisk in the mustard, butter and honey, and season with salt and pepper. Cover and keep warm.
5. Slice each rabbit saddle into eight equal slices. Squeeze the roasted garlic cloves out of the skins. Arrange the garlic cloves around the rabbit and spoon the sauce on top.

tips **Roasting Garlic**
The roasted garlic cloves add an amazing complexity to this dish. They have a much more mellow flavour when roasted for a long period of time.

Roasted Grouper with Tomatoes

3 tbsp olive oil

2 dried hot peppers

2 cloves garlic, peeled and lightly
   crushed

2 cups tomatoes (fresh or tinned),
   peeled, seeded and chopped

1 tsp dried rosemary

Salt and freshly ground black pepper
   to taste

1 large or 2 small grouper fillets,
   about 454g (1lb) total

30g (1oz) fresh parsley, chopped

Freshly grated Parmesan cheese

Serves 4	
Carb Level: Moderate	
Per serving:	
Carbohydrate:	18.4 g
Protein:	16.9 g

Lightly stewing the tomatoes enhances the flavour of the sauce.

1. Heat the oil in a large sauté pan over medium-high heat. Add the hot peppers and garlic, and cook, stirring, until the garlic is golden brown. Remove and discard the peppers and the garlic.

2. Add the tomatoes to the same pan and cook, stirring, until the tomatoes begin to liquefy. Add the rosemary, salt and pepper; cook for about 5 minutes, then gently place the fillets in the pan. Cover the sauté pan and cook over medium heat for about 7 minutes or until the fish is done. To check, insert a thin-bladed knife into the thickest part of the fish. The flesh should be white, opaque and flaky; no translucence should be apparent.

3. Carefully remove the fillets from the pan and set them on a warm platter. Add some of the parsley to the sauce along with the cheese. Allow the cheese to melt. Spoon the sauce over the fish and garnish with the remaining chopped parsley.

Veal Saltimboca

Serves 2
Carb Level: Moderate

Per serving:	
Carbohydrate:	17.1 g
Protein:	39.6 g

This recipe serves two as a starter course or one as a main dish.

Two 60g (2oz) veal cutlets
Salt and freshly ground black pepper
   to taste
2 fresh sage leaves, chopped
30g (1oz) mozzarella cheese, sliced
1 thin slice of prosciutto
2 large eggs, lightly beaten and seasoned with parsley, nutmeg,
   Parmesan cheese, salt and pepper
60g (2oz) bread crumbs, seasoned
   with salt, pepper and Parmesan
   cheese
1 tbsp butter
1 tbsp extra-virgin olive oil
125ml (4fl oz) veal stock

60ml (2fl oz) Marsala wine
60ml (2fl oz) vermouth
1 tbsp tomato paste
1 tbsp finely chopped fresh parsley
1 sprig fresh parsley for garnish

1. Beat the veal between two sheets of cling film with the flat side of a meat mallet to a uniform thickness of about 3mm (⅛in).
2. Lay the cutlets on a cutting board and season them with salt and pepper and the fresh sage. Lay a slice of mozzarella followed by a slice of prosciutto on the cutlet, and top with the second veal cutlet. Seal the edges by pressing them together with your fingers.
3. Carefully dip the veal packet in the beaten egg and then the bread-crumbs. Press the breadcrumbs firmly into the veal so the packet stays together.
4. Heat the butter and oil in a medium-size sauté pan over medium heat. Cook the veal on both sides until golden brown and cooked through, about 7 minutes.

(recipe continues on the next page)

Veal Saltimboca (continued)

5. Combine the stock, Marsala, vermouth, tomato paste, salt, pepper and parsley in a medium-size non-reactive saucepan. Bring to a boil, reduce the heat to low, and simmer until reduced by half.
6. Spoon some sauce on the bottom of a warm plate and lay the veal on top. Spoon a bit more sauce on top of the veal and garnish with the parsley sprig.

Making Veal Stock

Veal stock is a very tasty stock made from simmering roasted veal bones, vegetables and herbs together for 8 hours. The end result is a viscous and rich stock that can be used as a base for any sauce, soup or braising liquid. Demi-glaze is when veal stock is reduced by half its original volume. It has a very intense taste and usually needs to be diluted with some water. You can buy demi-glaze in specialist food stores.

Marinated Grilled Steak Strips

Serves 4

Carb Level: Low

Per serving:

Carbohydrate:	1.4 g
Protein:	8.3 g

An outdoor grilling favourite. Serve with roasted assorted vegetables and a crispy salad for a summer night treat.

Four 225g (8oz) sirloin steaks,
    trimmed of all visible fat
Salt and freshly ground black pepper
    to taste
Fresh herbs for garnish

Marinade

180ml (6fl oz) dry red wine
1 tsp chopped garlic or
    2 cloves garlic, crushed
1 tbsp dry sherry
½ tsp dried thyme,
½ tsp dried basil

1. For the marinade, combine all the ingredients in a small saucepan. Simmer uncovered over medium heat for 15 minutes. Remove from the heat and allow to cool to room temperature. Refrigerate in a sealed container until ready to use. Marinade can be prepared up to 48 hours in advance.
2. Place the steaks in a large plastic storage bag with a leak-proof seal. Pour the marinade over the steaks and squeeze out as much of the air as possible before sealing the bag. Refrigerate for at least 4 hours, up to 24 hours.
3. Preheat the grill. Lightly oil the grilling rack to ensure the steaks do not stick. Remove the steaks from the marinade, reserving the marinade for basting.
4. Season the steaks with salt and pepper. Grill, basting frequently with the marinade. For steaks of approximately 38mm (1½ in) thickness, grill 8–12 minutes per side for medium-rare. Increase the cooking time by 3 minutes per side for medium, 5 minutes for medium-well and 7 minutes for well-done.
5. Transfer the steaks to a warmed platter and let the steaks stand for about 5 minutes before serving to allow the natural juices to reabsorb. Adjust seasoning to taste. Serve immediately, garnished with fresh herbs if desired.

Grilled Swordfish
with Olive Tapenade

Eight 220g (7oz) swordfish steaks
6 small leeks, washed well
Salt and freshly ground black pepper
*   to taste*
125ml (8fl oz), plus 1 tbsp extra-
*   virgin olive oil, plus more for*
*   brushing*
15g (½oz) pitted oil-cured olives

1 small clove garlic, peeled
45g (1½ oz) rocket leaves
15g (½oz) fresh flatleaf parsley
*   leaves*
¼ tsp dried oregano

Serves 8	
Carb Level: Moderate	
Per serving:	
Carbohydrate:	15.5 g
Protein:	36.4 g

A great recipe for an evening barbecue with friends

1. Prepare a charcoal grill or preheat a grill to high. Make sure the grill grate is clean and lightly oiled to prevent sticking.
2. Season the swordfish and leeks with salt and pepper, and coat with 3 tablespoons oil. Allow the fish and leeks to marinate at room temperature for about 1 hour or until ready to grill.
3. To prepare the tapenade, combine the olives, garlic, rocket, parsley, oregano, salt and pepper in a food processor. With the machine running, drizzle in the remaining oil. Add 1½ tablespoons of hot water, and purée until smooth.
4. Place the fish and the leeks on the grill. After cooking the leeks for 5 minutes, remove from the grill and turn the fish over. Cook the fish for another 5 minutes until it is cooked through. Remove the fish from the grill and place on a plate. Arrange the leeks on a platter and place the fish on top of the leeks. Spoon the tapenade over the hot fish and serve immediately.

tips   If You Don't Have Access to a Grill

If the weather ruins your outdoor grilling plans, use the kitchen grill for this recipe. Grill the fish about 75mm (3in) from the heat source and turn once. Finish cooking the fish in a preheated 190°C, 375°F, gas mark 5 oven if needed.

Pecan-Crusted Catfish

Serves 8	
Carb Level: Moderate	
Per serving:	
Carbohydrate:	17.2 g
Protein:	32.4 g

A crispy Southern-USA method for fish preparation – add greens to this dish to make a perfect combination.

225g (8oz) ground pecans
225g (8oz) pecan pieces
60g (2oz) plain flour
Salt and freshly ground black pepper
    to taste
1 tsp cayenne pepper

1 large egg
3 tbsp milk
Eight 185g (6oz) catfish or red
    snapper fillets

1. Preheat the oven to 230°C, 450°F, gas mark 8.
2. Combine the pecans and spread them out on a plate. Mix together the flour, salt, pepper and cayenne. Spread this out on a plate. Whisk together the egg and the milk in a shallow bowl.
3. Coat each fillet with the flour, dip in the beaten egg, then firmly press the pecans onto the fish, coating them completely.
4. Arrange the fish in a single layer on an oiled baking tray. Be careful not to overlap. Place in the oven and bake for about 15 minutes. To check it is done, insert the tip of a thin-bladed knife into the thickest part of the fish. The flesh should be opaque and flaky. Serve immediately.

tips **Cheese Platters Are Great for Parties**
A nice selection of cheeses is a great addition to any get-together no matter how formal. Vary the intensity of flavours, and include a sheep's milk cheese, a cow's milk cheese and a goat's milk cheese, available at most supermarkets. Serve the cheese at room temperature with nuts and marinated olives. You can also add a roasted vegetable spread and wholegrain crackers. Garnish with fresh greens and serve on a wooden cheese board.

Roasted Salmon
with Goat's Cheese and Tarragon

Six 220g (7oz) salmon fillets,
  skin on
60ml (2fl oz) fresh-squeezed lemon
  juice
Salt and freshly ground black pepper
  to taste
2 cloves garlic, crushed
6 tbsp olive oil

185g (6oz) soft, creamy goat's
  cheese, at room temperature
3 tbsp chopped fresh tarragon,
  divided
3 tbsp chopped fresh chives, divided

Serves 6	
Carb Level: Low	
Per serving:	
Carbohydrate:	2.0 g
Protein:	42.8 g

The tang of quality goat's cheese goes perfectly with the rich taste of roasted salmon.

1. Place the fish in a shallow baking dish in a single layer; do not overlap.
2. In a small bowl, whisk together the lemon juice, salt, pepper, garlic and oil; pour over the fish. Cover and refrigerate for 2 hours, turning the fish several times.
3. Preheat the oven to 230°C, 450°F, gas mark 8.
4. Lay the marinated fish skin side down on a baking tray lined with baking paper. Bake the fish for about 10 minutes or until just done.
5. Meanwhile, beat the cheese with the back of a rubber spatula until soft and smooth. Mix with 1½ tablespoons each of the tarragon and chives.
6. Remove the fillets from the oven and discard the skin. Transfer to a platter. Sprinkle a bit of salt and pepper on top of the fillets. Place a large dollop of the cheese mixture on top of each fillet. Garnish with the remaining herbs.

Mussels Steamed in White Wine

Serves 4

Carb Level: Moderate

Per serving:

Carbohydrate:	20.0 g
Protein:	37.3 g

This is a traditional method for preparing fresh mussels.

1.3kg (3lb) fresh mussels
1½ tsp olive oil
3 small shallots, chopped
2 cloves garlic, chopped
375ml (12fl oz) dry white wine
2 bay leaves

4 very ripe tomatoes, peeled, seeded, cored and chopped
Salt and freshly ground black pepper to taste
2 tbsp chopped fresh flatleaf parsley for garnish

1. Wash the mussels very well in three changes of clean water. Scrub off any grit and remove the beards. Discard any open mussels.
2. Heat the oil in a large sauté pan over medium-high heat. Add the shallots and cook for about 1 minute or until tender. Add the garlic and cook until it just starts to brown. Add the wine and the bay leaves, then stir in the mussels. Cover and cook for about 4 minutes or until the mussels open. Discard any that do not open. Remove the pan from the heat. Using a slotted spoon, transfer the mussels to shallow soup bowls. Strain the cooking liquid through a fine-mesh sieve into a medium-size saucepan.
3. Add the tomatoes to the saucepan and bring to the boil. Season with salt and pepper. Ladle the sauce over the mussels and garnish with chopped parsley. Serve immediately.

Entertaining

❖ **Indicates Easy Recipe** ❖

Lemon Chicken Drumettes

Serves 10

Carb Level: Low

Per serving:

Carbohydrate:	7.4 g
Protein:	20.0 g

This makes a tasty appetizer for any get-together.

1.8kg (4lb) chicken drumettes
Salt and freshly ground black pepper
*   to taste*
60ml (2fl oz) orange juice
1 tbsp grated fresh ginger
3 tbsp vegetable oil
5 cloves garlic, finely chopped
60g (2oz) very finely chopped fresh
*   coriander*

1–2 fresh jalapeño peppers, seeded
*   and very finely chopped*
1 tsp ground cumin
1 tsp ground coriander seeds
Lemon wedges for garnish (optional)

1. Preheat the oven to 240°C, 475°F, gas mark 9. Line two baking trays with aluminium foil.
2. Cut off the wing tips from the wings to make drumettes if necessary. Arrange the drumettes on the foil, trying not to overlap them. Season with salt and pepper. Place the baking trays on the top rack of the oven until brown, about 5 minutes. Turn the drumettes over and return to the oven to brown for another 3 minutes. Transfer the drumettes to paper towels and set aside, saving the trays.
3. Bring 60ml (2fl oz) of water to a boil, then stir in the orange juice. Combine this mixture with the ginger and 250ml (8fl oz) of water in a blender or food processor; purée to a smooth consistency.
4. In a large, heavy frying pan, heat the oil over medium-high heat. Add the garlic and cook until softened, about 2 minutes (be careful not to burn the garlic; reduce the heat if necessary). Reduce the heat and stir in the coriander, jalapeños, cumin, coriander and about 1 teaspoon salt. Add the orange-ginger mixture to the pan and stir to mix. Turn up the heat, bring to the boil and reduce the liquid until the sauce is thick, like salsa. Adjust the seasoning to taste.

(recipe continues on the next page)

Lemon Chicken Drumettes (continued)

5. To serve, arrange the drumettes on a serving platter and top with the warm sauce. Garnish with lemon wedges surrounding the drumettes.

Anatomy of a Chicken Wing

Chicken wings are separated into three joints. Drumettes are the top joint of the wing and are like miniature drumsticks. They may be purchased precut, or the whole wing may be separated at the joints. The wing tips can be discarded or used for chicken stock. The middle section may be also used for this recipe, but the drumettes are much easier to eat as an appetizer.

Spanish Marinated Olives

36 large good-quality green olives (held in brine, but not marinaded), unpitted
½ tsp cracked peppercorns
1 tsp fresh thyme
1 sprig fresh rosemary
½ tsp dried oregano

3 bay leaves
4 cloves garlic, crushed
Finely grated zest from 1 lemon
60ml (2fl oz) balsamic vinegar
About 250ml (8fl oz) extra-virgin olive oil to cover

Serves 12
Carb Level: Low

Per serving:

Carbohydrate:	2.3 g
Protein:	0.6 g

These will keep in the refrigerator for up to four weeks.

Drain the olives. Place several at a time on a flat surface and crush them slightly with a large wide-blade chef's knife, without altering their shape. This opens them up just enough to marinate throughout. In a large bowl, toss together the olives with all the ingredients *except* the olive oil. Place them in a preserving jar or plastic container with tight-fitting lid and cover the olives with the olive oil. Marinate for a least a week in the refrigerator. Keep refrigerated, but return to room temperature before serving.

Smoked Prawns
with Horseradish Cream

Serves 6
Carb Level: Low

Per serving:	
Carbohydrate:	6.4 g
Protein:	12.6 g

This is a great recipe for making in advance.

1 seedless cucumber, unpeeled
125ml (4fl oz) crème fraîche or sour cream
60g (2oz) prepared horseradish, drained and squeezed
1 tbsp Dijon mustard
1 tbsp fresh-squeezed lemon juice
1 teaspoon fresh chopped dill
¼ tsp freshly ground white pepper
Salt to taste
454g (1lb) smoked prawns, chopped
Snipped fresh chives for garnish
Lemon wedges for garnish

1. Cut the cucumber into 12mm (½ in) slices. Use a small measuring spoon or melon baller to make a hollow in the centre of each slice.
2. Mix together the crème fraîche, horseradish, Dijon, lemon juice, dill, white pepper and salt in a bowl. Place the chopped smoked prawns in a medium-size bowl. Add half the horseradish dressing and toss to lightly coat. Add more dressing if needed: be careful not to overdress.
3. Use a teaspoon to spoon a small portion of the dressed prawns into the hollow of each cucumber slice. Top with the snipped chives. Refrigerate until ready to serve. Serve with fresh lemon wedges.

(tips) How Many Carbs in My Wine?

A bottle of wine will yield 4 to 5 servings per bottle. A bottle of champagne will yield 5 to 6 servings per bottle. A 160ml (5fl oz) serving of white wine contains 1.2g of carbohydrates; 160ml (5fl oz) of red wine contains 2.4g; and a 160ml (5fl oz) glass of champagne contains 4.3g.

Hard-Boiled Eggs
Stuffed with Mushrooms and Cheese

1 tsp vegetable oil
½ tsp unsalted butter
2 shallots, chopped
125g (4oz) finely chopped button
    mushrooms
Juice of 1 lemon
1 tsp finely grated lemon zest
Salt and freshly ground black pepper
    to taste
5 large hard-boiled eggs, peeled

3 tbsp mayonnaise
45g (1½oz) shredded Gruyère
    cheese, divided
Pinch of cayenne pepper
Pinch of ground nutmeg
1 tbsp chopped fresh flatleaf parsley,
    plus 4 extra leaves for garnish

Serves 4
Carb Level: Moderate

Per serving:	
Carbohydrate:	16.0 g
Protein:	14.5 g

Serve these platter-style as an hors d'oeuvre, or on a bed of spring greens as an appetizer.

1. Warm the oil and butter in a medium-size non-stick sauté pan over medium heat. Add the shallots and cook slowly for 3 minutes, until soft but not brown. Stir in the mushrooms, lemon juice and lemon zest. Season with salt and black pepper. Cover and cook, stirring frequently, for 10 minutes or until the mushrooms are very soft and all the liquid has evaporated. Remove from heat.
2. Slice four hard-boiled eggs longways. Remove the yolks and carefully slice a small piece from the bottom of each egg white half so that it will stand flat and steady on a platter.
3. Chop the remaining egg. Using a spatula, press it through a fine-mesh sieve into the pan with the mushrooms. Stir in the mayonnaise and add 2 tablespoons of the cheese, cayenne, and nutmeg. Add the chopped parsley, and season with salt and pepper. Cover and keep warm.
4. Preheat the oven to 190°C, 375°F, gas mark 5. Place an equal portion of the mushroom mixture in each egg-white half, mounding it slightly. Place the filled egg halves in a baking dish and sprinkle the tops with the remaining Gruyère; bake for 4 minutes, then turn on the grill (on low) and cook for about 2 minutes, until golden brown and bubbling. Serve hot.

Mussel Salad with Green Beans

Serves 4
Carb Level: Moderate

Per serving:	
Carbohydrate:	19.9 g
Protein:	23.2 g

Fresh farm-raised mussels are available at most fish counters.

375g (12oz) small green beans, trimmed and cut into 38mm (1½ in) pieces
Salt
680g (1lb 8oz) fresh mussels
2 tsp butter
3 medium shallots, chopped
60ml (2fl oz) dry white wine
1 large ripe tomato, peeled, seeded, cored and diced

2 tbsp chopped fresh flatleaf parsley, divided
125ml (4fl oz) olive oil
Juice of 1 lemon
2 tbsp rice wine vinegar
Freshly ground black pepper to taste
½ cucumber, sliced paper-thin

1. Place the green beans in a medium-size saucepan and add cold water to cover by about 25mm (1in). Add 1 teaspoon of salt. Bring to the boil over medium-high heat. Reduce the heat to medium-low and simmer for 3–5 minutes, until the beans are very tender; drain well. To stop the cooking, immediately plunge the beans in a bowl of ice water or run under very cold running water. Drain well and place in a medium-size bowl.
2. Wash the mussels very well in three changes of clean water. Scrub off any grit and remove the beards. Discard any open mussels.
3. Melt the butter in a large saucepan over medium heat. Add half of the shallots and sauté for 3 minutes, without browning. Add the mussels and wine, and raise the heat to high. Cover and cook for 3 minutes, or until the mussels open, shaking the pan while they are covered. Discard any mussels that do not open. Remove from the heat.
4. Toss the tomato, 1 tablespoon of parsley, olive oil, lemon juice, rice wine vinegar and remaining shallots in a small bowl; mix to combine and add salt and pepper to taste. Arrange the cucumbers around the edge of each of four chilled salad plates or on a medium-size platter. Place equal portions of the salad in the centre and sprinkle with the chopped parsley. Arrange the mussels around the salad. Drizzle the vinaigrette over the beans, cucumbers and mussels. Serve immediately. (As the green beans sit in the tossed vinegar, they will slowly begin to change colour due to the acid in the dressing. Don't dress the salad until just before serving.)

Mexican Prawn Cocktail

250ml (8fl oz) tomato ketchup
160ml (5fl oz) orange juice
2 tbsp fresh-squeezed lime juice
2 tbsp dry white wine
2 tsp Worcestershire sauce
1 tsp hot pepper sauce

Salt and freshly ground black pepper
to taste
275g (9oz) prawns, cooked, peeled
and de-veined
6 lime wedges for garnish

Serves 6	
Carb Level: Moderate	
Per serving:	
Carbohydrate:	14.8 g
Protein:	25.8 g

Easy to do in advance, and takes just minutes to prepare. Serve in chilled martini or margarita glasses.

Whisk together the ketchup, orange juice, lime juice, wine, Worcestershire sauce and hot pepper sauce in a large bowl. Season with salt and pepper. Taste and add more lime juice or salt if desired. Stir in the prawns. Cover and marinate in the refrigerator for 5 minutes or up to 4 hours before serving. Divide the prawn mixture among six martini or margarita glasses. Garnish each with a lime wedge.

Orange-Cucumber Salsa

Makes 4 cups

Carb Level: Moderate

Per serving:

Carbohydrate:	19.1 g
Protein:	2.9 g

Great as a dipping salsa or as an accompaniment to fish or shellfish.

4 large oranges
4 seedless cucumbers, washed
125ml (4fl oz) rice wine vinegar

2 tbsp olive oil
1 tsp red pepper flakes

1. Grate the rind of one or two of the oranges to yield 1 teaspoon grated zest. Trim the rind from the oranges, including as much of the white pith as possible. Cut the oranges into segments, remove any seeds and dice the flesh. Place the diced oranges in a medium-size bowl along with any accumulated juices.
2. Peel two cucumbers. Split all the cucumbers longways and use a small spoon to scoop out the seeds. Cut all the cucumbers into 6mm ($^1/_4$in) slices. Add to the bowl with the oranges.
3. Whisk together the vinegar, oil and red pepper flakes. Pour the mixture over the top of the oranges and cucumbers, and add salt and freshly ground black pepper to taste. Cover and marinate in the refrigerator for 1–2 hours. Serve chilled.

Stuffed Courgettes

4 large courgettes
30g (1oz) butter
1 shallot, chopped
2 cloves garlic, crushed
60g (2oz) chopped button
   mushrooms
30g (1oz) chopped spinach, cooked
   and drained
125g (4oz) smoked mozzarella
   cheese, grated

1 tbsp tomato ketchup
1 tbsp chopped fresh parsley
Salt and freshly ground black pepper
   to taste
1 tsp honey
1 egg, beaten
60g (2oz) toasted pine nuts

Serves 4	
Carb Level: Moderate	
Per serving:	
Carbohydrate:	13.6 g
Protein:	9.6 g

This recipe also works well with medium-size courgettes. You can also substitute yellow summer squash.

1. Trim off the ends of the courgettes, halve them longways and use a small spoon to scoop some out some of the seeded flesh to form hollow 'boats'. Bring a large pan of salted water to the boil and blanch the courgettes for 2 minutes. Drain well, then place them cut-side up in a greased casserole dish.
2. Heat the butter in a large saucepan over medium-high heat and sauté the shallot and garlic for 2 minutes. Add the mushrooms and spinach, and cook gently for 4 minutes to remove any liquid. Stir in the cheese, then the ketchup. Add the parsley, and season with salt and pepper; then stir in the honey. Remove the saucepan from the heat and stir in the egg and nuts.
3. Preheat the oven to 200°C, 400°F, gas mark 6.
4. Fill the courgette halves with this mixture. Cook uncovered for about 10 minutes until heated throughout. Serve hot, with a salad of thinly sliced tomatoes as a first course, or as a buffet item.

Mushrooms Au Gratin

Serves 4
Carb Level: Moderate

Per serving:

Carbohydrate:	18.5 g
Protein:	4.5 g

An excellent side dish that can be easily made in larger quantities.

454g (1lb) small button
   mushrooms, cleaned and stems
   trimmed
Juice of 1 lemon
2 tbsp brandy
60ml (2fl oz) vegetable oil
1 small shallot, chopped
2 tbsp sour cream
2 tbsp tomato paste

2 tsp honey
Salt and freshly ground black pepper
   to taste
Pinch of cayenne pepper
2 tbsp Dijon mustard
1 tbsp breadcrumbs
2 tbsp grated Gruyère cheese

1. Put the mushrooms in a medium-size bowl and stir in the lemon juice and brandy; let marinate for 10 minutes.
2. Heat the oil in a frying pan over medium-high heat and sauté the shallot for 1 minute, without browning it. Add the marinade juices to the shallot and cook for 2 minutes to reduce the liquid.
3. Add the mushrooms and cook for 2 minutes. Remove them from the pan with a slotted spoon and keep warm in a shallow ovenproof dish. Add the sour cream, tomato paste, honey, salt, pepper, and cayenne to the pan juices, stir to mix, and boil for 2 minutes to reduce further. Stir in the mustard, but do not allow the sauce to boil.
4. Preheat the grill on low.
5. Pour the sauce over the mushrooms. Combine the breadcrumbs and cheese, and sprinkle over the mushrooms. Brown under the grill until golden. Serve on a platter with toothpicks on the side.

Stewed Pepper and Tomato Purée

4 red peppers
2 tbsp olive oil
2 cloves garlic, quartered
½ tsp salt

Red chilli pepper flakes to taste
250ml (8fl oz) tomato sauce
1 tbsp tomato paste

1. Quarter the peppers, cut off the stems, and remove the seeds and the inner membrane. Chop the peppers into large pieces.
2. Heat the oil on medium-high in a non-stick sauté pan; stew the peppers with the garlic over low heat until very soft. Season with salt and red chilli flakes.
3. Transfer the peppers and garlic to a food processor or blender; process until puréed. Return the pepper mixture to the sauté pan and add the tomato sauce and tomato paste; stir to mix, and bring to a light simmer. Serve hot.

A Variation for Chicken

Whisk in a couple of tablespoons of goat's cheese to the hot sauce to make a great sauce for chicken.

Serves 4
Carb Level: Moderate

Per serving:	
Carbohydrate:	19.3 g
Protein:	3.1 g

Spoon one or two tablespoons on the centre of a dinner plate before serving with grilled or roasted meat or fish.

Aubergine Topped
with Gruyère Cheese

Serves 4

Carb Level: Moderate

Per serving:

Carbohydrate:	14.4 g
Protein:	19.3 g

A tasty dish that satisfies cravings for deep-fried food.

2 large aubergines
Salt
1.25l (40fl oz) vegetable oil
1 clove garlic, chopped
125g (8oz) Gruyère cheese or moz-
  zarella cheese, thinly sliced

Chopped fresh parsley for
  garnish

1. Cut the aubergines across into slices 12mm (½ inch) thick. Sprinkle each slice with salt and stand for 25 minutes (this extracts the bitter-tasting juices). Rinse the aubergines under cold running water, drain and dry thoroughly.
2. Preheat the grill on low.
3. Heat the oil and deep-fry each aubergine slice for 1 minute. Drain on paper towels. Arrange the slices in a single layer on a flat baking tray, sprinkle with the garlic, and place a slice of cheese over each slice. Grill until the cheese is bubbling and golden. Sprinkle with a little chopped parsley and serve immediately.

Avocado and Tomato Dip

2 ripe avocados
2 tomatoes, peeled, seeded and
    chopped
1 tbsp tomato paste
Juice and grated rind of
    1 lemon
1 clove garlic
1 small onion, chopped
2 tbsp chopped fresh parsley

225g (8oz) cottage cheese
1 tsp salt
Pinch of paprika
Freshly ground black pepper

Serves 4	
Carb Level: Moderate	
Per serving:	
Carbohydrate:	18.7 g
Protein:	10.6 g

Use this as a dip for vegetables or as a topping for shellfish – it also goes well with prawn and lobster dishes.

1. To peel the avocado, make a slice longways around the centre of the pit; twist the halves apart. To remove the stone, poke a fork into the seed and twist. Smash the avocado flesh with the back of a fork until quite creamy.

2. In a blender or food processor, blend together the tomatoes, tomato paste, lemon juice, lemon rind, garlic, onion, parsley and cottage cheese. In a large bowl, combine all the ingredients together and stir, seasoning with salt, paprika and pepper. Serve chilled or at room temperature. Note that avocados will turn brown as they are exposed to air, so this dish should be prepared just before serving.

Spicy Olive and Walnut Tapenade

Serves 4

Carb Level: Moderate

Per serving:

Carbohydrate:	15.9 g
Protein:	23.8 g

This tapenade works well as a garnish on grilled fish.

185g (6oz) large black pitted calamata olives, drained
375g (12oz) shelled walnuts
15g (½oz) large capers
2 tbsp sour cream
½ tsp red chilli pepper flakes
4 hard-boiled eggs, peeled and quartered
2 cloves garlic

2 tbsp soy sauce
1 tbsp chopped parsley
2 tbsp red wine vinegar
60ml (2fl oz) olive oil
Pinch of dried tarragon
1 tsp honey
Salt and freshly ground black pepper
   to taste

Place all the ingredients in a blender or food processor and blend to a paste. Adjust the seasoning to taste. Use as a filling for vegetables or as a hors d'oeuvre. Add a small amount of cream to thin if using as a dip for vegetables.

Crab Salad

Serves 2

Carb Level: Low

Per serving:

Carbohydrate:	7.5 g
Protein:	24.4 g

You can add fresh herbs, curry powder or Cajun seasoning for a different twist on this elegant salad.

225g (8oz) cooked, cold crabmeat,
   picked over for shells
3–4 tbsp mayonnaise
Juice of 1 lemon

1 shallot, chopped
Salt and freshly ground black pepper
   to taste

Combine all the ingredients in a medium-size bowl, mixing well. Adjust seasoning to taste. Serve as a centrepiece in a bed of crispy spring greens with a light citrus vinaigrette.

 Tinned Versus Fresh

You can use tinned crabmeat for ease and convenience, but the taste difference using fresh crabmeat is exceptional. Be prepared for the price of fresh meat – it is expensive.

Green Beans
with Shallots and Rosemary

*454g (1lb) green beans, ends
    trimmed*
2 tbsp butter
3 large shallots, chopped

1 tsp chopped fresh rosemary
*Salt and freshly ground black pepper
    to taste*

Serves 5	
Carb Level: Low	
Per serving:	
Carbohydrate:	8.3 g
Protein:	2.0 g

Use fresh green beans, which are available in abundance all year long.

1. Cook the green beans in a large pot of boiling salted water until crisp-tender, about 5 minutes. Drain and rinse with cold running water until the green beans are no longer warm; drain again. Pat dry with paper towels.
2. Melt the butter in a large, heavy frying pan over medium-high heat. Add the shallots and rosemary, and sauté until the shallots are tender, about 5 minutes. Add the green beans and toss until heated through, about 5 minutes. Season with salt and pepper. Transfer the green beans to a bowl and serve immediately.

Chicken Pâté

Serves 10

Carb Level: Low

Per serving:

Carbohydrate:	3.0 g
Protein:	11.4 g

This classic French recipe is easier each time you make it.

454g (1lb) boneless, skinless chicken breasts
2 large egg whites
80ml (2½ fl oz) sour cream
2 tbsp brandy
Salt and freshly ground white pepper
4 sprigs fresh tarragon
60g (2oz) pistachio nuts, crushed
2.5l (80fl oz) water

1. Cut the chicken into small pieces. Place three-quarters of the chicken in a food processor. Add the egg whites, sour cream and brandy. Season with salt and pepper. Process until the mixture is very smooth. Transfer to a medium-size bowl. Strip the leaves from the tarragon and add to the bowl; discard the tarragon stems. Fold in the pistachios and the reserved chicken pieces. Place a small sauté pan on medium heat and cook about a tablespoon of the chicken mixture thoroughly. Cool slightly and taste. Add more salt and pepper as needed.

2. Bring the water to the boil over high heat. Reduce the heat to medium-low. Place a large sheet of baking (not greaseproof) paper on a flat surface. Place the chicken mixture on the paper in a neat log shape approximately 255 x 50mm (10 x 2in), positioning it about 75mm (3in) from the long edge of the paper. Fold the 75mm (3in) of paper over the chicken mixture. Roll the paper around the chicken to form a neat cylinder. Twist the ends closed and tie firmly with butcher's twine.

3. Place the cylinder on a large piece of cling film. Use the same technique to enclose the cylinder. Tie the ends with butcher's twine. Place in the saucepan of simmering water. Place a Pyrex dish over the cylinder to keep it submerged. Simmer for 20 minutes. With a pair of tongs, carefully remove the cylinder and cool on a wire rack at room temperature.

4. Unwrap the log. Cut across into 6mm (¼in) slices. Arrange the slices in a decorative pattern on a chilled serving plate with whole grain and Dijon mustards on the side, or Spicy Olive and Walnut Tapenade (see recipe on page 268) on the side.

Tuna Tapenade

105g (3½ oz) tin tuna packed in
    water, well drained
30g (1oz) cream cheese, at room tem-
    perature
2 tbsp mayonnaise
1 tbsp sour cream
1 tbsp fresh-squeezed lemon juice
Freshly ground white pepper

30g (1oz) fresh baby spinach leaves
15g (½oz) chopped spring onions
2 tbsp capers, well drained
1 tbsp chopped fresh dill

In a food processor, combine the tuna, cream cheese, mayonnaise, sour cream, lemon juice and pepper; process until well blended. Add the spinach, spring onions, capers and dill; blend again until well blended. Serve as a spread for vegetables or as a garnish on a salad of mixed greens and a simple vinaigrette.

Serves 10
Carb Level: Low

Per serving:	
Carbohydrate:	1.5 g
Protein:	4.5 g

A versatile spread or salad garnish that requires no cooking.

Prawn Scampi

180ml (6fl oz) extra-virgin olive oil
2 large cloves garlic, slivered
454g (1lb) large prawns with tails on,
    shelled and de-veined
2 large cloves garlic, chopped
2 dried hot chilli peppers

1 tbsp grated orange zest
15g (½oz) chopped fresh parsley
Salt and freshly ground black pepper
    to taste
1 tbsp dry sherry

Warm the olive oil in a large frying pan over medium-low heat. Add the slivered garlic and cook gently until soft and just starting to colour, stirring occasionally. Place the prawns in the pan in a single layer. Add the chopped garlic, chilli pepper and orange zest. Cook undisturbed for 1–2 minutes. When the prawns are pink on one side, turn them over. Add the parsley, salt, pepper and sherry, raise the heat slightly, and cook until all the prawns are pink, about 2 minutes more. Serve immediately.

Serves 4
Carb Level: Low

Per serving:	
Carbohydrate:	2.3 g
Protein:	23.4 g

Chilli peppers and orange zest give this version of prawn scampi a kick.

Salmon Fillets with Basil

Serves 4	
Carb Level: Low	
Per serving:	
Carbohydrate:	5.7 g
Protein:	36.3 g

Use only fresh salmon and buy your basil during the summer, when it's cheapest, yet most tasty.

2 lemons
Four 185g (6oz) salmon fillets, cleaned and boned
4 tbsp unsalted butter, cut into 6 pieces
2 tbsp olive oil
1 tbsp shallots
2 tsp chopped garlic
30g (1oz) de-stemmed and torn fresh basil leaves
Pinch of cayenne pepper

Salt and freshly ground black pepper to taste
250ml (8fl oz) double cream at room temperature
15g (½oz) coarsely chopped fresh basil for garnish

1. Squeeze one lemon over the salmon, making sure to coat both sides. Melt 2 tablespoons of butter and the oil over medium heat in a sauté pan large enough to accommodate all the fillets. When the butter and oil mixture starts to foam, add the fillets. Cook for 3–5 minutes on each side; transfer to an ovenproof plate in an oven heated to 120°C, 200°F, gas mark ½.
2. Add the remaining butter to the pan a piece at a time, and melt until foaming. Add the shallots and garlic, and cook until soft, about 2 minutes. Add the juice from the other lemon, the basil leaves, cayenne, salt and pepper; stir to combine well. Add the cream very slowly to prevent curdling, and bring to a simmer. Cook until the sauce is reduced by a third. Adjust the seasonings to taste.
3. Place the fish on warm plates or a platter with a small pool of sauce underneath each fillet. Top each lightly with a little more sauce, and sprinkle with the basil.

Scallops
in Herby Tomato Sauce

15g (¹/₂oz) butter
1 clove garlic, chopped
1 shallot, chopped
125g (4oz) chopped tomatoes
   (tinned or fresh)
1 tsp balsamic vinegar
2 tbsp red wine
Salt and freshly ground black pepper
   to taste
1 tsp fresh tarragon, chopped, or 1
   tsp dried

1 tsp fresh thyme leaves
454g (1lb) large sea scallops, with
   hinges on the side of each scallop
   removed
1–2 tbsp olive oil
Fresh basil, chopped, for garnish

Serves 4	
Carb Level: Low	
Per serving:	
Carbohydrate:	7.3 g
Protein:	19.9 g

You can substitute fish such as cod, grouper or snapper for the scallops in this recipe.

1. Melt half the butter in a small saucepan over medium heat until foaming; cook the garlic and shallot, stirring occasionally, until softened. Add the tomatoes and cook about 10 minutes, stirring occasionally. Stir in the vinegar, wine, salt and pepper, tarragon, thyme and remaining butter. Cool slightly and purée in a blender or food processor; keep warm.

2. Heat a 305mm (12in) non-stick frying pan over high heat until almost smoking. Place the scallops on a plate, sprinkle them with some salt, and brush or drizzle them with a little olive oil. Add the scallops to the pan one at a time; turn them as they brown, allowing about 2 minutes on each side. Pour a little sauce onto each of four plates or a large platter, and top with the scallops and basil.

Beef with Cucumber

Serves 4
Carb Level: Low

Per serving:	
Carbohydrate:	4.9 g
Protein:	27.2 g

To present it as an appetizer, serve the steak on mini-skewers.

250ml (8fl oz) plain yogurt
15g (¹/₂oz) cucumber, coarsely
   shredded and unpeeled
1 tbsp finely chopped red onion
1 tbsp coarsely chopped fresh mint
¹/₄ tsp sugar
Salt and freshly ground black pepper
   to taste

454g (1lb) 12mm (¹/₂in) thick boneless beef sirloin steak
¹/₂ tsp lemon-pepper
   seasoning
Mint leaves for garnish

1. Preheat the grill. Make sure the grill grate is clean and lightly oiled to prevent sticking.
2. Combine the yogurt, cucumber, onion, mint and sugar in a small bowl. Season to taste with salt and pepper; set aside.
3. Trim the fat from the steak. Sprinkle the steak with salt and lemon-pepper seasoning on both sides. Grill the steak on the rack of an uncovered grill directly over medium heat for 12–15 minutes for medium, turning once. Let the steak stand at room temperature for 5 minutes before carving. Using a long straight-edge slicing knife, cut the steak into thin strips across the grain of the meat. Roll each slice and secure with a toothpick and place on a platter garnished with mint leaves. Serve the cucumber raita sauce on the side.

Eat Often

Don't go longer than six hours without having a protein meal or protein-rich snack. 'Fasting' will cause you to crave sugars. Planning your meal and snacks will allow you to manage your diet plan better.

Chicken with Nectarine Salsa

4 large boneless, skinless chicken
   breasts halves
1 tbsp lime juice
1–1½ tsp ground cumin
Salt and freshly ground black pepper
   to taste
60g (2oz) chunky salsa
45g (1½ oz) chopped nectarine

2 tbsp chopped fresh coriander
1 jalapeño pepper, seeded and finely
   chopped
1 tsp chopped garlic
Lime wedges for garnish

Serves 4
Carb Level: Low

Per serving:	
Carbohydrate:	5.0 g
Protein:	32.6 g

Adding a small amount of fresh, ripe fruit to quality pre-made salsa is a great time-saver. Also try peaches, mangoes or citrus fruits.

1. Preheat the grill. Make sure the grill grate is clean and lightly oiled to prevent sticking.
2. Rinse the chicken and pat dry. Brush the chicken with lime juice, and sprinkle evenly with cumin and salt and pepper. Grill the chicken on the rack of an uncovered grill directly over medium heat for 12–15 minutes, until the chicken is tender and no longer pink, turning once.
3. For the nectarine salsa, stir together the salsa, nectarine, coriander, jalapeño and garlic in a small bowl; spoon over the chicken, and serve with the lime wedges on the side for garnish.

Cooking Chicken Safely

tips

Chicken must be cooked to the following internal temperatures to ensure food safety and proper elimination of bacteria.

Boneless chicken   70°C, 165°F
Chicken pieces with bones   75°C, 170°F
Ground chicken   70°C, 165°F
Whole chicken with bones   80°C, 180°F

Sautéed Spinach with Pine Nuts

<table>
<tr><td colspan="2">Serves 2</td></tr>
<tr><td colspan="2">Carb Level: Low</td></tr>
<tr><td colspan="2">Per serving:</td></tr>
<tr><td>Carbohydrate:</td><td>6.4 g</td></tr>
<tr><td>Protein:</td><td>1.6 g</td></tr>
</table>

The sesame oil and bouillon granules add a twist to traditional sautéed spinach.

1 tbsp pine nuts
1 tbsp olive oil
30g (1oz) chopped onion
1 clove garlic, chopped
2 tbsp rice wine
⅛ tsp dark sesame oil
½ tsp chicken bouillon granules

Freshly ground black pepper to taste
300g (10oz) fresh spinach, washed, stemmed and chopped
1 tsp lemon juice

1. Toast the pine nuts in a small frying pan over low heat, turning often, until lightly browned (2 minutes or so); set aside.
2. Heat the oil in a large frying pan over medium heat; add the onion and cook until soft, about 4 minutes. Add the garlic and cook for another minute. Stir in the rice wine, sesame oil, bouillon granules and pepper. Add the spinach and reduce the heat to medium-low. Cover and cook until tender, about 6 minutes. Stir in the lemon juice; cook for 1 minute. Stir in the pine nuts and adjust seasoning to taste. Serve immediately on a serving platter or in a bowl.

tips
Roasting Vegetables the Right Way
Roasted vegetable platters are a colourful way to serve an assortment of delicious vegetables. The key is to start with a very hot oven– 200–230°C, 400–450°F, gas mark 6–8 is ideal. Toss the vegetables with a small amount of olive oil and season liberally with pepper and salt, and place on a baking tray in a single layer. Place in the oven and turn the vegetables about every 3 minutes, until just starting to caramelize on the outside but not overcooked. The vegetables should still have shape and texture. Roast each type of vegetable individually; mixing them all together to cook muddies the flavours. Roasted vegetables can be served warm or at room temperature.

Grilled Tomatoes

6 large ripe tomatoes
2 tsp olive oil

Salt and freshly ground black pepper
  to taste
1 tbsp fresh thyme

Preheat the grill to high. Make sure the grill pan is clean and lightly oiled to prevent sticking. Halve the tomatoes across. Gently squeeze each half to remove the seeds. Lightly brush the tomatoes with the oil and season with salt and pepper. Place cut side down under the hottest part of the grill; grill for 1 minute. Turn the tomatoes, moving them to the edge of the grill or to wherever the heat is reduced. Grill for 3 minutes or until charred. Remove from the grill and season with the fresh thyme. Serve warm or at room temperature.

Serves 12
Carb Level: Low

Per serving:	
Carbohydrate:	2.9 g
Protein:	0.5 g

Sprinkle a little grated Parmesan cheese over the tops as soon as they come off the grill to enhance the tomato and fresh herb flavours.

Grilled Radicchio

3 heads radicchio
1 tbsp extra-virgin
  olive oil
Salt and freshly ground black pepper
  to taste

Freshly grated Parmesan cheese
  (optional)

Preheat the grill to low. Make sure the grill pan is clean and lightly oiled to prevent sticking. Remove any damaged outer leaves from the radicchio. Trim the stem and quarter the radicchio longways, leaving the core intact. Lightly brush with the oil and season with salt and pepper. Place on the grill; grill for 8 minutes or until tender and lightly browned. Serve warm or at room temperature. If you like, drizzle a touch more olive oil over it and sprinkle with grated Parmesan cheese.

Serves 12
Carb Level: Low

Per serving:	
Carbohydrate:	0.1 g
Protein:	0.0 g

For a richer, sweeter taste, blanch the radicchio in lightly salted water for 1 minute, then drain well and grill.

Special Dishes

❖ **Indicates Easy Recipe** ❖

Oven-Roasted Winter Vegetables

Serves 6

Carb Level: Moderate

Per serving:

Carbohydrate:	20.0 g
Protein:	3.1 g

This colourful dish can be increased for larger parties.

225g (8oz) swedes, peeled and cut
 into 25mm (1in) pieces
225g (8oz) carrots, peeled and cut
 into 25mm (1in) pieces
225g (8oz) parsnips, peeled and cut
 into 25mm (1in) pieces
225g (8oz) Brussels sprouts,
 trimmed
1 tbsp unsalted butter
1 tbsp extra-virgin
 olive oil

2 tsp chopped fresh thyme
2 tsp chopped fresh sage
1/8 tsp freshly grated nutmeg
Salt and freshly ground black pepper
 to taste
125ml (4oz) Marsala

1. Preheat the oven to 230°C, 450°F, gas mark 8.
2. Bring a large pot of salted water to a boil. Add the swedes, carrots and parsnips, and simmer until they are somewhat tender when pierced with a fork, about 5–8 minutes. Drain well.
3. Place the swedes, carrots, parsnips and Brussels sprouts in a large roasting pan. Melt the butter in a small saucepan and stir in the oil, thyme, sage and nutmeg. Drizzle the butter mixture over the vegetables and toss to coat them completely. Season with salt and pepper. Pour the Marsala into the bottom of the roasting pan.
4. Cover tightly with foil and bake in the oven for 40 minutes. Remove the foil, toss the vegetables and continue to cook uncovered until the Marsala is evaporated and the vegetables can easily be pierced with a knife, 20–30 minutes. Place the roasted vegetables on a platter and serve immediately.

Pear and Pumpkin Soup

30g (1oz) chopped onion
125ml (4fl oz) chicken stock
454g (1lb) tin pumpkin purée
625ml (20fl oz) semi-skimmed milk
430ml (14fl oz) pear juice

¼ tsp ground ginger
¼ tsp freshly ground white pepper
Salt to taste

Serves 6	
Carb Level: Moderate	
Per serving:	
Carbohydrate:	20.0 g
Protein:	4.2 g

Top this dish with two very thin pear slices or a dollop of sour cream just before you serve it.

1. Combine the onion and chicken stock in a large saucepan; bring to a boil. Reduce heat and simmer covered for about 10 minutes or until the onion is very tender; let cool slightly.
2. Transfer the mixture to a blender or food processor. Add the pumpkin, cover and blend until smooth. Return the pumpkin mixture to the saucepan. Stir in the milk, pear juice, ginger and white pepper. Cook and stir until heated through. Taste and season with salt if needed. Ladle into soup bowls.

The Two Types of Dietary Fibre

Insoluble fibre is found in wholegrains and other plants. It absorbs water and creates peristalsis, the natural contraction of your intestinal wall to move solid materials through the digestive tract. Soluble fibre is found in forms such as pectin (in apples) and beta-glucans (in oats and barley). A diet high in soluble fibre helps reduce cholesterol, which offers protection against heart disease.

Sautéed Green Beans
with Shiitake Mushrooms

Serves 8

Carb Level: Moderate

Per serving:	
Carbohydrate:	12.7 g
Protein:	3.5 g

You can substitute button mushrooms to lower the carb count, but don't expect the same complex taste and textures.

900g (2lb) green beans, de-stemmed
3 tbsp olive oil
454g (1lb) Shiitake mushrooms,
    thinly sliced
1 small red onion, thinly sliced
2 cloves garlic, chopped
60ml (2fl oz.) rice wine
1 tsp chopped fresh thyme leaves

2 tbsp unsalted butter, softened
Salt and freshly ground black pepper
    to taste

1. Prepare a large bowl of iced water; set aside. Bring a large pot of salted water to a fast boil. Add the green beans and cook for 4–5 minutes, until crisp-tender. Drain the green beans, then submerge them in the iced water for 2–3 minutes. Drain well.
2. In a large non-stick frying pan, heat the olive oil over medium-high heat. Add the mushrooms, onion and garlic; cook, stirring occasionally, until the mushrooms are nicely browned, about 10–11 minutes. Add the rice wine and cook for 1 minute.
3. Add the green beans and thyme, and cook until heated through. Remove from the heat, add the butter and toss to combine. Season to taste with salt and pepper. Serve warm.

tips **Managing Carbs During Holidays**
Focus on foods that you can have, not those that you can't. It is more powerful to think 'substitute' instead of 'eliminate'.

Cornbread Stuffing

*100g (3½oz) white or yellow
    cornmeal*
125g (4oz) plain flour
2 tbsp sugar
1 tbsp baking powder
¼ tsp bicarbonate of soda
¼ tsp salt

*310ml (10fl oz) buttermilk or whole
    milk*
*60ml (2fl oz) unsalted butter,
    melted*
60ml (2fl oz) vegetable oil
1 large egg

Serves 8	
Carb Level: Moderate	
Per serving:	
Carbohydrate:	17.8 g
Protein:	12.1 g

Tastes best when eaten the same day it's made – allow it to cool, covered, in the refrigerator until ready to serve.

1. Preheat the oven to 100°C, 350°F, gas mark 4. Butter a 200mm (8in) square baking pan.
2. In a large bowl, whisk together the cornmeal, flour, sugar, baking powder, bicarbonate of soda and salt.
3. In another bowl, whisk together the buttermilk, melted butter, oil and egg until smooth. Stir the wet into the dry ingredients, and when smooth and well mixed, pour the batter into the prepared pan. Bake for 35–40 minutes, or until a toothpick inserted near the centre comes out clean and the cornbread begins to pull away from the sides of the pan, and the top is golden brown. Cool in the pan placed on a wire rack. When cool, crumble into large pieces. Stuff into a turkey that has been half baked, or serve just as is.

Rosemary Jus

Serves 8
Carb Level: Low

Per serving:	
Carbohydrate:	9.9 g
Protein:	2.2 g

This is a delicious accompaniment to sliced turkey.

Turkey wing tips, neck and giblets,
reserved from the turkey
2l (64fl oz) turkey or chicken stock
3 sprigs fresh rosemary
1 tbsp cornflour stirred into 2 tbsp
cold water

Salt and freshly ground white pepper
to taste
30g (1oz) butter, cut into pieces

1. Chop the turkey neck into large pieces. Transfer the neck pieces to a large, heavy saucepan and add the giblets, wing tips and stock. Bring to the boil over medium-high heat, skimming any impurities that foam and accumulate at the top. Reduce the heat to low and simmer for 3 hours.

2. Strain the stock through a strainer into a bowl. Chop the meat from the neck and the giblets, and transfer to a small bowl. Cover and refrigerate. Discard the bones. Pour the pan drippings from the turkey into a bowl. Skim off and discard the fat that rises to the surface, and set the drippings aside.

3. Set the roasting pan over two burners or hot plates and add 500ml (16fl oz) of the strained turkey stock (not the drippings). Bring to the boil and use a wooden spoon to scrape up any browned bits sticking to the bottom of the pan. Transfer the stock to a saucepan and add the reserved pan drippings, remaining stock and rosemary. Bring to the boil over high heat and cook until reduced to about 1l (32fl oz) and the sauce is richly flavoured. Whisk in the cornflour mixture, if necessary, to thicken. Cook for about 2 minutes. Add the reserved meat and giblets, and season with salt and pepper. Whisk in the butter to richen the sauce. Serve hot from the stove.

Smoked Whitefish Salad

¼ medium onion, finely chopped
½ whole smoked whitefish
1 hard-boiled egg, finely chopped
180ml (6fl oz) mayonnaise
1 tbsp fresh-squeezed lemon juice

1 tbsp Dijon mustard
Salt and freshly ground black pepper
*   to taste*

Serves 4
Carb Level: Low

Per serving:	
Carbohydrate:	4.2 g
Protein:	2.5 g

Smoked whitefish is usually available at Jewish delicatessens or speciality super-markets.

1. Place the chopped onion in a small bowl and cover with iced water. Let soak for 15 minutes. Drain and pat dry.
2. Use a small knife and your fingertips to remove and discard the skin, bones and any brown bits from the whitefish. Gently sort through the meat to ensure all small bones have been removed. Flake the fish into small pieces into a medium-size bowl, checking again for bones.
3. Add the egg and onion to the fish, and mash together with a fork. Blend in the mayonnaise, lemon juice and mustard. (For a smoother salad, blend the whitefish mixture in a food processor.) Season with salt and pepper to taste. Serve immediately, or store in the refrigerator for up to 3 days.

tips **Avoiding Caffeine**

Avoid coffee, tea and soft drinks with caffeine. Caffeine can lower your blood sugar, causing you to crave sugar and sweets.

Braised Brisket

Serves 8
Carb Level: Moderate

Per serving:	
Carbohydrate:	16.3 g
Protein:	50.4 g

This recipe is best when it's allowed to stand overnight in its own juices.

2.2kg (5lb) beef brisket, first cut, trimmed
3 tbsp vegetable oil
Salt and freshly ground black pepper to taste
1.3kg (3lb) onions, thinly sliced
6 medium carrots, peeled and cut into a large dice
5 cloves garlic, crushed

2 tsp peppercorns
Beef stock to cover brisket, approximately 1l (32fl oz)
Fresh parsley, chopped, for garnish

1. Preheat the oven to 170°C, 325°F, gas mark 3.
2. Pat the brisket with paper towels to dry. Heat the oil in a Dutch oven on high heat. Season the meat with salt and pepper. Brown the meat on all sides, then remove from the Dutch oven. Add the onions and carrots to the Dutch oven, and sauté until golden. Return the meat to the pan and add the garlic and peppercorns. Add beef stock just to cover the brisket. Bring just to a boil, cover, and place in the oven for at least 3 hours.
3. Season with salt and pepper, slice, and serve with its own juice. Garnish with the parsley.

tips **Slicing Braised Brisket**
Braised brisket is very tender. To make it easier to cut into slices without falling apart, use a very sharp slicing knife after the beef has been chilled thoroughly in the refrigerator. Once the chilled beef is sliced, gently reheat it with a small amount of the braising juices.

Matzo Ball Soup

Soup:

1 whole roasting chicken
3 whole carrots, cut into large
    chunks
4 celery sticks (stalks and tops), cut
    into large chunks
2 whole onions, quartered
30g (1oz) chopped fresh parsley
1 parsnip, peeled and cut into large
    chunks
4 sprigs fresh dill

Salt and freshly ground black pepper
    to taste

Matzo Balls:

3 large eggs, separated
2 tbsp chicken fat or vegetable oil
60g (2oz) matzo meal
1 tsp salt
2 tbsp soup stock (from above) or
    water

Serves 12
Carb Level: Low

Per serving:

Carbohydrate:	7.6 g
Protein:	23.5 g

This traditional Jewish soup tastes best when made the day before serving. Gently reheat the matzo balls in a small amount of the soup before serving.

1. To prepare the soup, use kitchen scissors to cut the whole chicken into quarters. Place the chicken into a stockpot and cover it with water. Bring the stockpot to the boil. Skim off any impurities that rise to the top of the water. Add the rest of the ingredients for the soup. Reduce heat and let simmer, partially covered, for approximately 1½ hours or until tender.

2. To prepare the matzo balls, mix the egg yolks with the chicken fat (or oil) in a medium-size mixing bowl. Mix together the matzo meal, salt and soup stock; add to the egg-yolk mixture, and stir to blend. Beat the egg whites to soft peaks. Fold the egg whites into the matzo mixture until just blended, and refrigerate for 40 minutes. Remove from the refrigerator and make heaped-tablespoon-size balls.

3. Strain the soup, reserving the chicken for another use. Reserve the carrots. Put the strained soup back into the stockpot, bring back to a low boil, and carefully drop the matzo balls into the soup. Cover and simmer for about 40 minutes. Serve the matzo ball soup in warmed soup cups with a few slices of the reserved carrots.

Chopped Liver

Serves 4

Carb Level: Low

Per serving:

Carbohydrate:	5.4 g
Protein:	13.8 g

Every Jewish family has their own version, but the ingredients for traditional chopped liver are pretty standard.

1 large onion, chopped
3 tbsp chicken fat or vegetable oil
1–2 eggs

225g (8oz) chicken livers
Salt and freshly ground black pepper
to taste

1. Fry the onion in the chicken fat (or oil) on low heat in a large frying pan with the lid on, until very soft and golden, stirring occasionally. Allow to cool.
2. Hard-boil the eggs by bringing them to a boil for 9 minutes, then cool them under running water.
3. Preheat the grill. Line a baking tray with aluminium foil.
4. Rinse the livers, pat dry and sprinkle with salt. Put the livers on the baking tray in a single layer and cook briefly, turning once, until they change colour and are cooked through. Let them cool.
5. Cut the hard-boiled eggs in half and chop them finely in a food processor; transfer them to a mixing bowl. Reserve 2–3 tablespoons of chopped egg to use as a garnish. Transfer the livers and onions to the workbowl of a food processor. Blend briefly, leaving the paste a little coarse. Mix the liver and onions with the rest of the chopped eggs by hand. Season with salt and pepper and mix well. Smooth the surface flat and sprinkle with the chopped egg.

Celery Root and Pear Purée

1 large celery root, peeled and cut into 25mm (1in) cubes
½ large onion, diced
2 ripe Anjou pears, peeled, cored and diced
180ml (6fl oz) double cream
3 tbsp unsalted butter

Salt and freshly ground black pepper to taste
Fresh watercress leaves for garnish
Crumbled goat's cheese for garnish

Serves 4
Carb Level: Moderate

Per serving:	
Carbohydrate:	19.1 g
Protein:	2.2 g

Makes a wonderful starter course to a special meal.

1. Place the celery root, onion and pears in a medium-size saucepan and cover with water; bring to the boil over high heat. Reduce the heat to a simmer and cook until the celery root is very soft, about 50 minutes. Drain, reserving 125ml (4fl oz) of the cooking liquid.
2. Place the celery root mixture in a blender or food processor and process until smooth. Add the cream, butter, salt and pepper; blend to combine. If necessary, reheat over low heat, stirring frequently. If the mixture seems too thick, add a little of the reserved cooking liquid. Adjust seasoning to taste. Garnish with watercress leaves and goat cheese. Serve hot.

Love Garlic?
Garlic is a wonderful flavouring agent. You can estimate about 1g of carbohydrate for an average clove of garlic. When using chopped garlic in a sautéed dish, be careful not to burn or allow the garlic to get too brown, as it will impart a bitter taste to your dish.

Beetroot Dip

Serves 10

Carb Level: Low

Per serving:

| Carbohydrate: | 8.1 g |
| Protein: | 2.3 g |

Serve with spears of endive radiating out from the centre of the platter for a special presentation.

6 fresh red beetroot
Splash of vinegar, lemon juice or red wine
60g (2oz) chopped red onion
180ml (6fl oz) sour cream
180ml (6fl oz) plain yogurt

45g (1½oz) chopped fresh dill
4 large cloves garlic, chopped
Salt and freshly ground black pepper to taste

1. Cook the beetroot in large pot of boiling salted water with a splash of vinegar, lemon juice or red wine until tender, about 35 minutes. Drain and leave to cool. Peel and chop coarsely. (You may want to wear rubber gloves while peeling, as beetroot stains your fingers.)
2. Combine the beetroot and onion in a blender or food processor; blend until smooth. Transfer the mixture to a medium-size bowl and mix in the sour cream, yogurt, dill and garlic. Season the dip to taste with salt and pepper. Cover and refrigerate for up to 2 days. Spoon the dip into a bowl and serve chilled.

tips Creating a Cheese Board

Cheese boards are an easy and elegant entertaining style. A cheese board should include a mix of goat's, cow's, and sheep's milk cheeses. Use a variety of textures, including soft cheeses such as brie or camembert; smoked cheeses such as mozzarella, gouda or provolone; hard cheeses such as manchego; and blue cheeses such as roquefort or gorgonzola.

Turkey Meatballs
with Tomato Sauce

2 tbsp butter
1 lightly beaten egg white
30g (1oz) fine dry breadcrumbs
2 tbsp plain non-fat yogurt
2 tbsp chopped fresh basil
1/4 tsp freshly ground black pepper
375g (12oz) ground raw turkey

454g (1lb) tin tomatoes, undrained
3 tbsp tomato paste
1/2 tsp sugar
1/8 tsp salt

Makes 36 Meatballs	
Carb Level: Low	
Per serving:	
Carbohydrate:	3.0 g
Protein:	4.3 g

A great dish to serve at parties.

1. Preheat the oven to 200°C, 400°F, gas mark 6. Spray a shallow baking pan with non-stick coating.
2. Combine the butter, egg white, breadcrumbs, yogurt, half the basil and pepper in a medium-size bowl. Add the ground turkey, and mix well. Shape into 25mm (1in) meatballs (should yield 36 meatballs). Place in the pan and bake for about 20 minutes or until no pink remains.
3. Meanwhile, for the sauce, combine the tomatoes and their liquid, the tomato paste, the remaining basil, sugar and salt in a blender or food processor. Cover and blend just until mixed and the tomatoes are slightly chunky. Transfer the mixture to a medium-size saucepan; bring to a boil. Reduce heat and simmer uncovered for 10–15 minutes or to the desired consistency. Serve the meatballs on wooden picks with tomato sauce for dipping.

tips **Entertaining with Olives**
Olives are a favourite for entertaining. Instead of serving tapenades, which require crisps, consider serving quality olives that have been marinated with peppercorns, dried rosemary and garlic cloves. Olives contain 2.8g of carbohydrates per 60g (2oz). Remember to include a small side dish for disposing of the olive stones.

Beef Sirloin in Red Wine-Peppercorn Sauce

Serves 6
Carb Level: Low

Per serving:

Carbohydrate:	2.3 g
Protein:	42.8 g

Serve with Creamed Spinach (see recipe on page 138).

2 tbsp olive oil
Six 215g (7oz) beef sirloin
    fillets
Salt and freshly ground black pepper
    to taste
310ml (10fl oz) beef stock

250ml (8fl oz) dry red wine
2 cloves garlic, pressed
3 tbsp green peppercorns
15g (½oz) unsalted butter, cut into
    pieces

1. Heat a large sauté pan on high, and add the oil. Sprinkle the steaks evenly with salt and pepper; place them in the pan and brown on both sides, about 3 minutes per side. Remove the steaks from the pan, place on a dish and set aside.

2. Add the beef stock, wine and garlic to the pan; cook over high heat for 15 minutes. Return the steaks to the pan and cook for 5–6 minutes on each side or to your taste. Remove the pan from the heat and remove the steaks, reserving the sauce in the pan. Add the peppercorns and gradually whisk in the butter. Serve the sauce over the steaks.

Safety Tip for Reheating
Reheated stews and casseroles must be heated to an internal temperature of 70°C, 165°F for at least 15 seconds to effectively kill bacteria growth and be considered safe.

Oysters Rockefeller Soup

2 tbsp butter
5 celery stalks, finely chopped
2 large onions, finely chopped
1 bay leaf
185g (6oz) chopped fresh spinach
185g (6oz) thinly sliced green onions
75g (2½oz) chopped fresh flatleaf
    parsley
1 clove garlic, chopped
1 tsp chopped fresh thyme leaves
½ tsp crushed dried oregano
2 tsp salt

⅛ tsp each: freshly ground black
    pepper, red pepper and white
    pepper
1 tbsp plain flour
30 oysters
250ml (8fl oz) chicken stock
180ml (6fl oz) Pernod
1.5l (48fl oz) whipping cream

Serves 12	
Carb Level: Moderate	
Per serving:	
Carbohydrate:	16.8 g
Protein:	6.7 g

Keep servings to no more than 180ml (6fl oz) each, as this soup is very rich.

1. Heat the butter in a Dutch oven over medium-high heat. When the butter starts to foam, add the celery, onion and bay leaf. Cook for 4–5 minutes or until the vegetables are tender. Reduce the heat to low, add the spinach, green onions and parsley. Cook, stirring constantly, for 3–4 minutes. Remove the bay leaf.

2. Add the garlic, thyme, oregano, salt and peppers. Cook, stirring constantly, for 4–5 minutes. Add the flour and cook for 2 minutes, stirring constantly and scraping the sides and bottom of the pan.

3. Drain the oysters, reserving the liquid. Add enough chicken stock to the oyster liquid, if necessary, to make 260ml (8fl oz); set aside.

4. Increase the heat to medium-high and carefully add the Pernod to the vegetable mixture. Cook, stirring constantly, for 4–5 minutes. Add the oyster and stock liquid, and cook for another 3–4 minutes. Let cool slightly. Transfer the vegetable mixture to a blender or food processor. Cover and blend or process to a smooth consistency.

5. Return the mixture to the Dutch oven. Stir in whipping cream and cook over medium heat for 4–5 minutes or until heated through, whisking occasionally. Add the oysters and cook for about 5 minutes or until the oyster edges curl. Serve immediately.

Lobster in Vanilla Sauce

Serves 4

Carb Level: Moderate

Per serving:

Carbohydrate:	17.6 g
Protein:	89.0 g

Fish glacé is made by taking 125ml (4fl oz) of fish stock and simmering it down to 30ml (1fl oz).

1 peeled carrot, coarsely chopped
1 large onion, coarsely chopped
1 celery stalk, coarsely chopped
A few parsley stems
1 clove garlic, peeled and chopped
4–5 black peppercorns
2 bay leaves
Pinch of thyme and tarragon
Salt to taste
1.7l (64fl oz) fish stock or water
1 vanilla pod, sliced in half longways
1.7l (64fl oz) dry white wine
4 lobster tails

Vanilla Sauce:

4 shallots, chopped
1 tsp unsalted butter
60ml (2fl oz) dry white wine
1 vanilla pod
860ml (32fl oz) whipping cream
Fish glacé
*Salt and freshly ground black pepper
   to taste*

1. To prepare lobster court bouillon, simmer all the ingredients up to and including the fish stock (or water) for 1 hour. Add the vanilla pod and white wine and bring to the boil. Add the lobster tails and boil for 8–10 minutes, until cooked. Remove the tails. When the lobsters have cooled, remove the meat from the tails, slice into medallions and reserve.

2. To prepare the vanilla sauce, briefly sauté the shallots in the butter in a large sauté pan over medium-high heat. Add the white wine and the vanilla pod. (Split the pod in half longways and scoop out the pulp with a small knife. The black specks hold all the flavour.) Simmer until almost dry. Add the cream and the fish glacé. Bring to the boil. Reduce the heat and simmer for about 5 minutes. Add salt and pepper to taste. Arrange the lobster meat on individual serving plates and top with the sauce.

Glazed Carrots
with Balsamic Vinegar

1.5kg (3lb 8oz) baby or medium
  carrots
30g (1oz) butter
6 tbsp sugar
80ml (2½fl oz) balsamic vinegar

Salt and freshly ground black pepper
  to taste
15g (½oz) chopped fresh chives for
  garnish

1. Peel the carrots and cut into 50mm (2in) pieces, halved longways.
2. Melt the butter in a large sauté pan over medium heat. Add the carrots and cook them for about 5 minutes. Cover and cook for another 7 minutes, or until slightly tender. Stir in the sugar and vinegar; cook uncovered until the carrots are tender and glazed and the liquid has reduced. Season with salt and pepper.
3. Serve in a warm bowl and garnish with fresh chives.

Serves 10
Carb Level: Moderate
Per serving:

Carbohydrate:	18.6 g
Protein:	1.4 g

A colourful and tasty side dish for a special meal.

Glazed Baked Ham with Rosemary

1.8kg (4lb) boneless ham
30 whole cloves
3 tbsp mango chutney
1 packed tbsp dark
  brown sugar

2 tbsp prepared horseradish mustard
2 tsp fresh rosemary leaves

1. Preheat the oven to 170°C, 325°F, gas mark 3.
2. Place the ham in a roasting pan set on a rack. Insert the whole cloves all over the ham, and bake for about 1½ hours or until the internal temperature reads 55°C, 130°F.
3. Meanwhile, in a small saucepan combine the chutney, brown sugar, mustard and rosemary. Cook over low heat until warm and liquified. Drizzle the sauce all over the ham and bake for an additional 30 minutes or until the internal temperature reads 60°C, 140°F. The outside of the ham should be crusty and sugary brown.

Serves 12
Carb Level: Moderate
Per serving:

Carbohydrate:	20.0 g
Protein:	27.6 g

This ham tastes great served either hot or cold. Use the next day in sandwiches.

Butternut Squash and Turnip
Gratin with Gruyère

Serves 8
Carb Level: Moderate

Per serving:	
Carbohydrate:	16.9 g
Protein:	6.9 g

The peak season for turnips is October to February.

900g (2lb) butternut squash
3 large turnips
1 tsp chopped fresh thyme
1 tsp chopped fresh marjoram
1 tsp chopped fresh sage

Salt and freshly ground black pepper to taste
3 garlic cloves, peeled and chopped
500ml (16fl oz) double cream
125g (4oz) Gruyère cheese, grated

1. Preheat the oven to 190°C, 375°F, gas mark 5. Grease a 305 x 230mm (12 x 9in) gratin dish.
2. Peel the squash and trim off the tops and bottoms. Cut off the seed-filled bottom halves, cut it in half longways and scoop out the seeds. Slice the necks of the squash into 3mm (1/8 in) rounds and slice the base into 3mm (1/8 in) half-circles.
3. Peel the turnips and cut them in half longways. Cut them into 3mm (1/8 in) half-moons.
4. In a small bowl, combine the thyme, marjoram and sage.
5. Beginning with the half-circles of squash, layer about a third of the squash slices into the gratin dish. Sprinkle with some of the herbs and season with salt and pepper. Layer the turnip slices over the squash layer. Sprinkle with some of the herbs and half the chopped garlic. Season with salt and pepper.
6. Spread another third of the squash slices on top of the turnips. Sprinkle with herbs and season with salt and pepper. Spread the remaining turnips in another layer over the squash. Sprinkle with herbs and the rest of the garlic. Top with the remaining squash and herbs, and season with salt and pepper.
7. Slowly pour the cream over the top and down the sides of the dish. Add enough to just barely cover the vegetables when pressed down.
8. Cover the dish with foil. Place the dish on a baking tray and bake for about 45 minutes. Remove the foil and sprinkle with the cheese. Continue to bake uncovered for about 25 minutes or until the cheese is lightly browned. Allow to rest for 10 minutes before cutting into it.

Fennel– and Garlic-Crusted Pork Roast

1 small head fennel, coarsely
    chopped
30g (1oz) coarsely chopped onion
2 tbsp olive oil
6 cloves garlic, peeled and sliced

15g (¹/₂oz) chopped fresh assorted
    herbs (thyme, sage, rosemary,
    parsley, oregano, etc.)
2 tsp fennel seeds
Freshly ground black pepper
2kg (4lb 8oz) pork rib roast, tied
Salt

Serves 6	
Carb Level: Low	
Per serving:	
Carbohydrate:	5.5 g
Protein:	58.8 g

Your butcher will prepare and tie your rib roast for roasting.

1. In a blender or food processor, combine the fennel, onion, olive oil and garlic; purée into a paste. Add the herbs, fennel seeds and pepper; blend to combine.
2. With a small sharp knife, make shallow diamond cuts into the skin of the pork roast. Season it all over with salt, rubbing it in well. Rub the garlic-fennel paste over the roast to cover it with a layer about 6mm (¹/₄in) thick. Cover and refrigerate for up to 8 hours. Remove from the refrigerator and let stand at room temperature for about 20 minutes.
3. Preheat the oven to 190°C, 375°F, gas mark 5.
4. Transfer the roast to a roasting pan with a rack. Roast for about 1 hour and 15 minutes or until the internal temperature reads 65°C, 150°F. Remove the roast from the oven and allow to stand for at least 20 minutes. Slice the roast into thick chops.

What Is Fennel?

Fennel is a broad, bulb-like vegetable cultivated throughout Europe It has long been believed by many cultures to have medicinal qualities. Both the base and stems can be eaten raw as a tasty addition to salads. Fennel can be cooked in a variety of ways, including braising, grilling, roasting and sautéing. Fennel is often mislabelled as 'sweet anise'. The flavour of fennel is much lighter and sweeter than liquorice-tasting anise. Fennel contains 4.3g of carbohydrates per 15g (¹/₂oz).

Spicy Chilled Prawns

Serves 12

Carb Level: Low

Per serving:

Carbohydrate:	5.7 g
Protein:	23.7 g

Keep the prawns chilled and put the serving bowl on ice while serving.

1.3kg (3lb) uncooked prawns with tail on, peeled and de-veined
180ml (6fl oz) olive oil
30g (1oz) chopped fresh coriander
60ml (2fl oz) white wine vinegar
3 tbsp fresh lemon juice
3 jalapeño peppers, seeded and chopped
3 large cloves garlic, chopped
$1/4$ tsp cayenne pepper
Salt and freshly ground black pepper to taste
3 large lemons, sliced
1 large red onion, sliced

1. Boil the prawns until pink and opaque, about 3 minutes. When done, chill the prawns in iced water; drain; put in the refrigerator.
2. Whisk the next eight ingredients. Pour the remaining marinade over the prawns; toss to coat. Layer the prawns, lemon slices and onion in a large glass bowl. Cover and refrigerate for 4 hours.

Egg Salad
with Endive Leaves

Serves 6

Carb Level: Low

Per serving:

Carbohydrate:	5.1 g
Protein:	10.1 g

Fan the endive spears in a star pattern around the egg salad for a special presentation.

6 tbsp mayonnaise
1 tbsp Dijon mustard
8 hard-boiled eggs, peeled and chopped
15g ($1/2$oz) finely chopped onion
15g ($1/2$oz) finely chopped celery stalks
15g ($1/2$oz) chopped fresh parsley
Salt and white pepper to taste
24 endive spears, separated
Paprika for garnish

Mix the mayonnaise and mustard in a medium-size bowl. Add the chopped eggs, onion, celery and parsley. Season with salt and pepper. Cover the egg salad with cling film and refrigerate until ready to serve. Place the egg salad in a serving bowl on a platter surrounded with the endive spears. Dust with paprika for colour.

Chilli Cheese Corn Casserole

680g (1lb 8oz) fresh corn kernels, or frozen, thawed and drained
125g (4oz) grated Cheddar cheese
225g (8oz) cream cheese, at room temperature

215g (7oz) tin diced green chillies
2 tsp chilli powder
2 tsp ground cumin

1. Preheat the oven to 180°C, 350°F, gas mark 4. Butter a 1.25l (40fl oz) baking dish.
2. Mix all the ingredients in a large bowl until well blended. Transfer to the prepared baking dish; bake until bubbling, about 30 minutes. Let cool, then cover and refrigerate up to 1 day. To serve, gently reheat, covered, in a 180°C, 350°F, gas mark 4 oven for about 30 minutes until heated throughout.

Serves 8	
Carb Level: Moderate	
Per serving:	
Carbohydrate:	17.9 g
Protein:	8.7 g

An easy dish to prepare the day before an outdoor picnic.

Spicy Cucumber Relish

2 seedless cucumbers
2 medium shallots, peeled and trimmed
1½ tbsp chopped jalapeño pepper
60g (2oz) fresh mint, chopped medium-fine

2 tbsp white wine vinegar or champagne vinegar
1 tsp salt
¼ tsp freshly ground black pepper
3 tbsp olive oil

1. Peel the cucumbers. Cut in half longways, remove any seeds and cut across into 3mm (⅛ in) slices.
2. Combine the cucumbers, shallots, jalapeño and mint. In a small bowl, combine the vinegar, salt and pepper. Whisk in the olive oil until combined. Pour over the cucumbers, and toss gently to combine. Serve.

Serves 10	
Serves 10	
Per serving:	
Carbohydrate:	4.7 g
Protein:	1.2 g

Smaller cucumbers have fewer seeds than larger ones.

Tandoori Chicken Kebabs

Serves 8
Carb Level: Low

Per serving:

Carbohydrate:	7.1 g
Protein:	24.5 g

The creamy yogurt sauce offsets the heat of the spices on the chicken.

500ml (16fl oz) plain low-fat yogurt
30g (1oz) chopped fresh coriander
60ml (2fl oz) fresh lemon juice
2 tbsp peeled and grated fresh ginger
2 large cloves garlic, chopped
4 tsp paprika
2 tsp curry powder
1 tsp ground cumin
1 tsp ground coriander
½ tsp cayenne pepper

900g (2lb) boneless, skinless chicken
breasts, cut into 25mm (1in)
cubes
4 medium-size red peppers, cut into
25mm (1in) pieces
16 bamboo skewers, soaked in water
for 30 minutes

1. Purée the first 10 ingredients in a blender or food processor. Pour 125ml (4fl oz) of the mixture into a small bowl, cover and chill. Pour the remaining mixture into a large bowl, add the chicken and toss to coat. Cover and chill for at least 1 hour or up to 24 hours.
2. Preheat a grill to medium-high. Make sure the grill grate is clean and lightly oiled to prevent sticking.
3. Thread the red peppers and chicken on skewers. Grill the kebabs until the chicken is cooked through, about 7 minutes per side. Serve with the reserved yogurt mixture for dipping.

Grilled Beef and Onion Kebabs

4 tsp finely ground coriander seeds
4 tsp finely ground anise seeds
1 tbsp chopped garlic
1 tbsp ground paprika
1/4 tsp cayenne pepper
125ml (4fl oz) olive oil, divided

Salt and freshly ground black pepper
    to taste
680g (1lb 8oz) boneless sirloin
    steak, trimmed, cut into 32mm
    (1 1/4in) cubes
12 red pearl onions, peeled and cut
    in half longways

Serves 4
Carb Level: Low

Per serving:	
Carbohydrate:	5.0 g
Protein:	13.1 g

An easy summer recipe that will please everyone!

1. Preheat the grill until hot.
2. Place the ground coriander and anise seeds in a medium-size bowl. Add the garlic, paprika, cayenne pepper and 60ml (2fl oz) olive oil. Season the marinade with salt and pepper, and stir until combined. Add the sirloin cubes, and stir to coat; set aside.
3. In a medium-size bowl, combine the onions and the remaining olive oil. Season with salt and pepper; toss to coat.
4. Divide the steaks among four skewers; thread, leaving 12mm (1/2 in) between each cube. Divide the onions among another four skewers and thread them.
5. Grill the sirloin kebabs until well-browned and medium-rare, and grill the onion until glistening, tender and slightly charred, 5–7 minutes for both. Serve on the skewers.

Summer Skewer Fun

Try some unusual twists on skewers: Fruit skewers – use colourful bites of strawberries, grapes and melon pieces. Greek island skewers – small pieces of feta cheese skewered with grilled cherry tomatoes (count 1g of carbohydrate per cherry tomato) and pitted calamata olives. This is an attractive presentation with fresh rosemary branches for the skewers. Trim the base end of the branch to a point and remove a portion of the rosemary needles, leaving the top of the branch intact.

Easy Dishes at a Glance

❖ ❖ ❖

Index